D0808036

ALYOSHA GOLDSTEIN *University of New Mexico*

MACARENA GÓMEZ-BARRIS *University of Southern California*

NOELANI GOODYEAR-KAʻŌPUA (Kanaka Maoli) *University of Hawaiʻi at Mānoa*

LISA KAHALEOLE HALL (Kanaka Maoli) *Wells College*

MICHAEL HAMES-GARCÍA *University of Oregon*

MARC LAMONT HILL *Morehouse College*

AILEEN MORETON-ROBINSON (Goenpul, Quandamooka First Nation) *Queensland University of Technology*

NADINE NABER *University of Illinois, Chicago*

MIMI THI NGUYEN *University of Illinois, Urbana–Champaign*

JESSICA BISSETT PEREA (Denaʼina) *University of California, Davis*

LEONI PIHAMA (Te Ātiawa, Ngāti Māhanga, Ngā Māhanga a Tairi) *University of Waikato*

JASBIR K. PUAR *Rutgers University*

SHERENE RAZACK *Ontario Institute for Studies in Education (OISE), University of Toronto*

KARYN RECOLLET (Cree) *University of Toronto*

JUANA MARÍA RODRÍGUEZ *University of California, Berkeley*

STEVEN SALAITA *American University of Beirut*

DEAN ITSUJI SARANILLIO *New York University*

LEANNE BETASAMOSAKE SIMPSON (Michi Saagiig Nishnaabeg) *Independent Scholar*

MISTINGUETTE SMITH *Black/Land Project*

HORTENSE SPILLERS *Vanderbilt University*

THOMAS MICHAEL SWENSEN (Tangirnaq Native Village) *Colorado State University*

ALEXANDER WEHELIYE *Northwestern University*

LISA YONEYAMA *University of Toronto*

Journal of the
Critical Ethnic Studies Association

VOLUME 2 · ISSUE 2
FALL 2016

Editor's Introduction

What Justice Wants

EVE TUCK AND K. WAYNE YANG

B efore we turn to the themes and threads of this issue on *what justice wants*, we pause to express our appreciation and intentions. We are so grateful to the many people whose labors and visions have brought this journal into existence, and into our hands. There is not space enough to name them all; however, we would like to especially acknowledge the work of the founding editors, John D. Márquez and Junaid Rana, and the first managing editor, Kelly Chung. The initial issues of this journal have laid the example for politically committed scholarship across the scope of what *Critical Ethnic Studies* is and can be.

We enter the scene as editors for a three-year term. We are delighted to be working with managing coeditor LeKeisha Hughes (University of California, San Diego) on this issue, and managing coeditor Sam Spady (OISE, University of Toronto) on our journal's blog and next issue. One of our early acts as editors was to invite members to the *Critical Ethnic Studies* Editorial Board, and all of them have been big-hearted with their guidance, critical feedback, and their intellectual and political weight. As authors returned final manuscripts imbued by the feedback of reviewers, they remarked again and again how generative and generous this particular review process had been for them, and we resoundingly agree. Something wonderful is happening.

This second phase of the journal under our leadership will no doubt carry our curatorial accents, and our particular perspectives on the field of critical ethnic studies (CES). The work of critical ethnic studies is far larger than our own particularities, and is taking off across activist intellectual spaces that include extra-academic and academic settings, anywhere that foments an open dialogue that brings together "Indigenous sovereignty, critiques of antiblackness, intersectional feminist and queer analyses, disability studies, border and migration studies, critical refugee studies, and more," in productive tension, and that is nurturing of ways of life that actively defy the impulses of "white supremacy, settler colonialism, capitalism, and heteropatriarchy, as well as militarism, occupation, Indigenous erasure, neocolonialism, anti-immigration, anti-Islam," and other structured harms.[1]

The organic intellectual work of organizing collectives who actively produce theory, like the Native Youth Sexual Health Network, Gallery of the Streets, the Palestinian Youth Movement and African Americans for Justice in the Middle East and North Africa, Third Eye Collective, We Charge Genocide, and Sogorea Te Land Trust; of independent research projects like Black/Land Project; of university-resourced resurgence projects like the University of Victoria's Indigenous Leadership Forum; and of lovingly radical media like Indian and Cowboy and This Is the Read are more influential than our journal in tending these open dialogues, even if their efforts are not named as "critical ethnic studies."[2] In academic settings, the first faculty positions that intentionally deploy the terminology "critical ethnic studies" have been created in the last few years, notably at the University of Minnesota, Kalamazoo College, and the University of California, Santa Cruz. The Critical Ethnic Studies Association (CESA) as an academic/activist organism of volunteer, past, present, and future members must be credited with expanding and naming this space, creating this journal, as well as a new book series just launched with Northwestern University Press coedited by Michelle Wright and Jodi Byrd, and a forthcoming anthology called *Critical Ethnic Studies: A Reader* by the Critical Ethnic Studies Editorial Collective.

Having said this about the state of the field, we must admit that we as editors are agnostic about field building. In part, this is because critical ethnic studies is itself an "interdisciplinary, and un-disciplinary" field that pushes back against the institutionalization of ethnic studies.[3] Also, it is because we, like many others, come to the CES conversation not to build a field but as sometime outsiders who find this node of convergence important, exciting, and resonant. Academically speaking, Eve and Wayne are coming to this work from education, a discipline not typically considered part of (critical) ethnic studies. Although Wayne is now in ethnic studies and Eve is in education and Indigenous studies, critical ethnic studies is for us, for now, a node of activist intellectualism committed to Indigenous land/life, Black life, queer life, and decolonization. We feel one of our main editorial commitments is to be caretaking of relationships between critical ethnic studies, Indigenous studies, and Black studies. We do not mean for this commitment to create another exclusive identitarian ordering of "importance" in ethnic studies but rather to provide space for critical dialogue currently underway—space that we do not see sufficiently provided for elsewhere. We mention this to be transparent about how we as editors might nurture vital topics of inquiry yet, in the process, leave gaps and missing persons and missing pieces. These priorities and gaps are not necessarily representative of CESA, nor of the field of critical ethnic studies. What we miss, we will try to name along the way, and we invite critical submissions that address them to this journal.

Beyond the themed issues we have planned and the selections we will make, we have also implemented some procedural-level interventions in order to cultivate radical citation practices, accountability to communities and community partners, and enhanced obligations of authorship. These interventions will continue to be seasoned over time and our hope is that this will be a journal that enacts a politics of relation that sets it apart from other journals but, better, informs the work of other journals. Of course, we are learning from the practices of other journals, particularly *Native American and Indigenous Studies* (published by the University of Minnesota Press) and *Decolonization: Indigeneity, Education & Society* (published online and open access), as we endeavor to foster a journal culture of generous criticality.

This special issue connects to currents in the field, largely named by terms like "justice" and, closely related, "social justice," yet sometimes insufficiently described by them. When formulating this issue and then again after the call for proposals was released, we received numerous affirming comments to the tune of "justice is the defining issue of our time." These comments resound with the spirit of resistance to the constant re/production of injustice. They also reveal how "justice" is one of those stalwart terms that can come to quickly dominate the terms of the radical agenda. This hegemony of justice is problematic, and that is why we see it as the job of this journal to interrogate it: making space for a critical conversation of what justice is, or more precisely what justice wants, what it produces, whom it fails, where it operates, when it is in effect, and what it lacks.

And because we do not see the interrogation of justice to begin nor end with this themed journal issue, we invite writers to submit future pieces on this theme of what justice wants, particularly addressing the gaps and generative openings of this issue. Articles in future issues might serve as rejoinders of what has been gathered here, or might take us to altogether different aims and urgencies of justice.

Our upcoming themed issue, "Late Identity," takes another topic of nearly unquestioned hegemony in ethnic studies—identity—to unpack its political impact and question its relevance, before it becomes simply propagated from an "old" ethnic studies canon into a "new" critical ethnic studies one.

We invite proposals for guest edited special issues, especially those that can prod the gaps in our curation of this journal. We also invite general submissions at any time, as well as contributions to our robust *Critical Ethnic Studies* blog, curated by our dynamic managing editors. The blog is a great incubator for ideas for future issues but also is more flexible and even a little irreverent of the types of ideas that can be addressed in a formal journal article. The website for our journal and blog is http://www.critical ethnicstudiesjournal.org/.

what justice wants

Before digging in to the rest of your reading of this introduction, and the articles in the issue, we invite you to go somewhere calm within your own thoughts to think about the notion of justice. Perhaps remember a time that you have been witness to this term being used or misused. Maybe let your eyes or fingers or ears linger on the word ::justice:: until it starts to dematerialize, to break down into no sense. Of course we can do this with any word, repeat it until it has lost its connotations, until it slides out of understanding; but to rebuild meaning for the word "justice," we can either believe what other fields say about it or invite it only as a placeholder word, a quick word for busy people doing so much good work. Indeed, justice may only be comprehensible when we do not get too bogged down by its commonly understood denotations. These definitions—a general sense of moral and ethical righteousness; a specific legal sense referring to the fair administration of punishments and rewards—do not in and of themselves inspire. Those accepted meanings do not necessarily satisfy, at least toward delivering their own promises of justice. They may fall apart at their seams when we pay close attention.

Yet justice is a catalytic concept in conversations like critical ethnic studies and among activists and organizers. The word circulates as a placeholder for actions and stances against dispossession, displacement, and death. Justice in this connotation takes many different forms, including holding power accountable to its abuses, pursuing revisions and expansions to civil rights law, and encouraging civil disobedience of the law. Some communities reject the very logics of (state) administration of justice and instead assert sovereignty of selves, communities, land, and living in ways that are right. These efforts exceed the formal meanings of justice. Many communities also use "justice" to call attention to the state of perpetual *in*justice, to the State or occupying nation's hypocrisy in claiming to administer justice, and indeed to the direct role of the State in the systemization of injustice. Much goes unsaid about what is meant by justice, but when considered from the perspectives of different communities and their concerns, justice takes on varying and sometimes contradictory meanings.

The lack of justice is overwhelmingly obvious in the face of specific wrongs, such as murdered and missing Indigenous women, girls, trans* and two-spirit peoples (#MMIWG2S), with more recent counts as high as four thousand since 1980.[4] The killings by police of Michelle Cusseux, Rekia Boyd, Michael Brown, Eric Garner, Tamir Rice, and Freddie Gray are also instances of justice ripped away.[5] We write at a time when trans* people of color and two-spirit people are often murdered; news stories about their deaths frequently misgender trans* and two-spirit people, and worse, depict their lives as likely to perish anyway. At the same time, mechanisms designed to facilitate justice almost always come up short; with this we are thinking of the ambivalence that some Indigenous public figures have expressed over the prospects of reconciliation after the convening of the Truth and Reconciliation Commission on residential schooling for Indigenous children in Canada; the non-indictment and not-guilty verdicts of police officers in the killings of unarmed Black people; and formal inquiries into Indigenous deaths in custody (see Latty et. al., this issue). At best, such mechanisms achieve only a "temporary armistice between me and my oppression."[6] Said another way, these mechanisms promise justice but often deliver deferrals.

When we put out a call for papers for this issue, we did so under the theme of "what justice wants," because to attend to what justice *wants* invites at least two potentially simultaneous rehearsals: considering what justice *desires* and/or considering what justice *lacks.*[7] To consider what justice desires, we might examine the role of the State and its functioning through promising, harnessing, and manufacturing hopes for justice. The State is a desiring-machine of justice in the Deleuze and Guattarian sense of an apparatus that consumes and produces and excretes justice. However, we might also consider how desire alludes to community and nonstate actors' desires for justice, which exceed those of the State, and their movements toward and away from the State. Desire includes hopes and disappointments with justice, the multiple lines of flight to and from justice.[8] To consider what justice lacks is one way to frame the horizons of justice, and to gesture at what is beyond justice. If justice cannot deliver itself, what does it actually deliver and what is lacking in its promise?

In these pages, we offer some definition to justice as comprised of limits and inherent wants. We begin by situating justice as a colonial temporality—

limited actions within a colonial moment against colonial structures. We lean heavily on the work of Saidiya Hartman and Stephen Best in order to frame justice as a "redress discourse" to understand why justice is both desirable and disappointing.[9] In a post on our journal's blog, we deconstruct "social justice" as a related idea developed within the modern colonial era of nation-states, colonies, and chattel slavery. With the limits of justice in mind, we then turn to places that exceed as outside elsewheres to the time and territory of justice. By territory, we mean the legal and political space of supremacist sovereignty normally attributed to states. By time, we mean the colonial application of justice to specific injured, living bodies (lives), and linear notions of past harm and present reconciliation and future irreproachability. These elsewheres include Indigenous concepts of the "good life,"[10] strategies for grounded normativity, self-determination, coalition building across movements and issues, transformative justice outside the pathologizing logics of the prison state (see Hwang, this issue), possibilities for art as resistance, the subversion of terms and language that limit our imagination, resurgence politics, the Black social life, and abolition.

This definitional introduction lays some groundwork for the ideas presented by the authors in this issue. We end with short descriptions of their remarkable contributions, which deconstruct and interrogate the wants of justice. Such critical intellectual work helps us understand how resistances to injustice can avoid being hoodwinked by the desiring machines of justice, and how alternatives to justice can name their own possibilities. At a practical organizing level, they help us understand where movements can contingently find objectives in justice and where they can define their own elsewheres beyond justice.

JUSTICE IS A COLONIAL TEMPORALITY

Justice is a colonial temporality, always desired and deferred, and delimited by the timeframes of modern colonizing states as well as the self-historicizing, self-perpetuating futurities of their nations. It is instructive to think of justice as a "redress discourse" as analyzed by Stephen Best and Saidiya Hartman, who build upon Hartman's framework on redress as developed in her profoundly impactful book, *Scenes of Subjection*.[11] Analyzing efforts to redress abuse during formal chattel slavery in the U.S. South, Hartman writes, "redress is a limited form of action aimed at relieving the pained body through alternative configurations of self and . . . the body as human flesh, not beast of burden."[12] The action of redress lies not just in demanding remedy and reparation from the State but also in redressing the Black body as human, and in re-membering the social body as Black life.

If we apply the lens of justice as a redress discourse, we gain several useful insights into its desires and limits:

Justice re-members. Drawing from Hartman, demands for justice re-member; they are a kind of ghosting that refuses to forget abduction, violation, displacement, dispossession, and death. They also re-member the fragmented social body back together as life that matters in ways beyond the ontological cages of pained plaintiff or object in need of subjection.[13] We might consider how #BlackLivesMatter is a re-membering in this double sense: a refusal to allow for the infliction of violence against Black bodies to be casually erased and forgotten, and the reminder that those bodies count beyond body counts. Black lives matter beyond the accounts of racial capitalism, where they only count as bodies for exchange and disposal.[14] Black lives matter beyond their neoliberal mattering as im/proper subjects who can/not govern themselves into peaceful acceptance of the social order.

Justice is a limited form of action. However, to say that Black life is human and thus matters is at once a re-membering that provides some relief but will always bear repeating. This very rearticulation of the Black body as human is problematic, because the "human" is already predicated on antiblackness.[15] Antiblackness is characterized by the "regularity of domination and terror."[16] In other words, antiblackness is already a present event taking place, and always a future event under white supremacist rule—a political reality that "engenders the necessity of redress, the inevitability of its failure, and the constancy of repetition yielded by this failure."[17] Thus, "no justice, no peace" in the liberal reckoning might seem to imply that justice will afford peace. However, another meaning is that both justice and peace are impossible desires bound in the repetition of redress.

The limit of justice is the state. The state asserts its monopoly on justice, particularly through its monopoly on the "administration" of violence. To enact justice, the state insists on its right to exceptional power, such as exile, imprisonment, dispossession, arbitration, redistribution, and murder—the very exceptional powers that give rise to the sovereign (in Giorgio Agamben's treatment) and thus the state as we know it.[18] This monopoly is a claim to supremacist sovereignty, that which we have come to know as the State. Yet let us remember that claims to sovereign power derive from empires' insistence of supremacy over an (Indigenous) territory. State sovereignty is the continual product of war. In settler-colonial nations, it is a reproduced claim over land and life not one's own—a claim that has evolved into the State "over here." Moreover, in the permanent arena of war "over there," the very state logic of justice is suspended and replaced by empire's exceptionalized right to commit mass murder, dispossession, and displacement.[19] This is a reality too well understood by Indigenous peoples on Turtle Island whose presence falls under the exceptional legal order of war rather than under the State. The State is the ultimate representation of the possibility for and limit of achieving justice. Justice is delimited by the borders of empire and colony, by the temporalities of "peacetime" and wartime. Thinking through what we learned in our interview with Leanne Betasamosake Simpson (this issue), we wonder if "justice" ought to be considered only within efforts that negotiate the State. Perhaps we do not have to rescue justice; perhaps justice is not rescuable from the limits of state-based forms of justice. If we take this intervention to heart, we would do better to strategize with the understanding that the very limit of justice is the state.

Justice is an impossibility. For Hartman, because redress fails and repeats, because the aim of redress is impossible, and because blackness is already configured as outside the human, demands for justice comprise a limited form of action, one that awaits "an event of epic and revolutionary proportions—the abolition of slavery, the destruction of a racist social order, and the actualization of equality."[20]

Justice as in between grievance and grief. Even though this "constancy of repetition" means a constant deferral of justice, it also means an unyielding of desire for redress that "is itself an articulation of loss and longing for remedy and reparation."[21] In other words, the chickens will come home to roost; the ghost will not fail to haunt.[22] Justice expresses desires between "grievance and grief; between the necessity of legal remedy and the impossibility of redress."[23] Indeed, in demanding justice for those killed, legal remedy against state-condoned killings is necessary, yet redress for the dead is impossible. The demands we make are part grievance and part grief. Considering justice as a redress discourse allows us to take desire seriously; we recognize the productive work of desire, of freedom-dreaming (to borrow similar notions from Robin D. G. Kelley's work on the audacity to imagine the impossible conditions of liberation).[24] Even if the desire for justice is unrequited, it produces futures beyond the current political moment.

Justice is a political interval. Redress is a "political interval . . . between the no longer and not yet,"[25] an insight that places in sharp relief the colonial temporality of justice: it is desired, deferred, haunting, always past and promised but never delivered. It is a set of political possibilities for limited relief, for continual resistance, *until.* The temporality of redress is inverted by Indigenous decolonizing temporalities, which Tuck has described as "involved with the *not yet* and, at times, the *not anymore.*"[26] Juxtaposing these two temporalities, we see how justice is framed *within* colonial time, while decolonizing *elsewheres* contest colonial time and territories.

ELSEWHERES BEYOND JUSTICE

As Leanne Betasamosake Simpson points out in this issue, Indigenous resurgence is about forms of life that do not take oppression as their defining referent. Discussing Black life, Fred Moten writes, "Everything I love survives dispossession, and is therefore before dispossession," even while Black life is already an effect of a past dispossession and future dispossession to come.[27] Such epistemologies precede and exceed injustice and, by the same token, justice.

Beyond justice, there are terms that articulate their theories of change: rematriation, reparations, regeneration, sovereignty, self-determination, decolonization, resurgence, the good life, futurisms.[28] Each approach is born of specific material concerns that refuse the abstraction of justice and its limits in the nation-state.

Glen Sean Coulthard's *Red Skin, White Masks: Rejecting the Colonial Politics of State Recognition* closes with a discussion about the future of Indigenous activism. He presents five theses of Indigenous resurgence and decolonization, each of which unmakes a fundamental co-optation of working within Western forms of systemic change. For example, Coulthard calls us to leave behind the routes of economic development offered through capitalism and to foreground gender justice. The fifth of the five theses is "beyond the nation-state." Writing from an Indigenous context of engaging the Canadian settler state, he observes that these efforts have "served to subtly reproduce the forms of racist, sexist, economic, and political configurations of power" that decolonizing efforts have intended to dismantle.[29] In much North American critical scholarship and activism, "white supremacy" is sometimes taken to be that zero-point of injustice to which social justice efforts are calibrated. This offers many possibilities for "already available" solidarities,[30] in seeing white supremacy as a "common enemy," so to speak. However, Coulthard's work suggests that the more pressing concern is to see how white supremacy creates common tools that are often picked up, reused, and recycled by efforts considered otherwise as "social justice." This is what is meant when resurgence is said to start from an "elsewhere" from injustice.

Likewise, these terms, and the articles in this issue, are also refusals of the inherent story-arc of justice (which begins with injustice). Justice as a story-arc falls back on temporality as its major mode, as highlighting a pained plaintiff, and promising redress that it never delivers. These other modes are not trying to tamper with its temporalities but root themselves in elsewheres. The authors in this issue, in our view, do their most difficult and rewarding work when they look beyond the zero-point of white supremacy and discuss the work before and surviving it.

ARTICLES ON WHAT JUSTICE WANTS

Articles in this issue sometimes offer a critique of justice, offer explanations of the impossibility of justice, offer dreams of justice that perhaps exceed the very term "justice," and offer radical alternatives to justice. We also sometimes see in these articles that "justice" is the meeting ground for politics of solidarity, where incommensurabilities are negotiated, where contingent collaborations are battle tested.

Our opening article, "Indigenous Resurgence and Co-resistance" by Leanne Betasamosake Simpson, was crafted from a set of written correspondences between Simpson and Eve Tuck. This was a way to invite Simpson to write directly to the concerns of this themed issue and to learn about how ideas Simpson has attended to across other writings and interviews come together. Simpson highlights the contributions of Indigenous scholars including Sarah Hunt, Jarett Martineau, Glen Coulthard, Audra Simpson, and Jeff Corntassel toward articulating (both naming and putting into related motion) understandings of justice that take shape outside the frames occupied by the settler state. Simpson's refusal of the notion of justice does important work for this issue, intervening on its very terms and its limits. As always, refusal is not just a no but generates other possibilities, other futures.[31]

Lena Carla Palacios's article, "Killing Abstractions: Indigenous Women and Black Trans Girls Challenging Media Necropower in White Settler States," describes solidarities at the intersections of Indigenous and Black organizing to address murdered and missing Indigenous women and murdered Black trans and nonconforming girls, in a Canadian and U.S. transnational context. Palacios highlights the strategies for mobilizing the State justice apparatus while avoiding state and media co-optation, and in so doing, for refusing the necropolitics that mark theirs as deserving deaths.

Leigh Patel and Alton Price conduct an important critique of "racial justice" in an unpacking of its histories of use and its effects in use. Their article, "The Origins, Potentials, and Limits of Racial Justice," expands on the pedagogies of Black radical traditions from W. E. B. Du Bois to contemporary antiracist pedagogies and questions the deployments of race to critique injustice and their elisions with race as a basis for justice.

In "Accounting for Carceral Reformations: Gay and Transgender Jailing in Los Angeles as Justice Impossible," Ren-yo Hwang describes the multiple routes taken by overincarcerated gay and transgender communities in Los Angeles to challenge strategic abolition and curtail the expansion of the prison system when reforms are undoubtedly predetermined by the hegemonic power of the criminal justice system. Examining K6G, the gay men and transgender women's unit within the largest jailer in the world, the Los Angeles County Men's Central Jail, Hwang critiques the advent of "abolitionist reforms" whose calculus of alleviating suffering are exchanged for increased carceral power and authority.

"Unjust Attachments: Mourning as Antagonism in Gauri Gill's '1984'" by Balbir K. Singh is a haunting analysis of the 1984 Sikh genocide on the Indian subcontinent. Leveraging Gauri Gill's 2014 artistic notebook as a counter-archive, Singh connects mourning as gendered methods for remaining and remembering to political models for resistance and militancy—including contemporary calls for Sikh sovereignty. In this way, Singh's work explores the affective work of mourning—as ontological and epistemological future-making—in imagining justice beyond the current Indian nation-state.

Juxtaposing the inquest proceedings into the suspicious deaths of Indigenous youth in Thunder Bay, Ontario, and the continual denial of clean drinking water to residents of Flint, Michigan, Stephanie Latty, Megan Scribe, Alena Peters, and Anthony Morgan take on the concept of the category "human," asking how these divergent events present deep similarities in the way they reveal who is and is not considered "human." Their article, "Not Enough Human: At the Scenes of Indigenous and Black Dispossession," considers how the neglect of what would be considered basic human rights to certain populations reveals the "deferral of justice" as a mode of racialization, genocide, and antiblackness. Indeed, their analysis resounds with

Hartman's observation of redress as bound to fail and repeat. Deferral and cyclical redress indicate the ways that desires for justice are channeled and recirculated in state justice systems, where deaths in custody also connect to concepts of certain populations as not human enough; they are so close to death, thus not worth saving.

In "On Rocks and Hard Places: A Reflection on Antiblackness in Organizing against Islamophobia," Délice Mugabo examines antiblackness and Islamophobia in the Quebecois political terrain, unearthing the complicities of organizing against Islamophobia with antiblackness on the one hand, and on the other hand, the anti-Black basis of Islamophobia to begin with. Writing from an activist intellectual perspective as a Muslim Black woman organizer, her goal is to "awaken us to some of the limits of coalition politics" and to be cautious of alliances with "dreams and projects that cannot imagine Black life." Mugabo's attention to the importance and timbre of Black life as inclusive of Black religiosity, joy, and indispensability resonates with the contributions throughout this issue.

To meaningfully close this set of articles, Denise Ferreira da Silva has generously contributed another paradigmatic piece, "The Racial Limits of Social Justice: The Ruse of Equality of Opportunity and the Global Affirmative Action Mandate." Da Silva brings attention to the global phenomenon of the rise of affirmative action (which may be surprising to some readers) and concomitant rise of the global security apparatus. She uses these twin global phenomena to illustrate how the racial is yet to satisfy—and likely cannot—as the horizon for equality.

What's not in this issue: We acknowledge the labor and efforts of the many people and thoughts not present nor immediately recognizable as present in this issue. In particular, we received numerous submissions for this issue, many of which were carefully reviewed and commented upon; in the interest of favoring activist intellectual work from nonacademic settings, we asked for creative writers to serve as reviewers to provide feedback for forms of writing that perform their theory in ways that are different from academic performances of theory. Despite these layers of review and revision and conversation, some of these pieces were not ready in time for publication. The coincidence of curation and creative timing makes for critical gaps in this issue. We feel that it is important to point to these gaps to gesture toward conversations that are happening about justice beyond the scope of these articles, and to foreshadow what is to come in future issues.

In particular, there is a marked absence on contributions from the conversations in Chicana/o studies and Asian American studies, and important transnational arenas from Latin American studies, European, and African/ diaspora studies. Hartman's description of justice as repetition resonates with Indigenous and decolonizing descriptions of colonial time (e.g., Scott Lyons, Frantz Fanon), and also resonates with Chicana feminist writings on the in-betweenness of colonial time (and space), of desires that are bounded in borderlands, and how their connections to past, present, and future leak beyond them. Works in Asian American studies and critical refugee studies that interrogate justice as impossible and/or irrelevant in the ontologies of permanent war also excite the thinking represented in this issue. Thus, these gaps engender possibilities for further thinking and writing, but a thinking and writing that we hope will be in conversation with articles that did become part of this publication. We know from our participation in the Critical Ethnic Studies Association conference and annual meetings of the American Studies Association (to name just two examples) that there is much exciting and rich work that is ongoing and exceedingly relevant to the issues described herein.

EVE TUCK (Unangax̂) is a member of the Aleut Community of St. Paul Island in Alaska. She engages in theories of decolonization in a series of collaborations, including with K. Wayne Yang, The Black/Land Project, The Super Futures Haunt Qollective, and the newly formed Land Relationships Super Collective. Her work often returns to the theories of change that (do not) operate in social science research, and moves of refusal needed for life in the undercommons of the university.

K. WAYNE YANG writes about decolonization and everyday epic organizing, particularly from underneath ghetto colonialism, often with his frequent collaborator, Eve Tuck, and sometimes for an avatar called La Paperson. Currently, he has an appointment as a professor of ethnic studies at UC San Diego. He is excited to collaborate with the Land Relationships Super Collective, the Black Teacher Project, and Roses in Concrete.

NOTES

Thank you, Nisha Toomey, for your close and elegant reading of much of the work in this issue. Thank you, reviewers, for your patient and passionate feedback. Thank you, authors, for your inspired and inspiring work. Thank you, Eric Ritskes and Rubén Gaztambide-Fernández, for ongoing advice.

1. "Critical Ethnic Studies," http://www.criticalethnicstudiesjournal.org/; "Why CESA? Why Now?," *Critical Ethnic Studies Association,* https://www.criticalethnic studies.org/content/why-cesa-why-now.

2. See the websites for these organizations: http://www.nativeyouthsexualhealth
.com/, http://galleryofthestreets.org/, blackpalestiniansolidarity.com, http://thirdeye
montreal.com, http://wechargegenocide.org/, http://sogoreate-landtrust.com/, http://
www.blacklandproject.org/, https://sites.google.com/site/indigenousleadershipforum/
program (the 2013 program), https://sites.google.com/site/indigenousleadership
forum/ilf2013-mixtape (the mixtape from the 2013 forum created by Jarrett Martineau), http://www.indianandcowboy.com/, http://thisistheread.com/.

3. "About," *Critical Ethnic Studies Association,* https://www.criticalethnicstud
ies.org/content/about.

4. John Paul Tasker, "Confusion Reigns over Number of Missing, Murdered
Indigenous Women," *CBC News,* February 16, 2016, http://www.cbc.ca/news/poli
tics/mmiw-4000-hajdu-1.3450237.

5. Emma Margolin, "Which #BlackLivesMatter? The Killings No One's Talking
About," *MSNBC,* February 2, 2015, http://www.msnbc.com/msnbc/which-blacklives
matter-the-killings-no-ones-talking-about.

6. Audre Lorde, *The Cancer Journals* (San Francisco: Aunt Lute Books, 1980),
12–13.

7. For a discussion of differences between desire in the Deleuzian sense as productive and desire in the Foucauldian sense as lack, see Eve Tuck, "Breaking Up
with Deleuze: Desire and Valuing the Irreconcilable," *International Journal of Qualitative Studies in Education* 23, no. 5 (2010): 635–50.

8. Gilles Deleuze and Félix Guattari, *A Thousand Plateaus: Capitalism and
Schizophrenia* (Minneapolis: University of Minnesota Press, 1987).

9. Stephen Best and Saidiya Hartman, "Fugitive Justice," *Representations* 92, no.
1 (2005): 3.

10. Leanne Betasamosake Simpson, *Dancing on Our Turtle's Back: Stories of
Nishnaabeg Re-Creation, Resurgence and a New Emergence* (Winnipeg: Arbeiter
Ring, 2011), 13.

11. Best and Hartman, "Fugitive Justice"; Saidiya V. Hartman, *Scenes of Subjection: Terror, Slavery, and Self-Making in Nineteenth-Century America* (New York:
Oxford University Press, 1997).

12. Hartman, *Scenes of Subjection,* 77.

13. Ibid., 76–77.

14. Nancy Leong, "Racial Capitalism," *Harvard Law Review* 126, no. 8 (2013):
2153–226; Tiffany Lethabo King, "Labor's Aphasia: Toward Antiblackness as Constitutive to Settler Colonialism," *Decolonization: Indigeneity, Education & Society,* June
10, 2014, https://decolonization.wordpress.com/2014/06/10/labors-aphasia-toward
-antiblackness-as-constitutive-to-settler-colonialism/.

15. For differing analyses of "human," in terms of "man" as white, propertied,
and so on, and thus predicated on colonial anti-Indigenous/antiblackness, see Sylvia Wynter, "Unsettling the Coloniality of Being/Power/Truth/Freedom: Towards
the Human, after Man, Its Overrepresentation—An Argument," *New Centennial
Review* 3, no. 3 (2003): 257–337; and Denise Ferreira da Silva, *Toward a Global Idea
of Race* (Minneapolis: University of Minnesota Press, 2007).

16. Hartman, *Scenes of Subjection,* 76.

17. Ibid., 77.

18. Giorgio Agamben, *Homo Sacer: Sovereign Power and Bare Life*, trans. Daniel Heller-Roazen (Stanford: Stanford University Press, 1998).

19. Jodi A. Byrd, *The Transit of Empire: Indigenous Critiques of Colonialism*, First Peoples (Minneapolis: University of Minnesota Press, 2011); Steven Sailata, *Anti-Arab Racism in the USA: Where It Comes from and What It Means for Politics Today* (London: Pluto Press, 2006).

20. Hartman, *Scenes of Subjection*, 77.

21. Ibid.

22. Malcolm X, "God's Judgement of White America (The Chickens Come Home to Roost)" (speech, December 4, 1963), http://www.malcolm-x.org/speeches/spc_120463.htm; Avery F. Gordon, *Ghostly Matters: Haunting and the Sociological Imagination* (Minneapolis: University of Minnesota Press, 1997); Eve Tuck and C. Ree, "A Glossary of Haunting," in *Handbook of Autoethnography*, ed. Stacey Holman Jones, Tony E. Adams, and Carolyn Ellis (Walnut Creek, Calif.: Left Coast Press, 2013), 639–58; Angie Morrill, Eve Tuck, and the Super Futures Haunt Qollective, "Before Dispossession, or Surviving It," *Liminalities* 12, no. 1 (2016): 1–20.

23. Best and Hartman, "Fugitive Justice," 3.

24. Robin D. G. Kelley, *Freedom Dreams: The Black Radical Imagination* (Boston: Beacon Press, 2002).

25. Best and Hartman, "Fugitive Justice," 3.

26. Eve Tuck, "Suspending Damage: A Letter to Communities," *Harvard Educational Review* 79, no. 3 (2009): 417.

27. Fred Moten, "The Subprime and the Beautiful," *African Identities* 11, no. 2 (2013): 242.

28. On rematriation, see Eve Tuck, "Rematriating Curriculum Studies," *Journal of Curriculum and Pedagogy* 8 (2011): 34–37; ReMatriate, Twitter, https://twitter.com/ReMatriate. On reparations, see Ta-Nehisi Coates, "The Case for Reparations," *Atlantic*, June 2014, http://www.theatlantic.com/magazine/archive/2014/06/the-case-for-reparations/361631/. On sovereignty, see Joanne Barker, ed., *Sovereignty Matters: Locations of Contestation and Possibility in Indigenous Struggles for Self-Determination* (Lincoln: University of Nebraska Press, 2005). On decolonization, see Maile Arvin, Eve Tuck, and Angie Morrill, "Decolonizing Feminism: Challenging Connections between Settler Colonialism and Heteropatriarchy," *Feminist Formations* 25, no. 1 (2013): 8–34. On resurgence, see Glen Sean Coulthard, *Red Skin, White Masks: Rejecting the Colonial Politics of State Recognition* (Minneapolis: University of Minnesota Press, 2014); Jeff Corntassel, "Re-envisioning Resurgence: Indigenous Pathways to Decolonization and Sustainable Self Determination," *Decolonization: Indigeneity, Education & Society* 1, no. 1 (2012): 86–101.

29. Coulthard, *Red Skin, White Masks*, 179.

30. Dylan Rodríguez, *Suspended Apocalypse: White Supremacy, Genocide, and the Filipino Condition* (Minneapolis: University of Minnesota Press, 2009), 31.

31. Audra Simpson, *Mohawk Interruptus: Political Life across the Borders of Settler States* (Durham, N.C.: Duke University Press, 2014).

ESSAYS

Indigenous Resurgence and Co-resistance

LEANNE BETASAMOSAKE SIMPSON

This article was created by a correspondence between Leanne Betasamosake Simpson and Eve Tuck between December 2015 and February 2016. Simpson was writing from Peterborough and Montreal, and Tuck was writing from Atlantic City and then Toronto. Tuck worked with K. Wayne Yang to develop an initial set of prompts, and the conversation launched from there. We have presented a tidied-up version of the correspondence here, keeping back parts that were just for us, and fine-tuning other portions for a public audience. We are grateful to K. Wayne Yang, LeKeisha Hughes, Eric Ritskes, and Nisha Toomey, who did some filling-in on references, formatting, notes, and editing of this correspondence to bring it into manuscript form.

Leanne Betasamosake Simpson is a Michi Saagiig Nishnaabeg storyteller, scholar, and activist and a member of Alderville First Nation. In her acclaimed book *Dancing on Our Turtle's Back: Stories of Nishnaabeg Re-Creation, Resurgence and a New Emergence* (2011), Simpson critically and actively engages resistance and resurgence through the context of Nishnaabeg theories, philosophies, and stories. Utilizing storytelling as a decolonizing process with the power to recall, envision, and create modes of resurgence and contesting cognitive imperialisms, Simpson has utilized this power throughout her short stories and poetry. Along with actively writing on Nishnaabeg pedagogy through stories, notions of land, and collectivity, Simpson has written on a breadth of topics including Indigenous resistance and resurgence through and beyond the Idle No More movement, the estimated four thousand missing and murdered Indigenous women in Canada,[1] and the accompanying four hundred years of gendered colonial violence. Also a musician, songwriter, and performer, Simpson accompanied her first book of short stories, *Islands of Decolonial Love* (2013), with a full-length album featuring Indigenous musicians from across Canada. Simpson's publications include *The Gift Is in the Making: Anishinaabeg Stories* (2013),

Lighting the Eighth Fire: The Liberation, Resurgence, and Protection of Indigenous Nations (2008, editor), *This Is an Honour Song: Twenty Years since the Blockades* (2010, edited with Kiera Ladner), and *The Winter We Danced: Voices from the Past, the Future, and the Idle No More Movement* (2014, contributor, edited by Kino-nda-niimi collective). Simpson's next book of short stories and poetry, *This Accident of Being Lost,* will be published by the House of Anansi Press in the spring of 2017.

EVE TUCK: One of the things that K. Wayne Yang and I have learned in editing this themed issue of *Critical Ethnic Studies* on "what justice wants" is that writing as directly as possible about what is meant by social justice is a challenge. What is your sense of what is difficult about this task?

LEANNE BETASAMOSAKE SIMPSON: It's difficult because the state has co-opted narratives of justice in complex ways, especially against Indigenous and Black peoples. For example, the Canadian state land claims processes purport to be about righting the wrongs of the past, but they are really just a way of terminating Indigenous rights and bringing legal certainty to land conflicts. The criminal justice system is another narrative of justice that ends up not being about justice at all; it ends up murdering Black people and Indigenous peoples at high rates, and criminalizing our communities. "Social justice" work is often about righting some of these wrongs, and inequalities, but in my own mind, this is different than the movements that are built and maintained within marginalized communities. As Indigenous communities, we often have social justice groups wanting to help, but they fall into a white savior complex by centering whiteness or being unwilling to join in the ways that Indigenous peoples are already organizing at the community level.

Many of the scholars and activists reading these words likely work in social justice, and likely they are doing valuable work with the communities of which they are a part. My contribution here is not meant to challenge good work. In my life as a scholar, a writer, an activist, and a mom within the Indigenous community, I haven't ever been a part of a group that uses the frame "social justice" for its work. I trust that those working in social justice will take my thoughts here in the spirit that they are intended—to share different modalities of thinking and practicing. My experience lies in using Indigenous theory, thought, and processes to rebuild Indigenous conceptualizations of nationhood. I am interested in movement building and mobilization as a mechanism to dismantle settler colonialism, and in using Indigenous practices to do so. I am a member of Alderville First Nation and I work within the practices and ethics of Michi Saagiig Nishnaabeg people.

Justice is a concept within Western thought that is intrinsically linked to settler colonialism. Indigenous thought systems conceptualize justice differently. We have experienced four centuries of apocalyptic violence in the name of dispossession in the part of the Nishnaabeg nation I am from and live in. White supremacy, capitalism, and heteropatriarchy have targeted and continue to murder, disappear, attack, criminalize, and de-value our bodies, minds, and spirits. Several of the plant and animal nations we share territory with have been exterminated. "Justice" to me, in the face of all that, means the return of land, the regeneration of Indig-enous political, educational, and knowledge systems, the rehabilitation of the natural world, and the destruction of white supremacy, capitalism, and heteropatriarchy. "Justice" within the confines of settler colonialism gets paralytically overwhelmed in the face of that. So I don't think about justice very much. I think about resurgence and movement building.

I don't want to say a lot here about settler-colonial narratives around justice because there are scholars, public intellectuals, and activists who've spent much more time analyzing these narratives, but I think for Indig-enous peoples, when Canada or the United States talks about justice in terms of Indigenous peoples, it's never about justice for us. A lot of the time state justice is about white people feeling better about themselves. State narratives of justice are processes that are about injustice for us—a system that steals our people and locks them up so the state can access our land for the exploitation of natural resources. In Canada, we've just gone through a truth and reconciliation process around residential schools where the conversation focused on individual pain and suffering. We were unable to account for how residential schools were a strategic tool of dis-possession. We were unable to talk about regenerating the damage caused to Indigenous political systems, languages, or spirituality, for instance. Now we are about to embark on a national inquiry into missing and mur-dered Indigenous women and girls, and scholar Sarah Hunt recently asked on Twitter, "What does 'justice' look like within a [government]-led inquiry when violence against us continues to be a daily reality?"[2] Hunt's longer interview talks about the limitations of the national inquiry, the steps we can take to make it more meaningful to Indigenous women, and the concrete short-term steps that can be taken right now to improve things.[3] Hunt was also questioning the state's ability to address the root causes of violences against Indigenous women, when it is actively engaged in violences against Indigenous women in order to maintain dispossession. Mohawk scholar Audra Simpson's work on the murdering, disappearing, and erasing of Indigenous women's fleshly bodies because they are symbols of Indigenous political orders that call into question the legitimacy of state sovereignty is crucial to this set of ideas because it points directly to the limitations of government-led inquiries into obtaining justice for these kinds of violence.[4] Audra's work seems to me to be so important right now. To me, dispossession is a structural relationship Indigenous peoples have to the state. The destruction of Indigenous bodies takes place to remove us from our physical, mental, emotional, and spiritual relationships to land primarily so that the land can be exploited for natural resources. How can we utter the word "justice" in Canada and not be talking about that?

JUSTICE THAT STARTS FROM GROUNDED NORMATIVITY

My thinking starts with reflecting on the idea of justice within Michi Saagiig Nishnaabeg thought, because this is the area I work in. It starts with how we live in the world. Relationships within Indigenous thought are paramount. I think for Indigenous peoples, whether we are talking about justice or solidarity or whatever, we need to start within our intelligence systems, or what Dene scholar Glen Sean Coulthard calls "grounded normativity"—the systems of ethics that are continuously generated by a relationship with a particular place, with land, through the Indigenous processes and knowledges that make up Indigenous life.[5] For me, it's these theories and practices that form Indigenous constructions of reality, of life, and of how to ethically relate to the plant and animal nations, our families, the waters, the skyworld, communities, and nations. Decolonizing, to me, means centering grounded normativity in my life and in the life of my community, while critically analyzing and critiquing the ways in which I'm replicating white supremacy, antiblackness, heteropatriarchy, and capitalisms—structures that are ethically horrific and profoundly unjust within Nishnaabeg grounded normativity. Indigenous resurgence, in its most radical form, is nation building, not nation-state building, but nation building, again, in the context of grounded normativity by centring, amplifying, animating, and actualizing the processes of grounded normativity as flight paths or fugitive escapes from the violences of settler colonialism. This resurgence creates profoundly different ways of thinking, organizing, and being because the Indigenous processes that give birth to our collective resurgence are fundamentally nonhierarchical, nonexploitative, nonextractivist, and nonauthoritarian.

Grounded normativity generates nations as networks of complex, layered, multidimensional, intimate relationships with human and nonhuman beings. Our societies work very well when those relationships are balanced. Our legal system isn't a series of "laws" based on authoritarian power with punishments for when the laws are broken. It is an embedded and interwoven spiritual, emotional, and social system of intelligence that fosters independence, community, and self-determination in individuals. It is centered around individuals, a diversity of individuals acting in a way that promotes and brings about more life, and more creation. This way of living in individuals amplifies out into families, communities, and nations. The well-being of individuals is directly linked to the well-being of collectives. When an individual is hurt or sick or having a hard time, there is impact throughout the system, and the community has the obligation to respond.

When there is conflict or something goes wrong, we have processes to hear from everyone involved. These processes allow the community of people impacted by the imbalance to learn the context of the individuals directly involved. It allows the individuals to account for themselves and their actions. It focuses on repairing and regenerating relationships and this restoration is something that happens repeatedly across scales with individuals, their interactions with plants and animals, and their families, communities, and nations. It is a supportive system of processing trauma, of taking measures spiritually, and of accounting for loss or hurt. These are the same processes of Nishnaabeg diplomacy we use in conflicts internationally.

PLACE-BASED INTERNATIONALISM

EVE: One idea that Wayne and I floated in our call for papers is that how a person or community understands the roots or source of injustice will have implications for how they go about undoing that injustice. Does this make sense to you? Might it be too simplistic or problematic?

LEANNE: I think we need to be a bit careful here, particularly in the academy. I think Indigenous peoples understand pretty well injustice in their own lives whether or not they can articulate it using the language of colonialism or decolonization. I think movements that link social realities with political systems and focus on creating real-world-on-the-ground alternatives are powerful. I worry that too much of our energy goes into trying to influence the system rather than creating the alternatives. It matters to me how change is achieved. Change achieved through struggle, organizing, and creating the alternatives produces profoundly different outcomes than change achieved through recognition-focused protest, and pressuring the state to make the changes for us. That is a recipe for co-option.

I think it is important to understand root causes of injustice, but it is also important to understand think strategically and intelligently about approaches to undoing that injustice. I think that diagnosis and strategic action must be done within grounded normativity. Indigenous thought has a tradition of place-based internationalism that I think is this beautifully fertile spot because it links place-based thinking and struggle with the same decolonial pockets of thinking throughout the world. Nishnaabeg have been linking ourselves to the rest of the world since the beginning of time, and throughout our resistance to colonialism we have our people traveling throughout the world to link with other communities of resistors. Grassy Narrows First Nation comes to mind in their nearly four-decade fight against mercury poisoning in their river system and the relationship they have made with the Japanese community in Mnimata.[6]

We need to use our experiences in the past to think critically about how we respond to injustice today. Right now, Indigenous peoples in Canada need to be thinking critically about the implications of seeking recognition within the colonial state because we have a government that is very good at neoliberalism and seducing our hope for their purposes. Again, Glen Sean Coulthard, in *Red Skin, White Masks,* using the Dene nation's experience in the 1970s, provides a blistering critique of the pitfalls of seeking political recognition within state structures. He makes the point that continually seeking recognition with the settler-colonial state is a process of co-option and neutralization, and is a way of bringing Indigenous peoples into the systems that guts our resistance movements, for instance, and we get very little in return.[7] In fact, in terms of dispossession—that is, the removal, murdering, displacement, and destruction of the relationship between Indigenous bodies and Indigenous land—this serves only to facilitate land loss, not improve things. Engagement with the system changes Indigenous peoples more than it changes the system. This can be destructive in terms of resurgence because resurgent movements are trying to do the opposite—we are trying to center Indigenous practices and thoughts in our lives as everyday acts of resistance, and grow those actions and processes into a mass mobilization.

I think it is useful to apply this same critique of recognition to orga-nizing and mobilizing with the purpose of making a switch from mobi-lizing around victim-based narratives—that is, publically demonstrating the pain of loss as a mechanism to appeal to the moral and ethical fabric of Canadian society (which has over and over again proven to be morally bankrupt when it comes to Indigenous peoples)—to using that same pain and anger to fuel resurgent actions. This organizing from within grounded normativity has always fueled Indigenous resistance and con-tinues to happen all the time in Indigenous communities—it is just often misread by others. The community of Hollow Water First Nation created the Community Holistic Circle of Healing as a Nishnaabeg restoration of relationships, or a restorative justice model to address sexual violence in their community.[8] Christi Belcourt's *Walking with Our Sisters* exhibit has created a traveling display of 1,800 moccasin vamps as a way of honoring and commemorating missing and murdered Indigenous women and children in Canada and the United States. The exhibit does not rely on state funding.[9] Thousands of volunteers made the vamps. The exhibit works with local communities and their cultural and spiritual practices to install the exhibit and do the necessary ceremony and community processes. *Walking with Our Sisters* works with local organizers a year in advance of installation, using Indigenous processes to embed the art in community on the terms of the local community. There is also the work of countless urban Indigenous organizations supporting the families of MMIWG2S people. The Native Youth Sexual Health Network provides on-the-ground, community-embedded, peer-to-peer support around sex-ual health and addiction for youth.[10] The Akwesasne Freedom School provides Mohawk education for Mohawk children.[11] The Iroquois national and Haudenosaunee women's lacrosse teams travel using Haudenosau-nee passports instead of American or Canadian ones.[12] The Unist'ot'en Camp pursues land protection resurgent action and the reclamation of the original name of Mount Douglas, PKOLS, in the city of Victoria, British Columbia.[13]

COLLECTION OF COLLECTIVES

EVE: Might you also discuss the relationship between the personal and the collective with regard to justice? Particularly for Indigenous peoples, the collective is a fundamental unit of being and knowing—and the collective extends beyond human life. What do you think about the relationship between the personal and the collective when it comes to justice? Furthermore, might there be times when the personal and the collective desires for justice are incommensurable with one another? How might we rethink the personal and the collective in imagining justice?

LEANNE: When I consider this within Anishinaabeg thought, my understanding is that we are more a collection of collectives, so I don't see a tension between individuals or collectives. Individuals are hubs of networks. When an individual is hurt, then the system is out of balance. These things are directly linked in Anishinaabeg thought. Of course we can push it to the point where an individual is having a huge negative impact on the community and something has to be done. We have processes for that, but I believe those situations are rare. In reality, if you set up a society that fosters individual diversity, promotes individual self-determination, encourages self-actualization and accountability, and nurtures intimate relationships among individuals, you might not ever encounter such a situation in your lifetime. The Nishnaabeg have a huge body of stories that surround us and provide so many different ways of solving problems and conflicts within our communities. I'm not sure that focusing on the rare occasions that an individual has to be removed from society is so important. I am much more interested in building the conditions that support the regeneration of these social, political, spiritual, and legal systems within our communities and creating a generation of individuals that has the intelligence to create the alternatives.

I don't want to be too prescriptive here because for Indigenous peoples this kind of knowledge has to be learned in a particular way. You can't read an academic paper or a book about it and think you know what you are talking about. That's not the way our intelligence systems work. This kind of knowledge needs to be learned in relationship to the place that generated it, with or in our languages, using Indigenous processes and expertise. It is different for unique Indigenous nations and communities. There are different ways of interpreting knowledge that collectives of people need to figure out. My point here is that I think it is important for Indigenous peoples to do this work individually and in community with others. The point of resurgence isn't to present case studies and then have them replicated in other communities. That won't work. It is for Indigenous peoples to regenerate the processes and ways of living of our ancestors, our practices, our grounded normativity, within an Indigenous criticality (so we aren't mistakenly replicating the logics of settler colonialism) and figuring out how to center this in our individual lives and in the collectives of which we are a part. This is a different way of living in the world. It changes us. Engaging in different processes and practices changes not only those involved but the outcome. Resurgence is an emergent and generative process.

RESURGENCE AND CONSTELLATIONS

I'm actually not interested in justice. I'm interested in Indigenous resurgence, nation building, addressing gender violence, movement building, linking up and creating constellations of co-resistance with other movements. I'm interested in making sure the movement around Indigenous resurgence is not replicating gender violence by placing bodies at our center. I'm interested in making sure we are not replicating heteropatriarchy or antiblackness by learning how to engage in constellations of co-resistance. I'm interested in freedom and creating a social, economic, political, artistic, spiritual, and physical space for futures of Anishinaabe people to be Anishinaabe on our land, unharassed and undeterred.

I'm in the process of writing a new book on resurgent mobilization and I've been thinking a lot about constellations within Nishnaabeg thought. Dene/Cree scholar Jarrett Martineau's dissertation, "Creative Combat: Indigenous Art, Resurgence, and Decolonization," uses the artistic practices of a diverse series of Indigenous provocateurs to examine the decolonizing potential of art-making to disrupt and interrogate forms of settler colonialism and advance the project of resurgence and Indigenous nation building.[14] He really advances this idea of the constellation drawing upon the work of Indigenous artists' collectives and folks like Black Constellation. Jarrett uses particular concepts and theories to create constellations that are flight paths or doorways out of settler-colonialist representation and thought. That's interesting to me. What happens when we make a constellation out of, say, Audra Simpson's work on the politics of refusal, Glen Coulthard's work on recognition, and Jarrett Martineau's work on constellated relationships in the context of my own work on Nishnaabeg resurgence? I'm trying to figure that out.

To me, in terms of organizing, this idea resonates both within Nishnaabeg thought but also in the aftermath of Idle No More. It is clear to me that we need to think about what resurgent mobilizing looks like. What does solidarity look like within grounded normativity?[15] How do we use Indigenous place-based internationalism to build constellations of co-resistance with non-Indigenous communities who are fighting different

aspects of the same system? This idea that you can bring particular theories or concepts together fits so well with Nishnaabeg star mapping and
story. I'd like to apply this on the ground in terms of organizing—
individuals or small collectives (stars) organizing within grounded normativity and connected to other individuals or collectives (stars) through
Indigenous internationalism makes a lot of sense in terms of creating
doorways out of settler colonialism.

EVE: I am particularly excited by this last set of ideas—I think it makes
sense to continue the rest of our discussion with the terms that you have
laid out, including resurgence, nation building, addressing gender violence and antiblackness, movement building, and creating constellations
of co-resistance. Jeff Corntassel and others have been writing/speaking
about everyday acts of resurgence—these are acts that are usually land
based and/or language based, which enlivens Indigenous sovereignty.
Can you address the everydayness of resurgence, but also the more occa-
sional, the *not everydayness* of resurgence?

LEANNE: I first began thinking about resurgence in a serious way when I
was working on *Dancing on Our Turtle's Back*.[16] I thought of resurgence
as a new theory or lens through which to think about Indigenous liberation. I set out to explore the idea of turning inward and rebuilding Indigenous nations on Indigenous terms using our intelligence and political
thought. Through the course of thinking about resurgence from within
Nishnaabeg thought I came to understand that it is an assemblage of
meta-processes that encapsulates how one constructs and lives in the
world. Indigenous worlds aren't institutions or states, they are relationships, movement, processes—life itself. I came to understand that the
theories or stories or philosophies of resurgence inherent in Indigenous
thought were the ways my ancestors had always lived. Recognizing this
was important for me. The emergent qualities of Indigenous intelligence
systems means that we have to be engaged with our physical bodies,
minds, emotions, and spiritual selves in processes for new ideas and the
alternatives to capitalism or heteropatriarchy or settler colonialism to
emerge. We have visions and then build the alternatives.

Cherokee scholar Jeff Corntassel's research on Indigenous pathways
of resurgence recently focused on identifying "everyday practices of renewal and responsibility within native communities today" by asking
"how will your ancestors and future generations recognize you as Indigenous?"[17] His challenge is for communities and individuals to reject state
affirmation and recognition and the performativity of the rights-based

discourse, to move beyond political awareness and symbolic gestures to everyday place-practices of resurgence. He warns against the politics of distraction—states' attempts to move us away from the renewal of place-based practices—and encourages us to center our individual and communal lives around renewal.

REAL-WORLD RELEVANCE OF COULTHARD'S CRITIQUE OF RECOGNITION

EVE: Glen Coulthard's book *Red Skin, White Masks* makes a critique of recognition that you seem to be engaging at different points in our correspondence so far. Might you say more about what you are learning from this important critique?

LEANNE: *Red Skin, White Masks* really changed the way I thought in the way George Manual's *Fourth World* did, Lee Maracle's *I Am Woman* did, and Taiaiake Alfred's *Peace, Power and Righteousness* did before.[18] Glen provides us with a stellar critique of recognition in Indigenous politics in relation to the Canadian state. *Red Skin, White Masks* is a book that I've thought constantly about over the past year and it's generated a lot of new thinking in me—especially the last chapter of that book, the resurgence that he gets to at the very end.[19] Indigenous peoples are often stuck in the position of having to make the best of things or of having to react to the state because the state holds power over our lives and our land. A great deal of our strategies for change hinge on state recognition and I think Glen really clearly and meticulously points out why that is problematic. As much as it is problematic, it is epidemic in how we think and organize, and I think that's likely what resonated with me so profoundly in this book. The idea that engagement with the settler-colonial political system changes you more than you can change it is something I continue to try and think very deeply about because while Glen confined his critique to politics, you can take his theoretical intervention and apply it to all of the intertwined systems of oppression that make up settler colonialism—including education, organizing, and mobilization. This is timely particularly in Canada because we have a government that is signaling (at least in superficial ways) that liberal recognition is the cornerstone of its interactions with Indigenous peoples. A number of radical scholars and organizers predict that in these situations of liberal recognition, mass movements that might have existed under Stephen Harper will all but collapse.

Some people have criticized *Red Skin, White Masks* as a book that is just for academics or that is too theoretical to be relevant to the real world. My reaction to the work was the opposite. To me it is shockingly real-world relevant. If we take Glen's analysis to heart, then what we should be doing right now is interrogating state recognition in our organizing and our responses to liberalism and figuring out what resurgent mobilization looks like. Perhaps Justin Trudeau is an opportunity, but how we use this opportunity and who benefits from it are important things to think about.

It is also significant to me that the Trudeau government, while signaling a new relationship with Indigenous peoples, has engaged in anti-blackness. This has happened through racist stereotypical comments on violence against women, the erasure of issues of concern to the Black community throughout the campaign, and in the complete absence of Black MPs in the "most diverse cabinet" in Canadian history.[20] Within Indigenous thought, within resurgence, it matters how change is achieved and with whom we achieve it. Indigenous nationhood cannot replicate heteropatriarchy or antiblackness.

CREATING MATERIAL BASES FOR THE NATIONS WE WANT

EVE: Every time I do a talk on theories of change, especially on Indigenous feminist theories of change, someone in the audience asks me to talk about what settlers can do to aid in Indigenous rematriation. This is not that type of question! But I do want to learn more from you about how you see your understandings of change in relation to other theories of change—more about Martineau's constellation that you mentioned. It seems that you are saying that theories of change/justice/injustice are specific—both historically and land specific. But is there anything to be said for how all of this specificity coheres with other specificities? Latches with other movements?

LEANNE: I get that first type of question about what settlers can do a lot and I hate it because it erases everything I've said in my talk and tries to recenter the talk on whiteness; we need to stop providing the space for that.

We have to create material bases for the nationhoods we want. We can't rely on the culture that capitalism creates. We just can't. We can't achieve Indigenous nationhoods while replicating antiblackness. We can't have resurgence without centering gender and queerness, and creating alternative systems of accountability for sexual and gender violence. Therefore, we need to create constellations of connections with other radical thinkers and doers and makers. We need to build mass movements with radical labor, with Black communities, with radical communities of color. We need to stop providing space for the "What can white allies do" questions and set up spaces where we can connect with other social movements and create constellations of mutual support and co-resistance. My experience as an Indigenous woman is with colonialism, settler colonialism, occupation and gender violence, and connecting with radical Black feminists, for instance, is rich ground for me because we have different but intimately related experiences with white supremacy. I watched the recent Black Radical Tradition conference online and I thought, wow, these comrades are thinking and writing similar things to me and my Indigenous comrades and maybe there is something in that.[21] Not that I want to take and exploit their intellectual work, but more of a, hey—they have their shit together, they have public intellectuals, they have movements on the ground. They aren't afraid to talk about the root of things.

That's why resurgence is so important. I am not particularly interested in holding states accountable because the structure, history, and nature of states is exploitative by nature. I'm interested in alternatives, I'm interested in building new worlds. That's not to say that movements that are working to hold states accountable should do something differently—only they would know that. It's not my place to critique that. I'm saying on a very personal level, this is not where my skills and thinking lie. I work exclusively with Indigenous peoples and theoretically my thinking and work is based in Indigenous resurgence.

Indigenous peoples standing up on our lands in a principled, strategic, and articulate way, embodying change, is a fundamentally different approach than begging the colonizer for their pity, or centering whiteness in solidarity or in allyship. We are not relying on victim narratives. We need to come at this from a place of principled strength having done the work, and we need to have the backs of other communities and movements, instead of continuing to dance for whiteness. There are other movements doing a better job of this right now than we are. Grounded normativity has no space for exploitation, heteropatriarchy, white supremacy, or antiblackness.

WHAT WE ARE MAKING THROUGH CONSTELLATIONS OF CO-RESISTANCE

EVE: Two of the ideas that you have described in other interviews have been deeply resonant with me—I think of them all the time with great appreciation. The first comes in an interview you did with Naomi Klein. Speaking about Mi'kmaq mothers, grandmothers, aunties, sisters, and daughters—armed with drums and feathers against the pointed rifles of the RCMP—and their choice to lay their bodies on their land to protest and protect their land from fracking, you said, "Our bodies should be on the land so that our grandchildren have something left to stand upon."[22]

The other idea came up in an interview-conversation between you, Glen Coulthard, and Eric Ritskes in which you talk about how your children have learned about being Nishnaabeg on Denendeh land—perhaps even more than when they are home. You said:

> One of the things I noticed with my kids when they're in Denendeh, is that they operate as Nishnaabeg people more so than I think they do at home sometimes. They notice different changes in traditions and different cultural changes, and I think they feel really, really proud of who they are at Dechinta. They have an opportunity to practice how to live respectfully in someone else's territory, according to Nishnaabeg traditions. They recognize Dechinta as a safe place to be who they are and express their opinions and perspectives.[23]

To close this correspondence, I wonder if you might bring these ideas together to talk about the kinds of present and kinds of futurities we might go about making for our children, and their children?

LEANNE: The primary way my ancestors and I have interacted with the state is through dispossession—the removal of Indigenous bodies from Indigenous lands. My disconnection from Indigenous thought, languages, and practices has been orchestrated by dispossession, as had the erasure of Indigenous bodies from the present. This is a dispossession of every meaningful relationship from my life. In building a radical resurgent movement—and by radical I mean one that addresses the root—I think we need to be centering our attachment to each other, the land, and our intelligence systems. We need to be creating a present that will inspire a radically different future than the one settler colonialism sets out for us. This means taking on heteropatriarchy, white supremacy, capitalism, and antiblackness, and actualizing Indigenous alternatives on the ground, not in the future but in the present. Indigenous alternatives that are rooted in Indigenous intelligence, or to again use Coulthard's term, grounded normativity. This means a land base, and nations that are physical, emotional, spiritual, artistic, and creative spaces where Indigenous peoples can be Indigenous. This means not centering white allyship but building relationships with our comrades in other commnities that are already doing this work in the context of their own communities and movement-constellations of co-resistance. And it means doing this work in the present so our kids know what freedom feels like, so they know what it feels like to be from a particular Indigenous nation whether they are in downtown Toronto, in the bush, or behind a blockade, so they know what to fight for.

NOTES

1. John Paul Tasker, "Confusion Reigns over Number of Missing, Murdered Indigenous Women," *CBC News,* February 16, 2016, http://www.cbc.ca/news/poli tics/mmiw-4000-hajdu-1.3450237.

2. Sarah Hunt, Twitter post, December 7, 2015, 5:32 p.m., https://twitter.com/ thesarahhunt/status/674037137059090433.

3. Sarah Hunt, "Do We Need an Inquiry to End Violence against Indigenous Women?," interview by Jim Brown, *CBC/Radio-Canada,* November 1, 2015, http:// www.cbc.ca/radio/the180/mmiw-inquiry-debunking-electoral-reform-and-what -is-the-west-1.3295363/do-we-need-an-inquiry-to-end-violence-against-indigenous -women-1.3295403.

4. Audra Simpson, *Mohawk Interruptus: Political Life across the Borders of Set-tler States* (Durham, N.C.: Duke University Press, 2014); Audra Simpson, "The Chief's Two Bodies" (keynote presented at "International R.A.C.E. Conference," Edmonton, October 2015).

5. Glen Sean Coulthard, *Red Skin, White Masks: Rejecting the Colonial Politics of Recognition* (Minneapolis: University of Minnesota Press, 2014), 60.

6. See, for instance, "Feds Waited 15 years to Act on Tainted Tap Water in Grassy Narrows," *Free Grassy Narrows,* September 2, 2015, http://freegrassy.net/feds-waited -15-years-to-act-on-tainted-tap-water-in-grassy-narrows; ICTMN Staff, "Mercury Poisoning Five Decades Later for Grassy Narrows and White Dog First Nations," *Indian Country Today Media Network,* June 12, 2012, http://indiancountrytoday medianetwork.com/2012/06/12/mercury-poisoning-five-decades-later-grassy-nar rows-and-white-dog-first-nations-117843; and Kelly Crowe, "Grassy Narrows: Why Is Japan Still Studying the Mercury Poisoning When Canada Isn't?," *CBC News,* September 2, 2014, http://www.cbc.ca/news/health/grassy-narrows-why-is-japan -still-studying-the-mercury-poisoning-when-canada-isn-t-1.2752360.

7. Coulthard, *Red Skin, White Masks,* esp. 51–78.

8. Berma Bushie, "Community Holistic Circle of Healing," International Insti-tute for Restorative Practices, August 7, 1999, http://www.iirp.edu/article_detail.php ?article_id=NDco.

9. See the exhibit's website at http://walkingwithoursisters.ca/.

10. See the organization's website at http://www.nativeyouthsexualhealth.com/.

11. Louellyn White, *Free to Be Mohawk: Indigenous Education at the Akwesasne Freedom School* (Norman: University of Oklahoma Press, 2015).

12. Sam Laskaris, "Passports Rejected: Haudenosaunee Women's LAX Withdraws from World Championships," *Indian Country Today Media Network,* July 20, 2015, http://indiancountrytodaymedianetwork.com/2015/07/20/passports-rejected-haudenosaunee-womens-lax-withdraws-world-championships-161139.

13. "Who We Are: Wet'suwet'en Peoples (Yinka Dini—People of this Earth)," Unist'ot'en Camp, http://unistotencamp.com/; Leanne Betasamosake Simpson, "The PKOLS Reclamation: Saturating the Land with Our Stories," rabble.ca, May 22, 2013, http://rabble.ca/news/2013/05/pkols-reclamation-saturating-land-our-stories.

14. Jarrett Martineau, "Creative Combat: Indigenous Art, Resurgence, and Decolonization" (PhD diss., University of Victoria, 2015).

15. Glen Coulthard and Leanne Betasamosake Simpson, "Grounded Normativity/Place-Based Solidarity," *American Quarterly* 68, no. 2 (2016): 249–55.

16. Leanne Betasamosake Simpson, *Dancing on Our Turtle's Back: Stories of Nishnaabeg Re-Creation, Resurgence and a New Emergence* (Winnipeg: Arbeiter Ring, 2011).

17. Jeff Corntassel, "Re-envisioning Resurgence: Indigenous Pathways to Decolonization and Sustainable Self-Determination," *Decolonization: Indigeneity, Education & Society* 1, no. 1 (2012): 86, 88.

18. George Manual, *The Fourth World: An Indian Reality* (Toronto: Collier-Macmillan, 1974); Lee Maracle, *I Am Woman: A Native Perspective on Sociology and Feminism* (Vancouver: Press Gang Publishers, 1996); Taiaiake Alfred, *Peace, Power and Righteousness: An Indigenous Manifesto* (Toronto: Oxford University Press Canada, 1999).

19. Coulthard, *Red Skin, White Masks,* 178–79.

20. Robin Levinson King, "Justin Trudeau Called Out for Statements Made about Music Causing Violence against Women," *Toronto Star,* September 22, 2015, http://www.thestar.com/news/federal-election/2015/09/22/justin-trudeau-points-finger-at-communities-for-causing-violence-against-women.html.

21. For more information on the January 2016 "Reclaiming Our Future: The Black Radical Tradition in Our Time" conference, see http://www.theblackradicaltradition.org/conference-info/.

22. Naomi Klein, "Dancing the World into Being: A Conversation with Idle No More's Leanne Simpson," *YES!* magazine, March 5, 2013, http://www.yesmagazine.org/peace-justice/dancing-the-world-into-being-a-conversation-with-idle-no-more-leanne-simpson.

23. Eric Ritskes, Leanne Simpson, and Glen Coulthard, "Leanne Simpson and Glen Coulthard on Dechinta Bush University, Indigenous Land-Based Education and Embodied Resurgence," interview transcript, *Decolonization: Indigeneity, Education & Society,* November 26, 2014, https://decolonization.wordpress.com/2014/11/26/leanne-simpson-and-glen-coulthard-on-dechinta-bush-university-indigenous-land-based-education-and-embodied-resurgence/.

Killing Abstractions

Indigenous Women and Black Trans Girls Challenging Media Necropower in White Settler States

LENA CARLA PALACIOS

We need, in our political organizing, to be aware of how impoverished our articulated agenda is in comparison with the suffering that we actually experience.

—Frank B. Wilderson III, "'We're trying to destroy the world'"

I was first introduced to Cynthia Frances Maas as just another disposable, dead-to-others nonentity. Media described her as a five-foot-two Indigenous woman with a "'high-risk' lifestyle" who was reported missing for three weeks before her decomposing body was found in a remote wooded area just off Highway 16—the so-called Highway of Tears in northern British Columbia (B.C.)—where dozens of mostly Indigenous girls and women, living off-reserve, have systemically disappeared and been murdered.[1] Even when there was nothing to link Maas to the sex trade, both the police and journalists publicly identified her solely as a sex trade worker and labeled the area in which her remains were found as a space unequivocally "frequented by sex-trade workers."[2] Gladys Radek is an Indigenous activist whose own niece went missing in 2005, prompting her to cofound Walk 4 Justice to draw attention to the dozens of Indigenous girls and women whose bodies have been discovered in the past four decades along the same stretch of the Trans-Canada Highway. She publicly criticized the Royal Canadian Mounted Police's (RCMP) statement linking Maas's murder to her work in the sex trade as a form of discursive violence.[3] Underscoring the structural devaluation of the lives of Indigenous women who are exposed to "a lot of brutality, a lot of violence," Radek states, "They [the RCMP] should be treating that woman as a woman first."[4]

In a statement made later the same day, the Maas family also deplored journalists for highlighting gender and lifestyle descriptions, claiming this practice "numb[ed] public empathy" and detracted from focusing on the murder of their daughter as well as the many other unsolved cases of missing and murdered girls and women.[5] Speaking about the measure of societal indifference to the fate of Indigenous women, the Maas family writes, "Murders do not just harm families, but our society is harmed as we forget and are numbed by senseless violence perpetrated against women portrayed as deserving of death." Because she was a disabled, street-involved Indigenous woman, her family adds, "Cindy . . . was a poster child for vulnerability in society."[6] After stating how they would like to see Canada strengthen the human rights of women and craft policies that better protect multiply marginalized Indigenous girls and women, the Maas family closed by thanking the RCMP detachment in Prince George for their diligence and sensitivity. Maas's aggrieved family deftly refused to spin a normative narrative that ascribing value to the devalued often demands. A politics of respectability would necessitate that they claim their daughter was actually "the girl next door," thus disavowing other Indigenous women and women of color who worked in the street economy—and struggled with addictions, poverty, and violence—alongside Maas. Her family, however, did not have a viable choice to engage in the politics of respectability to begin with; for those already marked as socially degenerate, there can be no claims of innocence and deservingness.

The same day that the Maas family released their statement, a group of Indigenous feminist activists in Vancouver's Downtown Eastside continued their boycott of British Columbia's Missing Women Commission of Inquiry while still honoring the families of women murdered by convicted serial killer Robert Pickton. During the protest, activist Cee Jay Julian announced that Cody Alan Legebokoff, a twenty-one-year-old white man, had been charged with four counts of first-degree murder in the deaths of three women and a legally blind fifteen-year-old girl. Having personally known Maas and two other Northern B.C. women—who all reportedly worked in the sex trade while raising their children—Julian states, "Cynthia Maas was aboriginal, like many of the Highway of Tears victims, like many of Pickton's victims, and it seems like our deaths aren't investigated until it's right in the face of the police." Journalist Suzanne Fournier represents Julian as emotional, saying she "broke down in angry tears" and "plead[ed] for help at [the] inquiry" before shouting, "When will it stop? Who will stop these men preying on our women?"[7] Julian's intervention underscores a reality in which "violence against Indigenous women is a key index to a hollowing out of any Indigenous self-determination in Canada and the United States, as it poses a loss of integrity to women's and the Indigenous nation's body/ social body."[8]

It is in these spaces of death where Achille Mbembe's provocative question takes on new meaning: "But what does it mean to do violence to what is nothing?"[9] Even as Maas's friends and relations as well as Indigenous feminist antiviolence activists attempt to reclaim her personhood in story-based terms, Maas's life-in-death existence remains nothing more than a mere abstraction, "a killing abstraction."[10] According to Ruth Wilson Gilmore, such practices and processes of abstraction are violent and not in themselves abstract. Gilmore argues that "the process of abstraction that signifies racism produces effects at the most intimately 'sovereign' scale, insofar as particular kinds of bodies, one by one, are materially (if not always visibly) configured by racism into a hierarchy of human and inhuman persons that in sum form the category 'human being.'"[11] The violence of abstraction refers to the multiple ways that racialized and gendered Others are made vulnerable to premature death by carceral state violence and settler colonialism, and it references how they are positioned as "permanently criminalized people" who are "ineligible for personhood."[12] As Lisa Marie Cacho explains, groups ineligible for personhood are "subjected to laws but refused the legal means to contest those laws as well as denied both the political legitimacy and moral credibility necessary to question them."[13]

This article focuses on the theoretical interventions and movement building led by Indigenous feminist and race-radical trans and gender-nonconforming girls and women at the forefront of antiviolence movement building in Canada and the United States. Such a transnational critical ethnic studies intervention upholds the tensions and refuses to collapse the radical and revolutionary political traditions and approaches of Indigenous movements for sovereignty and Black race-radical liberatory traditions. This comparative focus helps to not only identify and understand but to create multiple strategies that dismantle media necropower and the racialized gendered violence that it mobilizes and sustains.[14] To this end, I pose the following questions: In the face of such killing abstractions, what positions are actually available from which to critique and contest these necropolitical logics? How can the aggrieved families and communities of missing and murdered Indigenous girls and women in Canada as well as murdered trans and gender-nonconforming Black girls in the United States acknowledge and challenge social death and the mass-mediated necropower that legitimates it?

I argue throughout this article that the answers lie not in a politics of recognition but in a politics of refusal. As activist-scholars, we must refuse to recuperate social value—the act of ascribing normative social value to one "object" over an "Other"—and repudiate these killing, abstracting practices and criminalizing stereotypes. Over-relying on this strategy of disavowal and vindication—of assigning social value to some and *not*-value to others—reproduces the same problems we mean to resolve. We should instead work to manifest a politics that dismantles the social value that dictates who does and does not matter, and who can and cannot live, let alone survive. In this article, I introduce multiple Indigenous feminist and Black race-radical trans critiques that effectively undermine discourses championing state-sanctioned liberal politics of recognition as the only feasible and pragmatic form of resistance offered to those victimized by hetero-patriarchal, white supremacist state violence. As Glen S. Coulthard argues, "The empowerment that is derived from [a] critically self-affirmative and self-transformative process of desubjectification must be cautiously directed *away* from the assimilative lure of the statist politics of recognition, and in-stead be fashioned toward our own on-the-ground practices of freedom."[15]

Importantly, the politics of refusal are also shaped by each group's particular relationship to racial slavery and settler colonialism. I advocate for a justice outside the normative neoliberal politics of justice and the mechanisms of the state that are more in line with a politics of refusal that understands on the one hand—in line with an Afro-pessimist approach or intellectual disposition[16]—how social death and blackness are fungible and how the "freedom drive that abolishes slavery unsettles both colonial and decolonial forms of sovereign determination";[17] and on the other, an Indigenous politics of refusal that rejects statist relations of sovereignty in favor of self-determination informed by Indigenous knowledges. While the aims of Indigenous sovereignty movements are to bring about the repatriation of Indigenous lands and resurgence of Indigenous life, the politics of abolition (of racial slavery) that "consists in the affirmation of the unsovereign slave" rejects the restoration of sovereignty and refuses "a politics of resurgence, recovery, or recuperation."[18] I say all this not to rank oppressions—as "to be anti-black is also to be fundamentally anti-Indigenous"[19]—but to trace some of the different positions and approaches that are actually available from which to critique and potentially dismantle necropolitical logics.

In particular, I explore two instances that demonstrate how Indigenous and race-radical Black feminists engage in innovative strategies that intervene in both dominant and oppositional discourses and official and alternative narratives that are complicit in sustaining social death and the "violence of [social value]."[20] Since Indigenous girls and women in Canada and Black trans and gender-nonconforming girls and young women throughout the United States are *differently* marked as "ineligible for personhood"[21] in both life and in their untimely deaths, the activists and movements I explore grasp the importance of not falling into the well-worn trap of ascribing normative value to those already devalued. I focus on two particular movements that employ outlaw vernacular discourses and media-justice strategies to subvert human and civil rights–based calls that advocate for a state-led missing and murdered Indigenous women's inquiry in Canada and for the expansion of federal hate-crime protection to include gays, lesbians, bisexuals, transgender, and queer people in the United States. Instead of legitimating calls for legal protection by the carceral state, Indigenous feminists and Black queer feminists are building new antiviolence movements that advance community accountability and transformative justice to prevent the interpersonal, sexual, and state violence that targets nonnormative racialized bodies and, in particular, the disproportionate criminalization, incarceration, and execution of Indigenous girls and women and Black trans youth.[22]

Throughout this article, I underscore both the outlaw vernacular discourses and media-justice strategies that have already been deployed in various antiviolence movements driven by Indigenous and Black race-radical, queer, and trans feminists.

OUTLAW VERNACULAR DISCOURSES AS MEDIA-JUSTICE STRATEGY

As Stuart Hall suggests, "Nothing *meaningful* exists outside of discourse."[23] Outlaw vernacular discourses are produced by marginalized communities; logically incommensurate with broadly accepted, dominant notions of judgment and justice; and have historically been outlawed by the carceral and settler state.[24] Ultimately, I am attempting a critical theoretical project that investigates outlaw discourses and utilizes their radically disjunctive and counterintuitive logics to dismember dominant understandings of social justice and value. After studying various forms of outlaw discourses and media-justice strategies, I reflect these judgments back to other activist-scholars to be "used as provocateurs for the social imagination, a way to disrupt existing systems and logics of judgement."[25] My goal is to participate in the process of social transformation, not simply to record its impacts. By drawing attention to and making meaning of outlaw vernacular discourses—no matter how contradictory or ephemeral—that unsettle logics legitimating the legal elimination and murder of racialized and gendered Others, I am attempting a "critical rhetoric with an attitude."[26] This work is valuable, in large part, because Cynthia Frances Maas—like the many other Indigenous women and Black trans youth who have been rendered ineligible for personhood and marked for social death—was not.

The Indigenous and race-radical feminist activists explored in this article advance radically disjunctive ways of speaking that reject governing logics, therefore privileging discussions about the interlocking forms of interpersonal and state violence in order to create discursive changes that shift overall cultural understandings and political solidarities. For example, a prime example of an outlaw vernacular discourse is when Indigenous feminists argue that Indigenous decolonization is not accountable to white, nonwhite, immigrant, and postcolonial settlers who are not interested in seeking national liberation outside the nation-state. Challenging the inevitability of settler futurity, Eve Tuck and K. Wayne Yang argue that "decolonization is not accountable to settlers or settler futurity" but is only "accountable to Indigenous sovereignty and futurity."[27] Reenvisioning a politics of solidarity that challenges both the discursive and nondiscursive structures of white-settler power, Tuck and Yang forward a call for an "ethic of incommensurability, which recognizes what is distinct, what is sovereign for project(s) of decolonization in relation to human and civil rights based justice projects."[28] Unable to provide a logic for all peoples and all communities, Indigenous sovereignty movements whose aims are to bring about the repatriation of Indigenous lands and resurgence of Indigenous life are reestablishing themselves as truly self-determining, that is, as the creators of the terms and values of their own recognition. Emerging from the "textual residue of daily life,"[29] these outlaw vernacular discourses are produced and circulated in the everyday conversations, community media, activist-scholarship, marches and protests, and sovereignty movements driven by Indigenous outlaws not beholden to a liberal politics of recognition, and they are therefore discourses that, if and when translated into dominant systems of judgment or procedures for litigation, are deemed illegal, illogical, and immoral.

A key movement that brings forth and forwards such outlaw discourses is the media-justice movement—couched within the U.S.-based Black liberation struggle—which has always understood that media access without discursive power is a losing battle in the long-term war for racial justice.[30] Media-justice activism led mainly by racialized and criminalized communities aims to build social movements capable of challenging the fundamental roots of media necropower—namely, how the media engage and create culture, representation, meaning, and structural, symbolic violence.[31] Such media-justice strategies do not privilege elite media or public-relations strategies at the expense of building the strategic capacity of directly impacted people to communicate with each other in order to push for change that will significantly improve their lives.

A key aim of media-justice movements is to advance particular outlaw vernacular discourses and transfer them to a zone of civic discourse and public knowledge without the outlaw logic becoming silenced, erased, or lost. Media-justice activists and practitioners are keenly aware that "choosing to engage a system in which dominant logics predominate is treacherous for those practicing outlaw logics."[32] As Kent A. Ono and John M. Sloop explain, once the outlaw logic moves out of localized contexts into areas of the general culture, three distinct and overlapping possibilities emerge: "(1) it becomes popularized and hence productively leads to social change, (2) it is disciplined to become part of the dominant discourse and thus loses what is resistant and challenging about it, thus rendering it unable to alter the status quo power relations, or (3) it remains Outlaw, which means it never becomes part of the larger civic discourse and is, in a sense, remarginalized."[33] Media-justice activists strive to create the conditions conducive for the first option; they work to bring issues of concern to Indigenous communities and communities of color before the public and to encourage and mobilize individuals and organizations that share those concerns, as well as to shift the public and media conversations around racialized and colonized communities and their concerns.[34]

In addition, media-justice activists understand that to drive discursive change and social transformation necessitates multiple, interconnected strategies as well as acknowledgement of the many positions available inside and outside the master's house from which to contest and challenge white supremacist, hetero-patriarchal institutions and logics.[35] Their work is premised on resisting the belief that getting that one "good" article about a racial justice issue in the *New York Times* will change the hearts and minds of voters and the general public, thus resulting in meaningful social change. Instead of aiming to achieve visibility and recognition for the most vulnerable from the liberal voting public, media-justice activism is premised on building the communicative capacity of movement organizations led by those most directly impacted by carceral state violence in order to create dense activist networks and mobilize mass movements capable of both transgressing the territorial-political boundaries of the nation-state and defending themselves against the threat and promise of state violence.

I dedicate the next two sections to highlighting particular outlaw vernacular discourses and media-justice strategies that find "a way out of the violence of value"[36] and conscientiously work against dominant logics of recognition, rights, and respectability. As Eric Stanley argues, "For national violence to have value it must be produced through the tangled exclusion of bodies whose death is valueless."[37] By highlighting outlaw vernacular discourses that challenge the symbolic and literal extermination of "valueless" Indigenous women and Black trans youth, I am privileging the politics that emerges from the spaces of social death in white-settler and carceral states. As Sharon Holland observes, "You can tell the strength of a nation by the way it treats its poor; today, one can also ascertain this relative strength by examining the way a nation treats its dead."[38] It is precisely because these outlaws and outlaw discourses emerge from spaces where state violence is not only a threat but a promise that they are the least beholden to the nation-state and can best articulate outlaw ways of knowing and decolonial praxis.

DISMEMBERING VALUE: AGAINST A POLITICS OF RESPECTABILITY

A paradigm that relies on individualized victimization and injury is rendered legible only if the violated subject—if they are even recognized as a victim—is deemed respectable or symbolic of settler societies' standards of normalcy. Such a politics of respectability and deservingness broadly describes how dominant groups secure their position of dominance through the margins. As Mary Louise Fellows and Sherene Razack argue, "How groups on the margins are positioned in relation to one another on the disrespectable, or more aptly, the degenerate side of the divide, is of central importance to understanding how the dominant group produces and sustains feelings of innocence for itself and groups on the margins."[39] Dynamics of social value and deservingness determine which queer and trans murder victims become icons in the battle for antidiscrimination and hate-crime legislation in the United States. The names of white victims and the struggles for healing and justice on the part of their aggrieved friends and family are in greater circulation than those of victims of color through media and nonprofit channels, even though people of color are killed at higher rates. Islan Nettles—a young Black trans woman killed in Harlem in August 2013—was one of twelve African American trans people to be murdered during the 2012–13 Transgender Day of Remembrance cycle.[40] Unlike Sanesha Stewart, Amanda Milan, Marsha P. Johnson, Duanna Johnson, and Ruby Ordeñana, who are just a few of the Black and Latina trans women whose murders have been mourned by local communities but mostly ignored by media, large nonprofits, and lawmakers, the significance of Nettles's murder is actively being contested at local and national levels. While usually reserved for white queer and trans victims, both mainstream media and legal advocates are struggling to portray the assimilable characteristics of this young Black trans woman in order to emphasize their deserving nature and their ability to be named in hate-crime and antidiscrimination legislation. As Dean Spade points out, the inclusion focus of antidiscrimination law and hate-crime law campaigns "relies on a strategy of simile, essentially arguing 'we are just like you; we do not deserve this different treatment because of this one characteristic.'"[41] Black trans activists and other trans activists challenge the reductionist quests for inclusion and visibility that erase all elements of Nettles's identity—her blackness, her youth, her poverty, her gentrifying neighborhood—except for her gendered self-presentation, in order to read the tragedy of her death as a hate crime, as if the crime was, in fact, the sole injury. The outlaw vernacular discourses that emerge among many engaged in queer and trans resistance also reject how Islan has been used as a poster child by journalists, legislators, and even members of their own kin to expand police surveillance in racially marginalized communities and to bolster the passage of criminal punishment-enhancing laws that purportedly address transphobic violence. Instead of rendering Nettles's life and death palatable and legible to representatives of the carceral state, outlaws and their discourses sought to lovingly remember Nettles by dismembering social value and replacing a politics of respectability with "a politics of deviance."[42] Instead of repudiating nonnormative ways of being, Cathy Cohen argues that a politics of deviance would read nonnormative practices as forms of "definitional power" that have the potential to force us to radically rethink how value is defined, (mal)distributed, and withheld.[43]

A suspect in Nettles's murder, twenty-year-old Paris Wilson—a "rising senior at Buffalo State University" who wouldn't "let up on Nettles, issuing blow after blow even after she hit her head on the pavement"[44]—was arrested on assault charges, but the case against him was later dismissed. So far, no one has been charged with Nettles's murder, which followed a spate of local antigay hate crimes and has been dubbed the "last flail of the homophobes" in New York City.[45] In the liberal framing of both mainstream and alternative media, Nettles emerges solely as a victim of Paris Wilson's alleged hatred and disgust toward trans women. This normalizing register, which is incapable of forwarding an intersectional analysis, equates Nettles's injury with that of other cisgender gays and lesbians who are vulnerable to hate violence by "bigoted thugs" like Wilson.[46] Couching Nettles's murder, which took place in "the more menacing stretches of Harlem," alongside the well-publicized murder of Mark Carson in Greenwich Village, "a normally peaceful and progressive part of Manhattan,"[47] functions to effectively bracket their shared blackness—as if gendered and sexualized violence is not also racialized—and to portray them as two of many LGBTQ murder victims rather than exceptional cases that implicate larger structural inequalities specifically targeting Black female, trans, and queer bodies. In this liberal framing, gentrifying neighborhoods signal proximity to tolerance, openness, and safety for LGBTQ people of color, instead of increased intolerance for perceived gender transgressions and open displays of non-hegemonic sexuality in what could be argued are the much-less-tolerant, now-gentrified Greenwich Village and currently gentrifying East Harlem.

In 2006 four working-class, young, Black self-identified lesbians, Venice Brown, Terrain Dandridge, Patreese Johnson, and Renata Hill, dared walk through the increasingly white and middle-class neighborhood of Greenwich Village and were violently targeted. For their nonlethal efforts to defend themselves against an overtly sexual and homophobic attack, the "New Jersey 4" was convicted by an all-white female jury and received sentences ranging from three and a half to eleven years in prison. Like these other queer Black women, Nettles's race, class, and nonnormative gender appearance, as well as her transgression of the boundaries of newly gentrified neighborhoods, rendered her undeserving of "the protection of a prison nation."[48] Couched in white supremacy, gentrification is in itself a systemic, intentional process of uprooting and displacing already marginalized working-class queer and trans communities of color. In both dominant and vernacular civic discourses circulating in protests and media in the wake of Nettles's murder, very little attention has been given to these larger structural inequalities that would enable a more holistic representation of the social implications of both Nettles's life and death. Nettles is effectively reduced to a slain, parenthetically poor and Black, trans body whose agency is realized through the state recognizing her as just another individual victim of a hate crime.

Discourses about the death of queer and trans of color youth are material practices that help affirm what bodies do, and do not, count. On January 30, 2014, a group of trans women of color representing the Trans Women of Color Collective (TWOCC) of Greater New York and their allies gathered outside the New York City Police Department headquarters to protest what they felt was an unsatisfactory investigation and prosecution after Nettles's murder. These are some of the voices of TWOCC activists, excerpted from a transcript of the rally, that both reproduce and challenge dominant logics of social value. While reading the following excerpts, I cannot help but think through how these activists navigate the perils of being "'always already' pulled into governing logics in order to take part in the conversation":[49]

DANIELLA CARTER: I'm living in New York City. And I'm as educated, and I'm as political, I'm as human—you know, because we're dehumanizing the trans community. And this is a prime example of dehumanizing someone and their rights.

LOURDES ASHLEY HUNTER: With Islan Nettles, she was beaten until she could move no more, outside of a police station. She was in a crux of three different police stations in a gentrified neighborhood of Harlem where 10 different cameras are not working. This goes beyond just brutality and discrimination and against trans folks. What about the safety of all New Yorkers? How could it be in the middle of Harlem and cameras don't work? This could happen to anyone. If it happened to a white woman, would we be standing out here right here in the freezing cold fighting for justice six months later? There is a target on the backs of trans women of color!

MADISON ST. SINCLAIR: He was arrested, but he wasn't charged. And I sat with his mom, who is actually right there, Islan's mom, in court to listen to them sort of just destroy her as a person. It was disgusting. And she was the victim.

LOURDES ASHLEY HUNTER: Unacceptable. We are tired. We are tired of waiting by lesbian and gay folk to champion their policies and what they're interested in. Marriage doesn't impact us. We're tired of being pushed away and discriminated against in housing, access to jobs, education. And we've had enough. And even with this particular murder, you know what I'm saying? This is continual. This is not something new. This is indicative of NYPD. This is indicative of politics in New York City.

MADISON ST. SINCLAIR: Trans people are no longer a marginalized community. We're no longer a disenfranchised community. We're doctors. We're lawyers. We're taxpayers. And we demand and deserve the exact same rights as everyone else. We're not asking for special rights; we're asking for human rights. And so, it's disgusting that this happens now. It's constantly happening. People are being killed all the time, and no one is being charged for it.[50]

Not only do these Black trans members of TWOCC daily act in opposition to dominant norms, but they also contradict members of established, middle-class queer and Black communities who are committed to mirroring perceived respectable behaviors and hierarchical structures. Upon first reading, Madison St. Sinclair and Daniella Carter appear to be also mirroring and championing a politics of respectability. Carter's plea to be recognized as worthy of consideration—"I'm as educated, and I'm as political, I'm as human"—presumably by the so-called respectable strata of New York City society, conforms to liberal understandings of what constitutes legitimate politics. Both trans women root their analysis in a logic of visibility and inclusion; both highlight the exceptionalism of tax-paying trans people with high-level professional jobs and, by extension, uncomplicated—not illegal, not criminal, not deviant, not immoral—status. In no way is my analysis here meant to negate the struggle of those with little access to dominant power, who are attempting to secure such human necessities as autonomy, recognition, bodily integrity, and a meaningful life. Such attempts at claiming respectability and assimilation, however, imply that trans communities of color deserve social resources, political rights, and professional employment because they, too, are just like everyone else who subscribes to the normative values of the neoliberal, carceral state. As Lisa Cacho reminds us, "Claims to empowerment through deviant and defiant behavior urgently unsettle the stubborn relationship between value and normativity, but they cannot always offer something more."[51]

For St. Sinclair, justice for Nettles and other trans women of color will be realized through the criminal legal and punishment systems. St. Sinclair focuses her disgust on Paris Wilson's arrest and subsequent release and the misrepresentation of Nettles as assailant and not victim in the courtroom. While St. Sinclair is not directly advocating for hate-crime laws, the constant violence against trans women she wants to target is that violence carried out by purportedly aberrant individuals who are motivated by bias and transphobia. Advocating for criminal-punishment-enhancing laws serves to strengthen and expand the criminal punishment system, a system that targets the very same people hate-crime laws are supposed to protect. In the context of hyper- and mass-incarceration and rapid prison growth targeting historically marginalized communities, what is sacrificed by relying on criminal legal and punishment systems to purportedly address violence against these groups? Given how mainstream cisgender lesbian and gay rights work has aligned itself with the neoliberal law-and-order agenda,[52] it is not all that surprising that St. Sinclair would repeat dominant logics and "neoliberal reframing of discrimination and violence that have drastically shifted and undermined strategies of resistance to economic exploitation and state violence," which collude "in the harm and violence faced every day by queer and trans people struggling against racism, ableism, xenophobia, transphobia, homophobia, and poverty."[53] St. Sinclair's deviant presence as a member of a collective of trans women of color at a rally protesting the lack of police accountability and the criminalization of Nettles in both the courtroom and the court of public opinion does, however, translate into open defiance of the carceral state. As Ono and Sloop remind us, "dominant vernacular discourses . . . can work defensively even as they are resistant; they often respond to arguments on the playing field of dominant logic, staying within the logic of litigation."[54]

Lourdes Ashley Hunter performs an outlaw stance that does not over-rely on securing respectability at the hands of the state or from the mainstream cisgender gay and lesbian political establishment. While Nettles's murder has renewed calls from liberal lawmakers to pass the Gender Expression Non-Discrimination Act (GENDA)—a bill that would outlaw discrimination in New York State based on gender identity or expression and would expand the state's hate-crime law to explicitly include crimes against transgender people[55]—Hunter condemns Nettles's murder as an act of racialized and gendered violence exacerbated by enforcement and administrative violence. Instead of reaffirming the central language of GENDA, Hunter critiques the implicit good of gentrification, increased police surveillance, and movements that fight for gay and lesbian marriage rights to the exclusion of addressing the root causes of queer and trans premature death. As Dean Spade argues, "The paths to equality laid out by the 'successful' lesbian and gay rights model to which we [trans people] are assumed to aspire have little to offer us in terms of concrete change to our life chances; what they offer instead is the legitimization and expansion of systems that are killing us."[56] Hunter furthers a critical trans politics by raising demands that exceed visibility, inclusion, and recognition. Her oft-repeated phrase "We are tired. We've had enough" reminds us that people often come to political work through their own immediate experiences and intimate knowledge of harm and need; the bottom-up mobilization of TWOCC and other organizations led by trans people of color, like New York City's Fabulous Independent Educated Radicals for Community Empowerment (FIERCE!) led by queer and trans youth of color, is evidence of this truism. The outlaw discourses articulated by Hunter suggest that those in power have produced an atmosphere of transphobic and racist intolerance that has magnified the vulnerability of the living. Hunter also recognizes the central role of racism in determining which bodies are designated as more important and worth saving by a racist and transphobic NYPD ("If it happened to a white woman, would we be standing out here right here in the freezing cold fighting for justice six months later?"). Instead of advancing a politics of respectability palatable to the new liberal NYC political establishment, Hunter's discourse here tends toward survival, not legal recognition, and serves as the basis for a mobilized politics of deviance "where not only oppositional ideas and discourse happen, but lived opposition, or at least autonomy, is chosen daily."[57]

Hunter's intervention works as an outlaw discourse and radical media-justice strategy precisely because she is not directing her analysis or energy toward educating the mainstream press, city hall, or organizers beholden to assimilationist or respectable politics; she is speaking directly to those "sisters" who intimately understand how their own identities impact their survival and what it means to live in the margins, to have their lived experiences challenged. Her statements ultimately fail, however, as an outlaw or renegade discourse. Hunter decries "10 different" inoperable police surveillance cameras that should have been functioning in order to ostensibly capture the murder of Nettles. While noting the hypersurveillance and overpolicing of Black-bodies-as-criminals (versus the hyperinvisibility of Black-bodies-as-victims), Hunter proceeds to reinforce dominant notions of safety, the state, and justice: "What about the safety of all New Yorkers? How could it be in the middle of Harlem and cameras don't work? This could happen to anyone." First, while interlocking forms of interpersonal and state violence could happen to *anyone*, this violence is targeting *in particular* low-income trans and queer girls and women of color. Second, Hunter inadvertently reinforces carceral state logics by calling on more effective state-driven surveillance mechanisms in gentrifying communities of color. A growing body of activist-scholarship in race-radical, trans, and queer critical prison studies argues that the police and representatives of the prison-industrial complex are the single largest perpetrators of antitrans, anti-gender-nonconforming, and antiqueer violence.[58] How do we reconceptualize safety in ways that address harm against us while resisting carceral build-up (the antithesis of trans and queer safety) as a solution? Christina Hanhardt addresses why individualized notions of protection, safety, and by extension safe space need to be critiqued even within our most radical and revolutionary movements:

> I, too, am not convinced that safety or safe space in their most popular usages can or even should exist. Safety is commonly imagined as a condition of no

challenge or stakes, a state of being that might be best described as protec-
tionist (or, perhaps, isolationist). . . . The quest for safety that is collective
rather than individualized requires an analysis of who or what constitutes a
threat and why, and a recognition that those forces maintain their might by
being in flux. And among the most transformative visions are those driven
less by a fixed goal of safety than by . . . freedom.[59]

The critique of what is lost when we support the weaponization of safety
and other carceral logics is not meant to challenge the authenticity and real-
ness of Hunter's voice, especially when all the voices of TWOCC discussed
above violate certain claims and codes of racial innocence, ideological purity,
middle-class respectability, and the logics of civility. Given the power of
dominant voices and discourses, I, too, do not presume that I will always
think, act, and speak non-oppressively. I admit to these imperfections in
order to tangibly demonstrate how fraught, messy, contradictory, and violent a process it is to move from wanting to see Paris Wilson murdered by
an avenging Black trans angel or incarcerated for life by the state to wanting
to collectively organize to achieve a "freedom from violence." Sometimes
the only way to conjure this freedom is to confront one's own complicity in
structures of domination, to admit that despite our best individual efforts to
further a prison abolitionist stance the "cops *are* in our heads and hearts."[60]
Such contradictory discourses help to reveal the disjunctive processes in
which I, a queer Chicana and survivor of both sexual and state violence,
and other Indigenous feminist and Black race-radical and trans women of
color have reassessed facile, axiomatic assumptions that posit us merely as
vulnerable victims—and not agents—of gendered, racialized, and carceral
state violence.

Complex discourses like those heard at TWOCC's rally both simultaneously reinforce and chafe against the "politrix of civility and respectability"
and attempt "to re-member the Other by dismembering value,"[61] thereby
"ensuring that no one rewrote the life that *she* [Nettles] brilliantly lived."[62]
The primary argument of each of these living narratives is that the human
rights of trans girls and women of color outweigh and trump governmental
legislative rights. The very question of rights granted by the state—while
not misplaced—is shaken up by their logics; these Black trans activists are
not arguing for human rights as envisioned by Western humanism and uni-
versalism, which have historically privileged "free" white men and women,
but for a critical trans politics that calls for collective *self*-recognition and a
"turning away" from the carceral state. As bell hooks argues, we need to

stop being so preoccupied with looking "to that Other for recognition"; instead, we should be "recognizing ourselves and [then seeking to] make contact with all who would engage us in a constructive manner."[63] Outlaw discourses that make contact within and across radical movements work as politically savvy media-justice strategies that build, strengthen, and sustain mass movements not privy to or reliant upon visibility, hand-outs, or recognition from liberal movements that exclude the most deviant while propping up the carceral state. This critical outlaw politics is part of a larger framework of resistance that must grapple with the complex, interlocking relationship between interpersonal, sexual, and state violence, and the co-optation of social movements through legal reform and the institutionalization of resistance.

OUTLAWS DISMANTLING THE STATE: AGAINST A POLITICS OF RECOGNITION

While the interpellation of Islan Nettles as a murdered trans woman by the carceral state and mainstream press has been viewed as a triumphant outcome by mainstream LGBTQ organizations that identify the hate crime as the sole injury, race-radical trans activists and their allies argue that hate-crime laws legitimate and expand the very administrative and enforcement systems that are killing the most marginalized among us. As many radical queer and trans activists have demonstrated, trans people of color are disproportionately harmed by police brutality, administrative systems, and mass incarceration.[64] Given the reality of carceral state violence, the significance of Nettles's experience of discrimination and violent death being mediated through the law, mainstream LGBTQ politics, and dominant media cannot be overstated. As Eric Stanley argues:

> Yet even with the horrific details, antiqueer violence is written as an outlaw practice, a random event, and an unexpected tragedy. Dominant culture's necessity to disappear the enormity of antiqueer violence seems unsurprising. Yet I suggest that mainstream LGBT discourse also works in de-politicized collusion with the erasure of a structural recognition. Through this privatization the enormity of antiqueer violence is vanished.[65]

The belief that being named in this way—as a victim of individual, random violence—has to be critically reexamined. An additional case of outlaw discourses emerging in the wake of interpersonal and state violence targeting

Indigenous girls and women challenge the settler, carceral state by refusing such naming premised on recognition, visibility, and inclusion. Instead of turning toward the carceral state for answers on how to dismantle hetero-patriarchal, racialized violence, they consciously turn *away* from it—privileging instead the lure of belonging to a community dedicated to individual and collective *self*-recognition (as opposed to *state* recognition).

Like race-radical Black trans feminists, Indigenous feminism centers antiracist and anticolonial praxis within its antiviolence organizing and challenges the heteronormative and patriarchal nation-state. As Sarah Deer argues, Indigenous feminists and survivors of sexual violence have long been at the forefront of the development of contemporary tribal remedies for rape that incorporate "a unique indigenous vision for justice . . . that transcends both the male-dominated adversarial model of justice and the male-dominated peacemaking model."[66] Currently, numerous Indigenous feminist organizations led by Indigenous girls and women have been challenging calls for a Canadian-based national inquiry on missing and murdered Indigenous women. Instead of conveniently sidestepping outlaw logics and discourses that resist state intervention and litigation out of respect for the other family members of murdered women who wish to engage the state, radical Indigenous community organizers foster a politics of Indigenous resurgence to respond to racialized, gendered, sexualized, and carceral state violence. Indigenous renaissance and resurgence is about reclaiming Indigenous contexts (knowledge, interpretations, values, ethics, processes) for their own political cultures and refocusing Indigenous-led organizing work "from trying to transform the colonial outside into a flourishment of the *Indigenous* inside."[67] As Indigenous activist-scholar Leanne Betasamosake Simpson further elaborates:

> We need to rebuild our culturally inherent philosophical contexts for governance, education, healthcare, and economy. We need to be able to articulate in a clear manner our visions for the future, for living as *Indigenous Peoples* in contemporary times. To do so, we need to engage in *Indigenous* processes, since according to our traditions, the processes of engagement highly influence the outcome of the engagement itself. We need to do this on our own terms, without the sanction, permission, or engagement of the state, western theory or the opinions of Canadians.[68]

Grassroots, volunteer-led, local, and transnational groups, like Families of Sisters in Spirit (FSIS), No More Silence (NMS), and the Native Youth Sexual

Health Network (NYSHN), embrace this politics of Indigenous resurgence and are interested in nurturing self-determined and community-led responses to racialized gendered violence targeting Indigenous girls and women rather than relying on the Canadian nation-state and further engaging with and appealing to state institutions and government bodies. In their joint statement, which lays the groundwork to support the resurgence of community-based responses to violence, these three Indigenous-led organizations name specific forms of state violence and identify the harms of going through "the proper channels" of state-led interventions—from providing testimonies to British Columbia's Missing Women Commission of Inquiry to making recommendations to the United Nations Committee for the Elimination of Discrimination against Women (CEDAW).[69] For these organizations, heightened calls for a national inquiry into the phenomenon of missing and murdered Indigenous women in the wake of the disappearance and murder of Loretta Saunders, a pregnant young Inuk graduate student who was writing her thesis on the murders of three Nova Scotia Indigenous women, is a waste of time.[70]

More than a waste of time, however, an inquiry, as Robyn Bourgeois argues, "allows the Canadian state to *appear* that it is doing something about violence against women *without ever having to actually do anything.*"[71] Establishing an inquiry or special committee to examine an issue that has successfully been defined in mainstream media and civic fora as a social problem has historically been a common strategy by the state to silence the voices of opposition. After warning other Indigenous women who are advocating for the inquiry about how the "colonial government can, and will, define, dictate, and decide the purpose, mandate, process, and outcome of that inquiry," Andrea Landry deploys an outlaw discourse that delegitimizes an inquiry "established by a structure meant to murder, rape, and annihilate the Indigenous self."[72] Landry writes:

Inquiries . . . only establish the facts of this crisis in our communities. Guess what? We know those facts, stories, stats, rates and names. We, as Indigenous women, are the facts, we are the stories, the stats, rates, and names. . . . If the colonial government were to put the dollars in to "fix" an issue that they continuously create and justify, and if we were to agree to work together, we would be shaking hands with and embodying the oppressor. This destructive relationship would . . . attempt to disregard and void the grassroots work occurring in our communities to define our own solutions. We are holding on so tightly to a line cast set out by the colonial government to be our saviors in establishing an inquiry that this line is digging deep into our hands and into our spirits, spilling more blood."[73]

Landry powerfully equates Indigenous women's falling prey to the "assimilative lure of the statist politics of recognition"[74] in the form of a national inquiry to that of the visceral pain induced by internalized oppression and violent victimization at the hands of the white settler state. While nothing can be gained from engaging in a liberal politics of recognition, inclusion, and visibility—for Indigenous women, in particular—everything can be lost. The state's inability to meaningfully address violence against Indigenous girls and women is not simply about a lack of political will but is demonstrative of the critical investment the state has in perpetuating dominant systems of hetero-patriarchy, racism, and colonialism. As Sarah Deer states, "Depending on an outside government, especially a government established and created by the colonizers (the historical perpetrators of rape), is not the solution to violent crimes committed upon Native women."[75] And as the joint statement authored by FSIS, NMS, and NYSHN argues, "As much of the violence we face as communities, nations, and families stems from colonial nation-states like Canada and the US and the laws themselves."[76]

Instead of engaging with carceral and settler states, these radical Indigenous feminists are "call[ing] attention back to ourselves; we have the answers and solutions . . . we always have."[77] The solutions in which communities are already actively engaged range from Indigenous resurgence, teach-ins and critical education, média-arts justice, "Native woman-centered model[s] of adjudication,"[78] community accountability and transformative justice, supporting Indigenous people in the sex trades and street economies, centering Indigenous youth leadership and intergenerational organizing, and Annual February 14th Memorial Marches for Missing and Murdered Women,[79] to the "countless acts of hidden resistance and kitchen table resistance aimed at ensuring their children and grandchildren could live as *Indigenous* Peoples."[80] In the meantime, we can delight in the outlaws and their outlaw discourses that manifest themselves at the most perfect of times, such as at the beginning of Commissioner Wally Oppal's statement at the public release of the final report of the Missing Women Commission of Inquiry in Vancouver, British Columbia. As Oppal began to speak about some particulars of his report—in which he emphatically repeated words like "forsaken women," "nobodies," "abandoned women," "marginalized women," "drug sick women," "sex trade workers," "poor women," "Aboriginal women," "missing and murdered women"—he was interrupted by drums and singing. This was the Women's Warrior Song, gifted to an Indigenous woman who asked for a song for the missing women during a ceremony. Sung to the beat of a traditional Aboriginal hand drum, the Women's Warrior Song has become an anthem of courage and strength for those demanding justice for the missing women.[81] By disrupting the proceedings, these singers and drummers did not just demand space within this "official" event for the voices of marginalized women; as outlaws, they refused to recognize the state's legitimacy, submit to the dominant logic by which it operates, or abandon their more-than-five-hundred-year "war of position" fought against colonization.

CONCLUSION: STRUGGLING AGAINST ALL ODDS

As Lisa Cacho argues, "Without the expectation of rights and recognition, we start from the reality of social death rather than the promise of a better life."[82] The space of social death is a hopeless space but one that is also conducive to producing outlaw vernacular logics and deviant ways of knowing—a space "always graced with hope, courage, and/or youthful idealism, where those who decide to take responsibility for the unprotected are always looking for and stepping on the pressure points that can barely manage the contradictions that their very presence, their very being inspires."[83] The outlaw discourses and actions mobilized by Indigenous and trans Black girls and women—the unprotected and socially dead—who are overwhelmingly the targets of interpersonal, sexual, and carceral state violence in white settler societies are direct responses to their subjection, devaluation, and ineligibility for personhood. When one has nothing left to lose, the fear of failure loses its power to keep one in line. Instead of toeing the line of dominant logics of governmentality, the outlaw discourses advanced by aggrieved friends, family, and community members who have lost yet another mother, daughter, sister, friend, and lover to state-sanctioned racialized and gendered violence articulate a politics that rejects the violence of social value and deservingness. Regardless of the ephemerality, desperateness, and contradictory nature of the outlaw discourses explored here, they draw upon a well-informed worldview—an Afro-pessimist approach—that intimately understands that victory against a world in which "black life is *lived* in social *death*"[84] is not rooted to winning but to struggling despite guaranteed failure. As Fred Moten has argued about what Saidiya Hartman terms the "afterlife of slavery," "objects can and do resist."[85]

The outlaws who deploy media-justice strategies to counter media necro-power acknowledge that there is no clear "winner" in the hypermedia environment except for the interests of white supremacy, the carceral state, and transnational capital. Instead of claiming that they do not reproduce the logic of dominant culture, some who advance outlaw discourses presume that they are complicit in the structures of white supremacy, settler colonialism, and hetero-patriarchy even while attempting to resist them. Advanced by outlaws and deviants working to carve out alternative meaning in the spaces of social death, we must take failure for granted without equating failure with defeat. Because revolutions are necessarily long discursive and ideological struggles,[86] we must actively seek out, listen for, speak aloud, and be transformed by those radically contradictory and disjunctive ways of thinking and being born in the fertile spaces of social death.

LENA CARLA PALACIOS'S research and teaching focuses on critical prison studies and prison abolitionism, Black, Indigenous, Chicana, and Latina queer and trans feminisms, girls' and girlhood studies, transformative justice and community accountability, media justice, as well as research justice. She is currently writing a book titled "Weaponizing Safety" focusing on the activism of Indigenous, Black, and Chicana/Latina girls and women who are at the forefront of transformative justice movements in Canada and the United States, particularly around sexual and carceral state violence. One chapter that she is revising for the book appears in *Girlhood and the Politics of Place* (2016) on young women's de-carceral transformative justice activism. Part of the project is based on her own experience as a survivor of sexual and state violence and a transformative justice activist, on which she has also been publishing (she has a forthcoming piece in a special issue of *philoSOPHIA*).

NOTES

1. "2 Prince George Women Missing: Police," *CBC News,* October 1, 2010, http://www.cbc.ca/news/canada/british-columbia/2-prince-george-women-missing-police-1.882635; Derrick Penner, "Another Tragedy along Highway of Tears," *Winnipeg Free Press,* October 17, 2010.

2. Derrick Penner, "Latest Highway of Tears Victim Identified; B.C. Police Confirm Sex Trade Worker Was Murdered," *Calgary Herald,* October 17, 2010.

3. Patrick Brethour, "Treat 'Highway of Tears' Victims as Women First, Police Told; Linking Area Where Latest Body Found to Prostitution Highlights Wrong-Headed Attitude, Missing Woman's Aunt Says," *Globe and Mail,* October 17, 2010.

4. Ibid.

5. "B.C. Man Accused of Being Serial Killer," *CBC News*, October 17, 2011, http://www.cbc.ca/news/canada/british-columbia/b-c-man-accused-of-being-serial-killer-1.1080350.

6. Ibid.

7. Suzanne Fournier, "'When Will It Stop?': Activist Breaks Down, Pleads for Help at Inquiry," *The Province*, October 17, 2011.

8. Dian Million, *Therapeutic Nations Healing in an Age of Indigenous Human Rights* (Tucson: University of Arizona Press, 2013), 23.

9. Achille Mbembe, *On the Postcolony* (Berkeley: University of California Press, 2001), 174.

10. Sharon Patricia Holland, *Raising the Dead: Readings of Death and (Black) Subjectivity* (Durham, N.C.: Duke University Press, 2000), 17.

11. Ruth Wilson Gilmore, "Fatal Couplings of Power and Difference: Notes on Racism and Geography," *Professional Geographer* 54, no. 1 (2002): 16, doi:10.1111/0033-0124.00310.

12. Lisa Marie Cacho, *Social Death: Racialized Rightlessness and the Criminalization of the Unprotected* (New York: New York University Press, 2012), 6.

13. Ibid.

14. Sarah Lamble, "Retelling Racialized Violence, Remaking White Innocence: The Politics of Interlocking Oppressions in Transgender Day of Remembrance," *Sexuality Research & Social Policy* 5, no. 1 (2008): 24–42, doi:10.1525/srsp.2008.5.1.24; Goldie Osuri, "Media Necropower: Australian Media Reception and the Somatechnics of Mamdouh Habib," *Borderlands* 5, no. 1 (2006); Lena Carla Palacios, "Racialized and Gendered Necropower in Canadian News and Legal Discourse," *Feminist Formations* 26, no. 1 (2014): 1–26.

15. Glen S. Coulthard, "Subjects of Empire: Indigenous Peoples and the 'Politics of Recognition' in Canada," *Contemporary Political Theory* 6 (2007): 456, doi:10.1057/palgrave.cpt.9300307.

16. Saidiya V. Hartman, *Scenes of Subjection : Terror, Slavery, and Self-Making in Nineteenth-Century America* (New York: Oxford University Press, 1997); Jared Sexton, "The Social Life of Social Death: On Afro-Pessimism and Black Optimism," *InTensions* 5 (2011): 1–47; Frank B. Wilderson III, *Red, White & Black: Cinema and the Structure of U.S. Antagonisms* (Durham, N.C.: Duke University Press, 2010).

17. Jared Sexton, "The *Vel* of Slavery: Tracking the Figure of the Unsovereign," *Critical Sociology* (December 19, 2014): 1, doi:10.1177/0896920514552535.

18. Ibid., 11.

19. Shona Jackson, "Humanity beyond the Regime of Labor: Antiblackness, Indigeneity, and the Legacies of Colonialism in the Caribbean," *Decolonization: Indigeneity, Education & Society*, June 6, 2014, https://decolonization.wordpress.com/2014/06/06/humanity-beyond-the-regime-of-labor-antiblackness-indigeneity-and-the-legacies-of-colonialism-in-the-caribbean/.

20. Cacho, *Social Death*, 31.

21. Ibid., 6.

22. Lena Palacios, "Indigenous and Race-Radical Feminist Movements Confronting Necropower in Carceral States" (PhD diss., McGill University, 2014); Leanne

Betasamosake Simpson, "Not Murdered and Not Missing: Rebelling against Colonial Gender Violence," March 8, 2014, http://leannesimpson.ca/not-murdered-not-missing/.

23. Stuart Hall, "Reality and Discourse," in *Representation and the Media*, produced and directed by Sut Jhally (Northampton, Mass.: Media Education Foundation, 1997), transcript, 12, emphasis added.

24. John M. Sloop and Kent A. Ono, "Out-Law Discourse: The Critical Politics of Material Judgment," *Philosophy & Rhetoric* 30, no. 1 (1997): 50–69; Kent A. Ono and John M. Sloop, *Shifting Borders: Rhetoric, Immigration, and California's Proposition 187* (Philadelphia, Penn.: Temple University Press, 2002).

25. Sloop and Ono, "Out-Law Discourse," 63.

26. Ono and Sloop, *Shifting Borders*, 19.

27. Eve Tuck and K. Wayne Yang, "Decolonization Is Not a Metaphor," *Decolonization: Indigeneity, Education & Society* 1, no. 1 (2012): 35.

28. Ibid., 28.

29. Ono and Sloop, *Shifting Borders*, 6.

30. Malkia A. Cyril, "Media and Marginalization," in *The Future of Media: Resistance and Reform in the 21st Century*, ed. Robert Waterman McChesney, Russell Newman, and Ben Scott (New York: Seven Stories Press, 2005), 97–104; Hunter Cutting and Makani Themba-Nixon, *Talking the Walk: A Communications Guide for Racial Justice* (Oakland, Calif.: AK Press, 2006).

31. Makani Themba-Nixon and Nan Rubin, "Speaking for Ourselves: A Movement Led by People of Color Seeks Media Justice—Not Just Media Reform," *Nation*, November 17, 2003; Makani Themba-Nixon, "Mainstreams and Margins: A Critical Look at the Media Reform 'Story,'" *International Journal of Communication* 3 (2008): 3.

32. Ono and Sloop, *Shifting Borders*, 17.

33. Ibid., 18.

34. Cutting and Themba-Nixon, *Talking the Walk*.

35. Audre Lorde, "The Master's Tools Will Never Dismantle the Master's House," in *Sister Outsider: Essays and Speeches* (Trumansburg, N.Y.: Crossing Press, 2007), 110–14.

36. Cacho, *Social Death*, 31.

37. Eric Stanley, "Near Life, Queer Death: Overkill and Ontological Capture," *Social Text* 29, no. 2 107 (2011): 7, doi:10.1215/01642472-1259461.

38. Holland, *Raising the Dead*, 18.

39. Mary Louise Fellows and Sherene Razack, "The Race to Innocence: Confronting Hierarchical Relations among Women," *Journal of Gender, Race and Justice* 1 (1998): 336.

40. Monica Roberts, "Black Trans Year in Review 2013," *ELIXHER*, December 23, 2013, http://elixher.com/black-trans-year-in-review-2013/.

41. Dean Spade, *Normal Life: Administrative Violence, Critical Trans Politics, and the Limits of Law* (Brooklyn, N.Y.: South End Press, 2011), 86.

42. Cathy J. Cohen, "Deviance as Resistance: A New Research Agenda for the Study of Black Politics," *Du Bois Review: Social Science Research on Race* 1, no. 1 (2004): 27, doi:10.1017/S1742058X04040044.

43. Ibid., 38.

44. "Transgender Woman Dies after Being Savagely Beaten by a Facebook Friend When He Learned She Was Born a Man," *Daily Mail,* August 24, 2013.

45. Raillan Brooks, "A Transgender Woman Dies after an Assault in Harlem [Update]," *Runnin' Scared* (blog), August 23, 2013, http://blogs.villagevoice.com/runninscared/2013/08/transgender_woman_dies_in_harlem.php.

46. Nicholas Wells Moore, "Hate & Horror: Transgender Man Fatally Beat Latest in Series of Bias Crimes," *New York Daily News,* August 24, 2013.

47. Michael Schwirtz, "Embarking on a New Life, Transgender Woman Has It Brutally Taken," *New York Times,* September 8, 2013; "Revealed: The 'Courageous' Man Shot in the Head in Hate Crime Murder after He Refused to Deny He Was Gay to Homophobic Attacker," *Daily Mail,* May 19, 2013.

48. Beth Richie, *Arrested Justice: Black Women, Violence, and America's Prison Nation* (New York: New York University Press, 2012), 24, 120, 124.

49. Ono and Sloop, *Shifting Borders,* 136.

50. Democracy Now!, "'Black Trans Bodies Are under Attack': Activist CeCe McDonald, Actress Laverne Cox Speak Out," February 19, 2014, http://www.democracynow.org/2014/2/19/black_trans_bodies_are_under_attack.

51. Cacho, *Social Death,* 167–68.

52. Christina B. Hanhardt, *Safe Space: Gay Neighborhood History and the Politics of Violence* (Durham, N.C.: Duke University Press, 2013).

53. Spade, *Normal Life,* 89.

54. Ono and Sloop, *Shifting Borders,* 142.

55. Gender Expression Non-Discrimination Act, S195B (2013), http://open.ny senate.gov/legislation/bill/S195-2013; Gender Expression Non-Discrimination Act, A4226B (2013), http://open.nysenate.gov/legislation/bill/A4226-2013.

56. Spade, *Normal Life,* 41.

57. Cohen, "Deviance as Resistance," 43.

58. Eric Stanley and Nat Smith, *Captive Genders: Trans Embodiment and the Prison Industrial Complex* (Oakland, Calif.: AK Press, 2015).

59. Hanhardt, *Safe Space,* 30.

60. Paula X. Rojas, "Are the Cops in Our Heads and Hearts?," in *The Revolution Will Not Be Funded: Beyond the Non-Profit Industrial Complex,* ed. Incite! Women of Color Against Violence (Cambridge, Mass.: South End Press, 2007), 198–214.

61. Lindon Barrett, *Blackness and Value: Seeing Double* (Cambridge: Cambridge University Press, 1999), 128.

62. Janet Mock, "A Letter to My Sisters Who Showed Up for Islan Nettles & Ourselves at the Vigil," August 28, 2013, http://janetmock.com/2013/08/28/islan-nettles -vigil-trans-women-of-color/.

63. bell hooks, *Yearning: Race, Gender, and Cultural Politics* (Boston, Mass.: South End Press, 1990), 22.

64. See Joey L. Mogul, Andrea J. Ritchie, and Kay Whitlock, *Queer (In)Justice: The Criminalization of LGBT People in the United States* (Boston, Mass.: Beacon Press, 2011); Stanley and Smith, *Captive Genders*; Spade, *Normal Life.*

65. Stanley, "Near Life, Queer Death," 7.

66. Sarah Deer, "Decolonizing Rape Law: A Native Feminist Synthesis of Safety and Sovereignty," *Wicazo Sa Review* 24, no. 2 (2009): 162.

67. Leanne Betasamosake Simpson, *Dancing on Our Turtle's Back: Stories of Nishnaabeg Re-creation, Resurgence and a New Emergence* (Winnipeg: Arbeiter Ring, 2011), 7.

68. Ibid, 17.

69. Families of Sisters in Spirit, No More Silence, and Native Youth Sexual Health Network, "Supporting the Resurgence of Community-Based Responses to Violence," March 14, 2014, http://www.nativeyouthsexualhealth.com/march142014.pdf.

70. "Loretta Saunders Homicide Sparks Call by Native Group for Public Inquiry," *CBC News*, February 27, 2014, http://www.cbc.ca/1.2552572.

71. Robyn Bourgeois, "National Inquiry on Missing, Murdered Women Not Best Answer," *Huffington Post*, December 21, 2012, http://www.huffingtonpost.ca/robyn-bourgeois/missing-women-inquiry-report-vancouver-pickton_b_2333262.html.

72. Andrea Landry, "Why We Don't Need a Missing and Murdered Indigenous Women's Inquiry," *Last Real Indians Blog*, March 13, 2014, http://lastrealindians.com/why-we-dont-need-a-missing-and-murdered-indigenous-womens-inquiry-by-andrea-landry/.

73. Ibid.

74. Coulthard, "Subjects of Empire," 456.

75. Deer, "Decolonizing Rape Law," 151.

76. Families of Sisters in Spirit, No More Silence, and Native Youth Sexual Health Network, "Supporting the Resurgence."

77. Ibid.

78. Deer, "Decolonizing Rape Law," 153.

79. See the following statements by the Native Youth Sexual Health Network: "For Each Bead, Moccasin Top & Ceremony for Our Missing and Murdered Indigenous Women and Families: NYSHN Statement of Support & Media Advisory for Walking With Our Sisters," October 1, 2013, http://www.nativeyouthsexualhealth.com/wwossupportnyshn.pdf; "Responding to the Violence of Ongoing Colonialism on December 17th: International Day to End Violence against Sex Workers," December 17, 2013, http://www.nativeyouthsexualhealth.com/dec172013.pdf; "February 14th Women's Memorial Marches—Not Forgetting the Legacy and Honoring through Action," February 14, 2014, http://www.nativeyouthsexualhealth.com/feb142014.pdf.

80. Kiera L. Ladner and Leanne Simpson, "This Is an Honour Song," in *This Is an Honour Song: Twenty Years since the Blockades*, ed. Leanne Simpson and Kiera L. Ladner (Winnipeg: Arbeiter Ring, 2010), 8.

81. Robyn Bourgeois, "Is Anyone Listening to the 'Forsaken,' Marginalized Women of Vancouver?," *Huffington Post*, December 18, 2012, http://www.huffingtonpost.ca/robyn-bourgeois/missing-women-inquiry-reaction_b_2319073.html.

82. Cacho, *Social Death*, 145.

83. Ibid.

84. Sexton, "The Social Life of Social Death," 29.

85. Saidiya V. Hartman, *Lose Your Mother: A Journey along the Atlantic Slave Route* (New York: Farrar, Straus and Giroux, 2007); Fred Moten, *In the Break: The Aesthetics of the Black Radical Tradition* (Minneapolis: University of Minnesota Press, 2003), 1.

86. Raymond Williams, *The Long Revolution* (New York: Columbia University Press, 1961).

The Origins, Potentials, and Limits of Racial Justice

LEIGH PATEL AND ALTON PRICE

In April 2015 thirty-five Black American teachers in Atlanta, Georgia, were indicted on criminal charges for falsifying school assessment data. Of those thirty-five, twelve were formally sentenced, with fines ranging from one thousand to five thousand dollars and jail time from one to five years. That same year, nine white teachers in New York were charged with grade changing and test coaching. To date, four have been dismissed from their jobs, and six in total have paid punitive fines, but none have been sentenced to prison time. The knots of (in)justice in these cases include interwoven threads of institutional anti-Black racism, racialized incarceration, and criminalization, all fomenting through the conduit of high-stakes assessment in public schooling. To ask what is just for these teachers requires an understanding of the sources of intertwined forms of injustice, particularly injustice as purposefully organized and delivered through racialized differences in societal institutions.

In 1903 W. E. B. Du Bois predicted "the problem of the Twentieth century is the problem of the color-line." It is controvertible that his assessment of "the relation of the darker to the lighter races of men in Asia and Africa" as the foundational issue facing modern society has proven true and extended into the twenty-first century with a tight grip.[1] Recent social movements, including Black Lives Matter and the Dream Defenders, indict systemic racism and speak back to the state-inflicted and extralegal violence enacted on Black people. These movements, like many movements before, address the mismatch between the nationalist rhetoric of a democratic society and the material machinery of racist capitalism. However, an indictment does not necessarily mean a theory of change. In the historical and ongoing role of racism to stratify peoples of disparate levels of well-being, there is little question about the existence of a color line; less clear is how to dismantle this line and its material effects, or even if dismantling the color line is part of the public imaginary when it comes to racism and racial justice. As in the case of the teachers in Georgia and New York, racism operates through racial categories and actively intertwines oppressive structures. Pursuant to this special issue on discerning versions of justice, then, we ask, in light of the creation of racial categorizations to deliver racism, do we have the conceptual tools to articulate what justice wants when it comes to racism?

Our inquiry is into the linguistic and analytic tools we have for disrupting and dismantling the color line Du Bois wrote of, or, as it is more ubiquitously named now, racism. Specifically, we explore how the term "racial justice" has been used and indexed in academic and public rhetoric in the United States. We approach racial justice as a term and construct out of a desire to not just know its shape but how it has come to take that shape. We situate this inquiry from the position that the sources of injustice must be adequately named and theorized to then determine how to interrupt those injustices and build realities beyond.[2]

Undergirding this inquiry are several foundational principles already firmly established in social science research and theorization of race. First, we work from the understanding that race is not a fixed characteristic of individuals but rather constructed for individual and population-level stratification and consequences through multiple intertwined structures, including policy, institutionalized practices, culture, and individual interactions.[3] Our analysis is situated within and limited to the uses of racism within the United States. This analysis, though, is not meant to imply that racial formation does not touch and shape many ethnicities and racialized realities in other parts of the world. In some areas of our analysis, we address how U.S.-based scholars and activists drew on movements for independence in other parts of the world, but we delimit our analysis to how ideas about racial justice have been shaped and leveraged in the United States, in part because dialectics of justice are often attached to projects of nationhood.[4] Further, race is discussed here as an outcropping of racism, a set of permeable yet durable stratified categorizations created and expressed to distinguish the "more human" from the "less than human."[5] These racial categorization projects have taken shape in distinct but related ways within and across geographies and disciplines.[6] In considering the roots and uses of terminology, we assume that all language is metaphorical and partial, that it stands in for ideas and objects but only some and then always incompletely and impermanently.[7] Finally, we view language as a contextual phenomenon. While language and ideas move and travel, they are always contextually shaped and entered with meanings, associations, and foreclosures of other meanings.

To explore what "racial justice" as a term can do and what it cannot, we investigate its appearances and uses, and consider these against the purposeful mechanisms of racism. We examine the origins of the term in the United States after European invasion created this settler structure. We also ask who has used the term, in what ways, and for what purposes. We work from a belief that justice wants a reimagination of society without a color line as arbiter of differentiated well-being, and we ask what "racial justice" as a term can do for that goal.

METHODOLOGY

The impetus for this inquiry was our anecdotal observation that the term "racial justice" had increased in popularity in many different social fields. A Google search for the term yields no fewer than 11.9 million results. It is found in academic texts, mission statements for nonprofit organizations, popular journalism articles, and, quite recently, some politicians' platforms. While we were certain that there was something "there there" when it comes to racial justice having become an unfixed yet still perceptible category and referent, our inquiry was what uses of the term afforded, with attention to what was being said as well as what was not defined. We sought to understand how references to racial justice have persisted and shifted over time to better understand these moments not as predictive of how the term is used in contemporary speech acts but more so as palimpsest. Understanding what came before current uses can aid in apprehending tangled histories, forcibly and temporarily holding still what former moments are etched in the shadows of contemporary uses. We engaged a genealogical inquiry out of the premise that understanding historical uses assists in analyzing current contextual shaping of the term.[8]

To systematically consider the shapes and histories of the term, we conducted a content analysis of referents to racial justice in academic texts, public speeches, and online statements of activist organizations. We narrowed our analysis to these groupings so that we might think more precisely about the terms relative to the social locations and purposes of those using it rather than run the risk of discussing uses of the term in a decontextualized manner. Our data sources included activist organizations' statements available on the Internet, academic articles, and speeches made by U.S.-based civil rights leaders addressing race and racism. Within each field, we used the key terms "racial justice," "inter-racial justice," "racial equality," "racial equity," "racial progress," and "racial injustice" to search for texts. Because of the sharp uptick in uses of the term in academic texts after the year 2000, we conducted a fine-grained analysis of the seventy-six articles that used the term between 2006 and 2015. Of each text, we asked the following questions:

- Is racial justice defined? If so, how?
- If not, how is the problem relative to racism defined?
- How then is solution or progress named relative to that problem statement?

This article presents a systematic content analysis of terms, referents, and omissions. Within this content analysis, we analyzed how accompanying categories and markers, such as brotherhood, humanity, justice, and progress, were given shape and boundaries. We considered the cultural context of the speech act and the role of the speaker and speech act relative to audience. Over the next sections, we provide overview, discussion, and analysis of the uses of the term "racial justice" and accompanying referents to justice, freedom, and reckoning with racism as a project of social domination. Along with the analysis of the published uses of these terms, we also provide a few snapshots of racism-related events that occurred in the same spatio-temporal environs. In providing genealogical analysis of the term "racial justice" and historical events, we do not imply that particular events caused or shaped the uses of the term but rather that language and meaning are always situated within contexts. To best apprehend the affordances, then and now, of racial justice, and to ask what it can speak to, we aver that it is necessary to consider sociopolitical and historical contexts.

ACTIVIST AND NOT-FOR-PROFIT ORGANIZATION USES

Using a content analysis of the top one hundred returns of a Google search for "racial justice," definitions were expressly articulated in less than half of the articles and organizational descriptions. Most often, the term was not defined but instead juxtaposed against descriptions of racial injustice, including disproportionate rates of incarceration, inequity in schooling, and disparate health outcomes. Of the forty-three organizations and articles that defined racial justice or used appositive phrases to expand on it, the terms "equity" and "equal" predominated, such as in the definition from Race Forward, a self-described center for racial justice innovation. Their statement reads: "We define racial justice as the systematic fair treatment of people of all races, resulting in equitable opportunities and outcomes for all."[9] References to equity, equal rights, and fairness were most commonly paired with the term "racial justice" but often without further detail on what ways and by which measures equity might be deemed attainable. In this social field, racial justice is a widely used term but precise definitions are infrequent, and therefore it is unclear, from public view, within activist organizations what kind of consensus exists for what racial justice means, what it would look like if it were achieved, and what it cannot address.

EARLY EXPRESSIONS OF INTERRACIAL AND RACIAL JUSTICE

"Racial justice" as a term first appears in U.S. publications under the related term "interracial justice." In 1911 Edwin D. Mead used this term in his article "International Organization for Inter-racial Goodwill."[10] Mead was a pacifist and social reformer of the United States and a member of several peace organizations, including the International Peace Bureau, the School Peace League, and the American Peace League. Mead used the term in his address to the Universal Races Congress, a four-day gathering in 1911 of delegates from fifty countries, convened so that "the representatives of the different races might meet each other face to face, and might, in friendly rivalry, further the cause of mutual trust and respect between the Occident and Orient, between the so-called white peoples and the so-called coloured peoples."[11] With an apparent transposition of peace for justice, peace was sought and contrasted with a racial conflict that had emerged out of misunderstandings with no mention of structural forces that deliberately created the construct of race. This initial use of the term "interracial justice" and its use in the context of a race relations congress raises questions of the term's referents and apparent, if not intentional, silences on the historical and current purposes of racism.

Although she did not use the terms "racial justice" or "interracial justice," journalist and activist Ida B. Wells spoke about racial violence in 1909. In a speech titled "This Awful Slaughter," Wells spoke to the first meeting of the National Association for the Advancement of Colored People about the ways that Black women, men, and children were being terrorized by a national campaign of lynching. Without uttering the terms "racial injustice" or "racial justice," she laid out a clear appraisal of the problem of this co-ordinated lynching campaign as well as a solution.[12] Wells noted that what would "resolve" this violence on Black people was neither education nor agitation but the nation delivering on its promise of rights to its citizens. Wells's words are a markedly different stance, then and now, from a stance on racial justice as peace. Wells, in essence, indicted the nation for proclaiming in word an expression of citizenship and then, in deed, denying citizenship to its own people, male, female, young, and adult. Wells's speech denotes the still pressing potential for justice to demand reconciliation of word and deed but also reifies the nation as the fulcrum for abrogation and deliverance from injustice.

Returning to explicit references to racial justice, after Mead's use in 1911, the term "interracial justice" appeared again ten years later when John White Jr. set out to challenge the conventional image of the ignorant white Southerner in the essay "Inter-racial Co-operation in the South." White wrote that the "frictions between the races" after Reconstruction were due to a more industrial society in which power and economic resources were being redistributed.[13] In the same essay, White drew positive attention to the Inter-racial Committee in Atlanta, Georgia. Founded in 1919, this organization, with its mostly white female leadership, promoted racial justice by decrying daily instances of racism, including lynching.

These early public uses of racial justice coincided with the modification of the nation's stratified durability from post–Civil War Reconstruction into the racial segregation of Jim Crow, which explicitly enforced racial segregation and disparities of resources and well-being through legal codes, housing, education, and cultural practices. In 1911, the year that the term "interracial justice" first appeared, sixty-six Black Americans were lynched. In 1919, often deemed the year of the "Red Summer," there were twenty-six protests between the months of April and October, and seventy-six Black Americans were lynched. In May and June of 1921, a group of whites attacked and burned to the ground the Greenwood District, known as the Black Wall Street because it was the wealthiest Black community in the United States.[14] The early twentieth century also witnessed a dramatic surge in white supremacist writings, such as Madison Grant's *The Passing of the Great Race*, as well as the Black centrist nationalist movement led by Marcus Garvey and the political and artistic surge of the Harlem Renaissance.[15] This historical context, alongside the emergence of the term "interracial," situates uses of "racial justice" and "interracial justice" amid a racialized reordering of society in the aftermath of slavery that does not necessarily speak to racism as a system created to benefit whites.

The terms "interracial justice" and "racial justice" cropped up again in the 1930s. In his 1937 publication *Interracial Justice: A Study of the Catholic Doctrine of Race Relations*, John LaFarge Jr. explores solutions to the "Negro factor" in national and religious processes through a Christian philosophy of social justice and social action.[16] The work is notable as the first complete treatment of the doctrine of racial justice from the Catholic viewpoint, but it is not unique in centering racial relations as the path to justice. George Edmund Haynes, a contemporary of LaFarge's and a Black Protestant social worker, was an educator and founder of the Urban League. Haynes published extensively on interracial relations, years before LaFarge, positing that interracial contact under amiable conditions would counteract growing Black nationalism. Historian David W. Southern posits that LaFarge neglected to cite Haynes's work out of the larger project to build the base of African Americans in the Catholic Church and refute perceptions that the church was for white people.[17] This contestation over the term "interracial justice" testifies to the ways that terminology around justice is in dynamic interaction with political economies of knowledge, status, and power. While not sentenced to any particular outcome, justice and its contestations are no less influenced by, and influential upon, power than any other social field.

These publications and the emergence of the term "interracial justice" occurred within a historical, political, and economic pursuit of religious following and whiteness-fueled concerns about the rise of Communism and Black nationalism. Interracial justice, within this context, included political goals that may today be characterized as interest convergence. This principle, put forward by critical race theorist Derrick A. Bell Jr., posits that partial release on restrictions is enacted by the dominant population only in order to further secure larger material investment.[18] Interracial justice referenced inequity but did not name the material investment in societal structures that amassed wealth for whites by restricting it from Black populations. We argue that the referents to interracial justice in the early twentieth century by white religious leaders and peace activists cordoned off materially transformative goals of justice and spoke of injustice as an almost happenstance product of diffusely shared separation. Further, the establishment of interracial justice set in motion the still-used trope of improving race relations, connoting that material inequity can be ameliorated through contact and/or that it is an equally shared burden irrespective of material investment in its perpetuation. Uses of interracial justice relied on ideas of proximity as the pathway to a better society, even though white and Black Americans had long lived in proximity to each other even when widely separated by policy and resources.[19] The contrastive words from Wells minimally display different affordances that emanate more critically indicted racialized violence.

The first time the term "racial justice" appeared without the prefix "inter" was in Hans Trefousse's 1969 publication, *The Radical Republicans: Lincoln's*

Vanguard for Racial Justice, which traces radicalism from its late 1840 beginnings to its decline in Ulysses S. Grant's administration. In the book, Trefousse explored the generation of radicals who "had been in the political struggle for human rights" and were the driving force within the Republican Party for the liberation of slaves and guaranteeing Black males the right to vote.[20] Trefousse maintained that the radicals laid the foundation for the subsequent achievement of their goals. Although "racial justice" is in the title of the book, it only appears three times in the text itself. Because the book is centrally an exploration of the abolishment of slavery and the advancement of civil rights, we infer that Trefousse meant those to be equivalent to racial justice. As with referents of interracial justice, how the problem and solutions are framed in the absence of explicit definitions still speaks to goals and theories of change. Although it can be maintained that racial justice is equivalent to the abolishment of slavery and the advancement of civil rights, stating so explicitly provides more opportunity to contest, agree with, or modify such definitions.

Following these scant handful of references first to "interracial justice" and then to "racial justice" in 1911 through 1969, the 1970s witnessed an exponential increase in the use of the term "racial justice" within academic and popular publications, with over twenty thousand academic references alone during the years 1967 to 2015 (see Figure 1). We argue that the first uses of the explicit term became something of a shorthand or placeholder

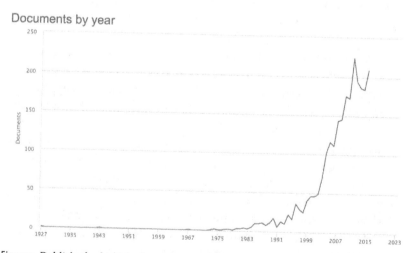

Documents by year

Figure 1. Published scholarly documents in English featuring the term "racial justice" between 1927 and 2015. The vast majority of documents were published beginning in 2003.

for mainstream justice agendas that meant to address race-based inequities but did not necessarily speak directly to the source of racialized injustice or the purposes of racism. Put more bluntly, it originated in projects that, intentionally or not, consciously or not, worked to protect white material investment in racism by not naming that investment.

USES DURING THE CIVIL RIGHTS MOVEMENT

An important corollary to mainstream texts, meaning of and for the dominant power group, are the theories that civil rights leaders provided about race and racism in the 1960s and 1970s. Speeches, as in the aforementioned one from Ida B. Wells in 1909, are a genre notably distinct from other political text genres. They serve many different purposes, but they generally share purposes of altering imaginations, setting forth action items, and/or rallying followers and potential followers. Speeches seek to effect particular peoples to act or think in particular ways, but those intentions do not predict their effects. This is particularly important to note in contextualizing the oft-quoted excerpt of Martin Luther King Jr.'s speech at the 1964 rally for dreams on Washington, D.C.'s mall, a speech that has become all but synonymous in its abridged ubiquitous form with racial progress as integration. Just before saying the words that have come to be the most quoted portion of the speech, King stated that this was the time to "lift the nation from the quicksand of racial injustice," situating his appeals within a project of nationhood. King's closing remarks then reference that now-familiar dream that all children be judged on the content of their character rather than their skin color. The widespread popularity of the few closing lines from a much longer speech and substantially larger movement and effort has taken on a life of its own. However, these remarks were not a planned portion of the speech but were added extemporaneously by King in the waning moments of his time at the podium.[21] That this speech is colloquially known as the "I Have a Dream" speech and not the name used for the rally in 1964 speaks to the ways that this excerpt from the speech, which served performative rallying purposes in 1964 in front of an audience of 250,000 people, has come to overshadow the other elements of this event that explicitly named and challenged the racialized condition of poverty. Further, this portion of a nation-referenced project of racial integration is starkly different from the multiple nation/state references King used in noting the "creative turmoil of a genuine civilization" in his 1964 acceptance speech for the Nobel Peace Prize.[22] In another speech, just three weeks before his assassination in

1968, King spoke in a small church in Mississippi and condemned the government subsidies set aside for white land-owning men and their reliance on unpaid and stymied compensation for Black labor. In that speech King proclaimed that Black Americans were "coming to get our check," a radically different point of content and tone than the speech he gave at the march on the Washington mall in 1964.[23] This is a markedly different speech and demands a contextually referenced engagement of King's words when considered alongside the "I Have a Dream" stanza that has become pablum for color-blind racism and benign projects of inclusion.[24] One portion of one speech has become a placeholder for appeals to color blindness while other speeches that address material inequities, by the same person, are drastically underreferenced. Racial justice and its referents to a snippet of a 1964 speech have shifted the fuller original contextualized meaning to become more closely aligned with colorblind ideals of racial justice, inclusion and harmony, and nation/state identity. We regard this winnowing of meaning as minimally an imperative to ask more pointedly what is obviated when colorblind versions of racial justice become most durable but also why ideas of integration prove more diffusely static than material analyses of gain wrought from harm. Further, we question how robust conceptualizations of justice are misassociated in the singular with two-dimensional views of speakers, obviating even the textured differences in the same speaker who communicates ideas of justice and change to different audiences. From our analytic view, whiteness is again perpetuated when color blindness is conflated with justice and reliant on singular tropes of public persona.

Black nationalists and pan-Africanist revolutionaries of the 1960s and 1970s often addressed racial terror, colonialism, and imperialism, but they rarely used the terms "racial injustice" or "racial justice." King, more than any other civil rights leader of this time, used the term "racial injustice" but not necessarily "racial justice." James Baldwin referred to the "racial nightmare" several times in his writings. He spoke to waking up from a nightmare and that being a painful process. Racial justice, in fact, does not appear in the speeches of the more revolutionary U.S.-based thinkers of the twentieth century, including Malcolm X, Ida B. Wells, Huey P. Newton, Marcus Garvey, or Elaine Brown, to name a few. This does not mean that racialized violence was not being addressed. Instead of "racial justice," "freedom" and "self-determination" were used. We interpret this difference in both nomenclature and project as tied to the strong influx and connection to Third World projects for national independence, the engagement with the writings of Karl Marx, and the responses and critiques to Marx that demanded a consideration of colonialism and racism along with class stratification.[25] These intellectual and praxis traditions, then, shaped a pursuit of freedom rather than justice. Many of the Black nationalist and internationalism speeches and platforms of the 1960s and 1970s speak of creating altogether different systems of interaction, sometimes nation based and sometimes not. For example, in 1970 Huey P. Newton, having just been released from federal prison for his actions on behalf of the Black Panther Party, commented that "the Black Panther Party will not accept the total destruction of the people. As a matter of fact, we have drawn a line of demarcation and we will no longer tolerate fascism, aggression, brutality, and murder of any kind. We will not sit around and allow ourselves to be murdered. Each person has an obligation to preserve himself."[26] Later in the same speech, Newton spoke not of building a new or more just nation but of intercommunalism to foster connection across and within Black communities. This project of survival in the face of fascism draws from a markedly different impulse for community and interreliability than the referents of interracial goodwill that Mead wrote about in 1911.

A discussion of racial freedom and justice is woefully incomplete without noting the significant contributions from then and still lesser-discussed Black feminists of the twentieth century. These contributions pushed forward the otherwise largely missing analysis of how projects of racism and racial injustice have always been gendered, with techniques of large-scale rape and conceptual divisions that highlight public realms of racialized violence at the expense of noting the connected private locations of violence. Many Black and Third World feminist thinkers, activists, and educators have illuminated the ways that projects of racial justice must attend to gender or they will have foreclosed addressing the lived realities of dispossession.

June Jordan wrote succinctly: "Freedom is indivisible or it is nothing at all besides sloganeering and temporary, short-sighted, and short-lived advancement for a few."[27] Before that, Anna Julia Cooper put forth ideals of how the "Negro" race could be delivered, and she asserted that it had to be sourced from the knowledges afforded by the liminal racialized and gendered location of Black women:

Now the fundamental agency under God in the regeneration, the re-training of the race, as well as the ground work and starting point of its progress upward, must be the *black woman*. With all the wrongs and neglects of her past, with all the weakness, the debasement, the moral thralldom of her present, the black woman of today stands mute and wondering at the

Herculean task devolving around her. But the cycles wait for her. No other hand can move the lever. She must be loosed from her bands and set to work.

Our meager and superficial results from past efforts prove their futility; and every attempt to elevate the Negro, whether undertaken by himself or through the philanthropy of others, cannot but prove abortive unless so directed as to utilize the indispensable agency of an elevated and trained womanhood.[28]

Cooper's, Jordan's, and Wells's words shed light on the ways that amid tendencies of many civil rights leaders to speak with varying precision to various constituencies about racial violence, too often, this did not feature an illumination of the connections between racialized and gendered injustice. The theorization of what constitutes justice and its limitations in race-only pursuits of freedom were borne of patriarchal logics that inconsistently locate women as strengths and threats to projects of equity and those of nationalism.[29] It is of note that we write this article and consider the project of racism as always having been gendered at a time when the contemporary social movement Black Lives Matter is demanding reckoning with systemic racism and patriarchy. This movement was started by three Black women. None of these facts mean anything static in and of themselves as transformative for what justice can do about race and racism, but we can and do ask how differing approaches to justice, race, and racism have circulated more and less widely. Neither does the presence of female-led movements mean that racism is being confronted for its purposes and then justice is shaped accordingly. We return to these points of assumptions of justice and progress based in social categories following an examination of uses of "racial justice" in academic texts.

ACADEMIC TEXTS

The societal institution of the academy is firmly rooted in the colonial racialized and gendered logics of property accumulation for some and dispossession for others.[30] This makes the pronounced increase in the use of "racial justice" in academic scholarly writing compelling as a point of analysis. As with any social field, the use begs the question of what trends and patterns these uses confer for imaginations and manifestations of justice.

Our analysis of references to "racial justice" in academic publications shows a small presence beginning in the early twentieth century and then a sharp uptick in publications around the late 1990s and 2000s (see Figure 1).

For a closer look at what kinds of framings were used in relation to social justice, we conducted a publication-by-publication content analysis of the one hundred most recent scholarly publications published in English that referenced "racial justice" in between 2005 and 2015. Of these, 70.8 percent are from the social sciences (see Figure 2).

As in other venues and genres of speech, references to "racial justice" and the problem of racism in academic discourse are malleable and linked to the positionality of its users. An analysis of one hundred articles from the arts and humanities and social sciences shows that racial justice is inconsistently, and rarely, defined. Orator F. Cook Jr. used the term "racial justice" in academic scholarship, with an appeal for American scholars to create distance from Afro-centered epistemologies: "Since our American negroes know nothing of Africa, teaching them to lament these imaginary 'destroyed values' is one way of teaching a resentment which otherwise might not be felt and for which there is no basis."[31] Cook's words have commonalities with the interracial justice meanings found in white organizers working from a framework of peace.

As with speakers in other fields, scholars have attempted to reckon with racial injustices and racism in varied ways. In fifty-nine of the articles, "racial

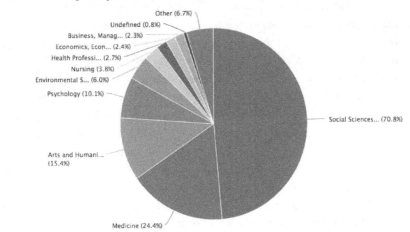

Documents by subject area

Other (6.7%)
Undefined (0.8%)
Business, Manag... (2.3%)
Economics, Econ... (2.4%)
Health Professi... (2.7%)
Nursing (3.8%)
Environmental S... (6.0%)
Psychology (10.1%)
Social Sciences... (70.8%)
Arts and Humani... (15.4%)
Medicine (24.4%)

Figure 2. Scholarly publications that use the term "racial justice," organized by scholarly area. The publications span from 1927 to 2015 (see Figure 1 for trend by year of publication) and are organized by academic discipline, showing the tendency for publications using the term to be in the social sciences, medicine, and arts and humanities.

justice" is mentioned in the title and abstract but not defined in the text itself. This finding is pivotal in and of itself, strongly manifest in academic texts and also prevalent in the other text genres we examined. As with other texts, the tendency was for examples of racial injustice to be articulated but with no explicit definitions of racial justice offered. A predominant framing in social science articles that refer to racial justice describes injustices and then proposes racial justice as the interruption, erasure, and/or cessation of racialized injustices.

One recent trend is to imagine racial justice as something that can be obtained through a prescribed set of actions that seek to redistribute justice or equality through dialogue and space for reflection. For example, eight articles published between 2013 and 2015 analyzed the impact of antiracist teaching. In 2013 Cheryl E. Matias, a noted authority on antiracist preparation of white teachers, wrote that educators must employ a resistive humanistic violence to racial injustice for true race dialogue to begin. Matias's argument, as in the majority of articles in our search, builds from a clear articulation of racial injustice, such as how children of color "play along" to appeal to white teachers and their projects. Importantly, as with four of the other articles examined, Matias cautions against the image or idea of the white teacher or social servant who is a savior and protector of justice, explaining how such images can ostracize teachers and students of color and weaken racially just projects.[32] However, as with forty-nine articles in the social sciences, what constitutes a racially just project is not articulated. In five of the articles that address how to reduce racial injustice, the prevailing concrete action to enact racial justice is to provide a "space." We contend that this tendency in the social sciences emanates from an applied aspect of the disciplines. Scholarship from these fields, including counseling psychology, education, and social work, have in common an appeal to praxis and impact on societal structures. In that vein, it makes sense that racial justice would include some actions relative to interrupting racial injustice even when default framing of racial justice prevails over explicit definitions.

In the group of articles that address racial justice and its relation to policy and the integrating of historically segregated spaces, four of the articles assert that a deep, calibrated, and cogent understanding of and discussion about the definition of race be had before discussions about racial justice emerge. In addressing the nuances and limitations of race as a concept, the group of articles under this category supports an audit of what it means to be assigned a race and the implications of such an assignment for policy. Examining the ways in which race has been used to stratify and subjugate people holds implications for what racial justice can and cannot do. For example, Blake Emerson, in "Dialectic of Color-Blindness," critiqued the idea of color blindness. He placed the right to racial justice on the individual and the law, referencing Theodor Adorno's social theory of emancipation. Racial justice here can only be achieved if the law helps the individual by becoming conscious of its own racist constructs and actively eradicates racism and racial inequality. Emerson wrote: "Law must stand against social structures that increase the salience of social and economic forces in determining individual thought and action."[33] From a critical race perspective, though, the law was codified precisely to enact racism, to create and preserve whiteness as property. As with the tendency in the social sciences to have applied redress to racial injustice in the form of dialogue and space, scholarship from the arts and humanities has shortcomings in its apprehension of the purposes of racism and how societal structures are intertwined and linked through these architectures. These inconsistencies and contradictions are not problems in and of themselves but hold more force for perpetuating racial injustice when clear goals and theories of change are forestalled.

RACIAL JUSTICE AND LIBERAL HUMANISM

The lack of explicit definition of "racial justice" in the vast majority of academic references and even in the statements of racial justice organizations does not mean that associative concepts are not communicating goals and theories of change. The term has been coupled with discussions of improving racial relations, removing barriers to civil rights, progress writ large, and redressing sites of racialized injustice. However, outside of the Black nationalist and Black feminist thinkers of the twentieth century and the current Black Lives Matter movement, we found that racial justice has been invoked as a form of liberal humanism, as a view of rights and human agency as metered through the nation/state project and largely individually accessed. From a liberal humanist perspective, the full development of societies should guarantee access to civil rights that transcends individuals' differences. As such, frames of racial justice, and justice more broadly, that are based in individuality are at cross-purposes with the population-level material structures and the fundamental aims of racism. As David Wills pointed out, "Compensatory justice cannot be appended to the liberal notion of racial justice as the non-discriminatory treatment of individuals as if it were a minor modification."[34]

The history of the term "racial justice," and its predecessor, "interracial justice," points to first church-centered and then state-centered interests to revise and modify how races are perceived but not to change material structures that organize using race as a category. In other words, the source of racial categories, racism itself, is not necessarily interrogated under most references to racial justice and certainly not in the origins of the term and its concerns for interracial dialogue. Furthermore, situating the emergence of the term with its first authors and the context of racism at those moments brings into question the ways the term was coined that served purposes of maintaining vested interest in material differential impacts of racism. That racial justice came into being through a concern for improving race relations while the nation was modifying its racial organization from reconstruction to the era of Jim Crow questions the function and effect of interracial dialogue against the shifting yet durable project of racial stratification. These questions become even sharper when considered alongside the charges of imperialism and appeals to survival and self-determination by many Black nationalists.

Under the onus of policies and practices that maintain a racial hierarchy, racial discord is to be minimally expected and perhaps quite rational in the face of structural racism. The racist capitalist structures of housing, labor, and education discrimination are not the result of a lack of dialogue. Juxtaposed to Ruth Wilson Gilmore's widely cited definition of racism, "the state-sanctioned or extralegal production and exploitation of group-differentiated vulnerability to premature death," racial justice that focuses on individual equity and interracial dialogue may do more to reseat material structures of inequity than to unhouse them as it forestalls population-level analyses of material profit for some predicated on material risk and harm for others.[35]

And yet the logic of racial justice in interracial dialogue shows signs of durability. In one recent example, in 2014, the chief executive officer of Starbucks issued an open letter outlining an initiative to "come together, in a safe space, and have a conversation about what was happening in our nation"; he went on to explain that a need for conversation "is why the Leadership Team and I have decided to expand opportunities for civil discourse within Starbucks, among our partner communities."[36] With little outline, guidance, or grounding in the historical and contemporary racial structure of the nation, let alone the crucial roles that coffee, sugar, and tea have played in the imperialist and colonial projects of the past several centuries, the initiative was a short-lived and much-critiqued break in the regular business of this multinational corporation. Echoing the origins of racial justice, the campaign, and its referents to safe spaces and universal ability to participate, is reflective of the genealogies of interracial dialogue. This history and still very much present work of racial justice reveals what its limits may be.

THE LIMITS OF RACIAL JUSTICE

Imani Perry grounds the title and focus of her 2011 book *More Beautiful and More Terrible: The Embrace and Transcendence of Racial Inequality in the United States* with a quote from James Baldwin: "American history is longer, larger, more various, more beautiful, and more terrible than anything anyone has ever said about it."[37] Both the quote from Baldwin and Perry's book bring much to bear on our analysis of the term "racial justice." Much has been written using the term, and its mere utterance is surely an improvement from a denial of racism as a fundamental and ongoing project of stratification in the United States and elsewhere. However, the phrase also has had untoward consequences. Without explicit definition, for there to be multiple and conflicting definitions, racial justice acts as a proxy for vague solutions to racism yet not necessarily transformation to its place as a tool for social categorization. Referents to equity, interracial justice, and equality all invoke egalitarian structures that propose to reorganize population-level realities of well-being through the category of race. It is a fair question to ask how justice can be achieved through a construct created in order to deliver injustice. The term "racial justice" is perhaps least strong when it assumes a common working definition by forestalling the important work of deliberating contesting views, goals, and theories of change.[38]

If racial justice is to interact productively with how racial categories are fomented and used to organize proximity to well-being and harm for entire populations, it requires language that is explicit about the origins of race relative to racism. As scholarship and study of racial formation, racism, and its structural elements builds, it should do so with an analysis commensurate with the sophistication of systemic racism captured in the profile of criminalized teachers offered at the start of our analysis. In other words, we call for a more sophisticated discussion of racial justice. Such a justice must be able to contend with not only how racism deeply needs racial categories but also how it coalesces with other vectors of oppression.[39] It should contend with how the killing of Eric Garner by a choke hold from a police officer was offset through attention to Garner's size, how Sandra Bland's death while in police custody was obviated by questions about her mental health, how the racialized difference in sentencing teachers under a neoliberal high-stakes testocracy was overshadowed by righteous but still limited vilification of testing regimes. Minimally, the language of justice should have capacity to describe how injustice happens in such ways that the primary arbiters of injustice maintain an appearance of neutrality and innocence.

Our analysis suggests that uses of the term "racial justice" must be much improved upon, beginning with baseline practices of defining the term. It should be defined differentially to approximate the ways that racism is enacted with different effects. Cumulatively, the term must be used for the job of confronting the ways that race was sociopolitically created as an organizing logic of humanity and more aptly put, less than human, and how it shapeshifts.[40] Denise Ferreira da Silva contends that "we fail to understand how the racial governs the contemporary global configuration because the leading account of racial subjection—the sociohistorical logic of exclusion—(re)produces the powers of the subject by rewriting racial difference as a signifier of cultural difference."[41]

CONCLUSION

In the same volume in which Du Bois made his prediction about the color line's material impact, he also explored ideas of progress. His essay "On the Meaning of Progress" recants through anecdote that the deeply entrenched project of white supremacy works systemically and in intertwined, nimble fashion. It is an essay in which Du Bois tells of his own reckoning with the ways that economic progress for the nation did not mean improvement for the lives of Black people, as capitalism and materialism overtook opportunities for the development of Black people as sentient, self-determining people in the United States. A few decades later, when the term "racial justice" was emerging from interracial justice, Du Bois distinguished between the long-term goal of interracial equity and the more immediate, short-term goal of segregation to develop opportunities within the Black community, among Black people, for Black people.[42] We return our analysis to Du Bois to learn from his technique of theorizing based on experience rather than on political economies.

Racism is an attack on humanness. Rather than ask how we can achieve racial justice, we ask what tools, perspectives, and practices can help to unhook the hold of this long-standing project from its anchor, if it is possible to wrest race away from its still operating bidding from racism. Or perhaps a lifting off from the project of race is necessary to imagine a global reality not filtered through the color line. What is apparent from just these two wonderings about possible futurities is that racial justice defined as the mere cessation of racialized injustice is proffered far too simplistically. Our analysis is offered in the hope of not resigning ourselves to a curtailed project of justice but to see the limits of what racial justice can do so that we might reach further to not just undoing injustice but to considering what freedom might entail.

LEIGH PATEL writes, teaches, and researches about the societally reproductive yet always potentially disruptive role of education in society. She is a board member of the Education for Liberation Network. She has worked as a journalist, teacher, policymaker, and academic. Across all of these roles and institutions, she tries to disrupt education as a colonial pursuit of property.

ALTON PRICE studies how the racialization of Black and Brown educators impacts school culture and student development. He has worked as a teacher and ministry fellow. As he pursues his graduate studies, he looks forward to learning more about school culture and its impact on students and teachers.

NOTES

1. W. E. B. Du Bois, *The Souls of Black Folk* (New York: Oxford University Press, 2007), 32, 15.

2. Robin D. G. Kelley, *Freedom Dreams: The Black Radical Imagination* (Boston, Mass.: Beacon Press, 2002); Audre Lorde, "The Master's Tools Will Never Dismantle the Master's House," in *Feminist Postcolonial Theory: A Reader*, ed. Reina Lewis and Sara Mills (London: Routledge, 2003), 25–28.

3. Michael Omi and Howard Winant, *Racial Formation in the United States* (London: Routledge, 2014).

4. Mae M. Ngai, *Impossible Subjects: Illegal Aliens and the Making of Modern America* (Princeton, N.J.: Princeton University Press, 2004).

5. Sylvia Wynter, "Unsettling the Coloniality of Being/Power/Truth/Freedom: Towards the Human, after Man, Its Overrepresentation—An Argument," *New Centennial Review* 3, no. 3 (2003): 257–337.

6. Leith Mullings, "Interrogating Racism: Toward an Antiracist Anthropology," *Annual Review of Anthropology* 34 (2005): 667–93.

7. Jacques Derrida, "Structure, Sign, and Play in the Discourse of the Human Sciences," in *A Postmodern Reader*, ed. Linda Hutcheon (New York: State University of New York Press, 1993), 223–42.

8. On genealogical inquiry, see Michel Foucault, "On the Genealogy of Ethics: An Overview of Work in Progress," in *The Foucault Reader*, ed. Paul Rabinow (New York: Pantheon Books, 1984), 340–72; Lisa Lowe, *The Intimacies of Four Continents* (Durham, N.C.: Duke University Press, 2015).

9. Race Forward: The Center for Racial Justice Innovation, "About Race Forward," https://www.raceforward.org/about.

10. Edwin Mead, "International Organization for Inter-racial Goodwill," *Advocate of Peace* 73, no. 9 (1911): 205–10.

11. G. Spiller, ed., *Papers on Inter-racial Problems Communicated to the First Universal Races Congress* (London: P. S. King & Son, 1911), xiv.

12. Ida B. Wells, "This Awful Slaughter" (speech, National Association for the Advancement of Colored People, Atlanta, Ga., May 8, 1909), http://www.blackpast.org/1909-ida-b-wells-awful-slaughter.

13. John White Jr., "Inter-racial Co-operation in the South," *Advocate of Peace through Justice* 83, no. 8 (1921): 300.

14. Scott Ellsworth, *Death in a Promised Land: The Tulsa Race Riot of 1921* (Baton Rouge: Louisiana State University Press, 1992).

15. Madison Grant, *The Passing of the Great Race; or, The Racial Basis of European History* (New York: Charles Scribner's Sons, 1916).

16. John LaFarge Jr., *Interracial Justice: A Study of the Catholic Doctrine of Race Relations* (New York: America Press, 1937).

17. David W. Southern, *John LaFarge and the Limits of Catholic Interracialism, 1911—1963* (Baton Rouge: Louisiana State University Press, 1996).

18. Derrick A. Bell Jr., "*Brown v. Board of Education* and the Interest-Convergence Dilemma," *Harvard Law Review* 93, no. 3 (1980): 518–34.

19. Kristen M. Lavelle, *Whitewashing the South: White Memories of Segregation and Civil Rights* (Lanham, Md.: Rowman & Littlefield, 2014).

20. Hans Trefousse, *The Radical Republicans: Lincoln's Vanguard for Racial Justice* (New York: Alfred A. Knopf, 1969), 407.

21. Gary Younge, *The Speech: The Story behind Dr. Martin Luther King Jr.'s Dream* (Chicago: Haymarket Books, 2013).

22. Martin Luther King Jr., "Nobel Prize Acceptance Speech," in *A Testament of Hope: The Essential Writings and Speeches of Martin Luther King, Jr.*, ed. James Melvin Washington (San Francisco: Harper & Row, 1986), 226.

23. Martin Luther King Jr., "Remaining Awake through a Great Revolution" (speech, National Cathedral, Washington, D.C., March 31, 1968), https://kinginstitute.stanford.edu/king-papers/publications/knock-midnight-inspiration-great-sermons-reverend-martin-luther-king-jr-10.

24. Eduardo Bonilla-Silva, *Racism without Racists: Color-Blind Racism and the Persistence of Racial Inequality in the United States* (Lanham, Md.: Rowman & Littlefield, 2006); Sara Ahmed, *On Being Included: Racism and Diversity in Institutional Life* (Durham, N.C.: Duke University Press, 2012).

25. Kelley, *Freedom Dreams*.

26. Huey P. Newton, "Speech Delivered at Boston College on November 18, 1970," in *The Huey P. Newton Reader*, ed. David Hilliard and Donald Weise (New York: Seven Stories Press, 2002), 161.

27. June Jordan, "A New Politics of Sexuality," in *Some of Us Did Not Die: New and Selected Essays* (New York: Basic/Civitas Press, 2003), 131.

28. Anna Julia Cooper, *A Voice from the South* (Oxford: Oxford University Press, 1988), 28.

29. Kelley, *Freedom Dreams.*

30. Joy James and Ruth Farmer, eds., *Spirit, Space & Survival: African American Women in (White) Academe* (London: Routledge, 1993).

31. Orator F. Cook Jr., "American Race Problems: Studies in America and Africa Lead to Conflicting Conclusions—Race Crossing and Racial Justice," *Journal of Heredity* 18, no. 11 (1927): 472.

32. Cheryl E. Matias, "Tears Worth Telling: Urban Teaching and the Possibilities of Racial Justice," *Multicultural Perspectives* 15, no. 4 (2013): 187–93.

33. Blake Emerson, "Dialectic of Color-blindness," *Philosophy & Social Criticism* 39, no. 7 (2013): 708.

34. David Wills, "Racial Justice and the Limits of American Liberalism," *Journal of Religious Ethics* 6, no. 2 (1978): 194.

35. Ruth Wilson Gilmore, *Golden Gulag: Prisons, Surplus, Crisis, and Opposition in Globalizing California* (Berkeley: University of California Press, 2007), 28.

36. Shaun King, "Starbucks CEO Writes an Open Letter on Race, Justice, Ferguson, and Open Communication," *Daily Kos,* December 18, 2014, http://www.daily kos.com/story/2014/12/18/1352776/-Starbucks-CEO-writes-an-open-letter-on-race -justice-Ferguson-and-open-communication.

37. Imani Perry, *More Beautiful and More Terrible: The Embrace and Transcendence of Racial Inequality in the United States* (New York: New York University Press, 2011), v.

38. Eve Tuck, "Suspending Damage: A Letter to Communities," *Harvard Educational Review* 79, no. 3 (2009): 409–28.

39. Barbara Ransby, "Black Feminism at Twenty-One: Reflections on the Evolution of a National Community," *Signs* 25, no. 4 (2000): 1215–21.

40. Wynter, "Unsettling the Coloniality."

41. Denise Ferreira da Silva, *Toward a Global Idea of Race* (Minneapolis: University of Minnesota Press, 2007), xxiv.

42. David Levering Lewis, *W. E. B. Du Bois: A Biography* (New York: Henry Holt, 2009).

Accounting for Carceral Reformations

Gay and Transgender Jailing in Los Angeles as Justice Impossible

REN-YO HWANG

We are in a state of war. But it's not enough to say that or understand that it seems to me. We need to understand what exactly it is the state is defending itself from. . . . So when we say that "Black Lives Matter" I think what we do sometimes is obscure that it's Black life that matters. That insurgent Black social life still constitutes a profound threat to the already existing order of things.

—Fred Moten, in "Do Black Lives Matter?"

The girls usually keep physical violence [by correction officers] to themselves. They might say something if they can tell us directly, but they don't write about it as much. The fact that people don't talk about it doesn't mean it doesn't happen. It means that people are scared. There's no way it can just be the inmates because the inmates don't have access all the time. It's the guards who have access. They see it and know what's going on. If it's happening, even if it's another inmate doing it, then the guards are involved, because flat out, they're in control.

—Miss Major Griffin-Gracy, quoted in Jessica Stern,
"This Is What Pride Looks Like"

The concept of justice invokes an endless flow of contradictions, whether in recitation, practice, or visions of equity and fairness. Justice, at its etymological English root, is "the exercise of authority in vindication of right by assigning reward or punishment," or, simply put, the administration of the law.[1] Whether in daily exchanges, commonsense notions, institutional policy, de facto / de jure legal practice, or even our most futuristic imaginations of a world not yet here, the call for justice often results from a lack. Through three avenues of justice—the criminal justice system, restorative justice, and transformative justice—it asks how these ideological and material interpretations of justice might inhibit and/or make life possible in both particular and abstract ways.[2] This article begins by considering the various ways in which "accountability" has been studied and used as an evaluative mode to define what is "just" or justifiable. Through discourses of "police accountability," it further argues that carceral logics have continued to control the reach of what justice could mean through spurious processes of accountability. The second section focuses on the case of K6G, the gay men and transgender women's unit inside the Los Angeles County Men's Central Jail. Interwoven with an ethnographic narrative, it argues that differentiating community power wielded against expansion of state law enforcement agencies versus being yielded as a "community-based partner or relation" controlled by state law enforcement agencies allows for clearer reflective pathways distinguishing abolitionist reform from carceral expansive reform. Moreover, in an effort to uplift the nuances of collective resistance to the entrapments of the criminal justice system, it argues that survival necessitates dealing with faulty options, ones that do not always result from or in strategic abolitionist reform, yet these contradictions are interlinked to visioning a world beyond just justice.

ACCOUNTING TO WHOM AND FOR WHAT?

Whether from institutions of financial management to studies of compliance in regulatory procedures and practices, accountability is broadly defined as a process of holding individuals or organizations responsible for their performance or actions.[3] Edward P. Weber defines the process of accountability as a "set of roles, rules, norms, decision-making procedures, and programs that serve to define social practices and to guide interactions of those participating in these practices."[4] In one sense, accountability is a process that does not necessitate public or social accountability but rather relies on the internal structural and performative mechanisms within a system itself, an interior relationalism. The system, however willfully negligent to the exterior—to relationships of moral, social, ethical, justice-based obligations—can still be, as is often the case, unquestionably founded in settler-colonial genocide, anti-Indigenous, anti-Black, institutional and structural racism, ableism, and gendered and sexual violence. Governing structures, such as the U.S. government, military, law enforcement, nongovernmental organizaions (NGOs), World Bank, International Monetary Fund (IMF), and international corporations, with internal mechanisms of accountability do not need to review their institutional impact beyond predesignated social partners and specified public sectors. However, most performance-based systems do not exist within a sphere of power unto themselves. Internal review and self-reporting practices promulgate narrow conceptions of accountability as a logical syllogism. Weber describes two critical threads of inquiry in accountability scholarship, asking "for what" and "to whom" as a means of promoting models of broad-based democratic accountability, which exists beyond dualities of internal or external governing structures.[5] Carol Chetkovich and Frances Kunreuther describe models of grassroots accountability as making possible sustainable community-led relations between governance, democratic internal structures, collectivity, consensus decision-making, and consistent commitment to community input and holistic engagement. Weber, on the one hand, and Chetkovich and Kunreuther, on the other, present two models of accountability: the reformation of a top-down hierarchical "above" model versus a grassroots bottom-up "below" accountability approach.[6] Social and public accountability, particularly when leveraged by players outside the system that's being challenged, can force new bottom-up accountability in even the most self-regulated and naturalized systems of power such as law, policing, and prisons.

Candace McCoy, editor of the 2010 anthology *Holding Police Accountable*, describes the subject of police accountability scholarship as a past fad, its previous heyday established in the wake of 1960s and 1970s professional reform that focused on regulatory cohesion and uniformity between local, state, and federal agencies, "standards of law and internal departmental rules in compliance with law."[7] At that moment where local "watchman" patrols transitioned rapidly into cooperating law enforcement agencies, the U.S. Constitution as a regulatory juridical device united the development of agency policies and procedures on a federal to local level. Accountability within this sector of internal law enforcement governance was distinctly approached through a top-down hierarchical framework, albeit with an acceptable range of autonomy and discretion as "justifiable" if avoiding noticeable violations to constitutional law. Following this original wave of traditional "police accountability"—alongside the expansive growth of the criminal justice system; rapid private and public prison construction; "tough on crime," "quality of life," and "broken window" policing and targeted incarceration; the "war on drugs"; extreme austerity measures via welfare reform inciting economic warfare on working-class inner-city people of color, particularly Black and Latinx families—neoliberal social science research on "accountability" took up interest in discrepancies in discretionary practices in racial profiling and "implicit bias."[8]

Current criticisms of police accountability not only name failures to comply with law and internal policy but also link racial profiling, unfair sentencing, and racially biased excessive and lethal force as systemic issues beyond individual misconduct. In 2011 the United Nations Office on Drug and Crime published its *Handbook on Police Accountability, Oversight and Integrity,* offering policy recommendations to which both the state and civil society are integral to ensuring the legitimacy of the policing system. This account of necessary international criminal justice reform presumes that a system of policing with oversight and accountability will create ever-better, ever-improving, and effective policing.[9] However, even in the realm of accounting for police misconduct on an individual officer basis, these discourses continue to naturalize the social contract and exponential expansion of the (post)modern police force, one that uses new invasive and sublimating technologies such as geolocation, biometrics, hyper-militarization, drone and identity surveillance, big data, and (c)overt intelligence gathering via "community participation" and NGO collaborative crime databases.[10] Policing, as Michel Foucault theorized nearly a half century prior at the birth of modern policing, in a coupling relation to the prison and the criminal justice system, seeks to seamlessly produce disciplinary power, naturalizing its ability to make accountability and justice a matter of perfecting crime control and the administration of punishment (euphemistically deemed rehabilitation).[11] Policing and prisoning, as a modernized system that must appear to always account for its parts and whole at all times, remains self-defending, self-justifying, self-surrounding, and thus mandating its indispensability to shared notions of (criminal) justice, even when admitting to corruption and/or crisis by its own rules.[12]

The issue of police accountability and U.S. police violence has remained front and center in national and international news since the blooming of #BlackLivesMatter in 2013.[13] Those who understood the necessity of the outcry of "Black Lives Matter!" often identified with one of two factions, those who understood the criminal justice system as a thing lacking accountability and need of repair and those who believed the system was perfected through the continual control and extermination of "insurgent Black social life."[14] The former is viewed as inhabiting a restorative justice or reformist approach and the latter as more aligned with an abolitionist/ transformative justice framework. Public discourses critiquing police brutality and law enforcement abuse have both invoked and challenged various processes of "accountability" inside and outside more familiar frameworks of justice.[15] Self-regulation in governance and most public institutions, like law enforcement, will always perform some modest interior/internal account-ability via reform of administration, and enforcement and revision of formal agency policies. With law enforcement, this normally involves agency-level and/or individual-level officer processes of self-regulated accountability that largely remain dependent on documented civil or supervisor-based com-plaints. Agencies such as Internal Affairs, police unions, and state investiga-tive bureaus might further become involved when mass outcries generate enough public pressure that police officers or departments then force the investigative hand of outside agencies. However, police unions often in the provisional fine print of their contracts prevent even the most modest forms of individual-level accountability.[16]

Criminal justice reform, even if reaching accountability par excellence, still cannot conceive of rule of law and "crime and punishment" as, in itself, a thing undignified, as that which can only offer a violently subjective objec-tivity. The analogous relationship between "poverty," "criminality," class, and contribution either owes or benefits from the exponential power and institutionalization of U.S. law and the criminal justice system. In *Debt to Society: Accounting for Life under Capitalism,* Miranda Joseph demonstrates the encompassing relation of crime and debt as measures and metrics in which we have come to know and inhabit forms of accounting for justice.[17] The rapid expansion of interstate-agency intelligence gathering, multiagency participation, and crime data naturalizes a white supremacist penal logic as evidenced by numbers narrating and mapping crime trends and social failures. Inversely, such data production also awards success to law enforce-ment for efficiency when, for instance, the number of reported crimes de-creases from one year to the next. These numbers are purposed both to account for trends from particular to abstract sets of typified crimes (e.g., violent hate crimes, property crimes, sex offenses) and to ensure the stock-piling of state-based data production year to year. Inversely, if crime report-ing is high, such accounting via numbers serves as objective evidence for state agencies to prove an increase in funding needs. Such accounting for "injustices" against the law or the state not only naturalize the need for accu-mulating and standardizing state data as an actuarial science of precrime profiling but has become the hardened receptacle for conservative to pro-gressive criminal reform (e.g., less insensitive or more inclusive categoriza-tion, streamlining, or making more autonomous data intake procedures and policies). Criminal justice reform via statistical accounting or processes of state accountability remains an unshakeable calculus of crime and debt, a sublimated calculus that has been perfected through historical and material atrocities of colonial and racial violence, capitalism, and accumulation.

Nonprofit foundations, policy institutes, NGOs, and social justice organizations seeking justice often participate in the production of state-based data as well as advocate for resources based on state-based statistical claims. Brokering coalitional partnerships with state agencies in order to gain access to federal funding and advocate for some version of law reform, such efforts regenerate the notion of state-based justice as justice incarnate.[18] Jennifer Wolch pointedly described in 1990 the very conglomerate role of the voluntary sector in institutionalizing what she calls the "shadow state" and what Treva Ellison has described as the phenomena of individuals being "serviceable yet unprotectable."[19] Such a voluntary sector, however focused on issues of "social justice," is compelled to account for injustices through contribution and application of state-mandated statistical crime reporting, what Lauren Berlant describes as the collusion between social justice activism and risk-management governance in producing an "actuarial imaginary of biopolitics."[20] In other words, the politics of identity-making and service provision create an image of abstracted yet particular peoples *as* risk, those who are most inherently a "debt to society."[21] These realities thus leave certain catch-all identities perhaps serviceable to a degree yet fail to guarantee safety from daily state or law enforcement violence.[22] Accountability of who receives protection at the expense of disposable others results not in a matter of increased safety but in permitting state-sanctioned safety as the very punishment of excessive social life.

The omnipresence of the criminal justice system (e.g., border patrols, Transportation Security Administration [TSA], juvenile and immigration detention centers, hate crimes task forces, school resource officers, highway patrols, sheriff's departments, departments of corrections, prosecutors, and public defenders) has largely continued to attempt to control and dictate what is meant by the pliable and bureaucratic term "accountability." Authorized forms of accountability by state apparatuses—as an ideological, practical, and sociohistorical process—therefore hide the flexible interiority that makes any such claims to "accountability" actually lifeless or selecting of what is left for living *(make live and let die)*.[23] Accounting for the productivity and generative possibilities *within* and *by* the criminal justice system can only attend to prescriptions and proscriptions of particular colonial and imperial notions of justice; such notions reproduced through the very mechanisms machined to control life abound (in excess and surplus) against a securitized and protectable life (universality or "the human" as intrinsically excluding/exclusive).[24] The task of criminal justice reform thus has remained an adjustment of the decibels in which the "administration of violence" has reached an unwarranted peak. Such accounting thus can only register the state's failure or our collective failure to conceive of a more just discipline, one in which intensity of punishment can be traded against a decrease of magnitude of projected social risks. Such a calculus always begins and ends with the deficit incurred by the risk—"the criminal"—and their relationship to the crime and society. Like a nonexpungeable criminal record, the "criminal" remains in eternal indebtedness to the state. Although the U.S. criminal justice system has reformed from sovereign power and corporal punishment to biopolitical discipline through "mass incarceration,"[25] the state, even in its decentralization of power, holds hostage our shared sense of value we attribute to one another. Joseph describes this deficit as debt to society, the "criminal" time paid to society through prison time.[26]

Fred Moten invites us to consider a new way of looking at the world beyond the "rubric of accounting, or accountability, or accountableness, or something, of calculation in that sense" through "the abolition of credit," one of the most violent and death-making structures of our time. He writes, "Anybody who's breathing should have everything that they need and 93% of what they want—not by virtue of the fact that you work today, but by virtue of the fact that you are here."[27] Life cannot be accounted for in terms of deserving or earning credit or imposed with debt. It is not work, labor, or one's inherited birthright that earns credit; rather, life is the thing that exceeds accountability. Life cannot actually be accounted for—life *just is* by virtue of *being*. Implemented policies and protocols such as the police-dispatched acronym and category of N.H.I. (*no humans involved*), brought to light following the Los Angeles uprisings in 1992, became a code to permit any discretion of force upon Black and Brown inner-city jobless youth deemed disposable. Routine practices such as these, approved by government agencies, loudly demonstrate how obeying internal organizing protocols of self-accountability exist as violent and empty signifiers of justice. Sylvia Wynter concludes in her 1992 letter, "No Humans Involved," that even with life counted as less or absent of humanness, no matter, life lived simply is the *Truth*. She states, "He is, they are, the Truth."[28] Wynter here challenges all systems of accounting, positivist logic, and knowledge-making in order to provoke us to consider our role as those who are in the business of "instituting this Truth" as the subject of adjustment and transformation, not the manufacturing of the criminal subject/object/figure of social control. How then might our conceptions of the value of life actually not be grounded in value *as* our adjustment to capitalism and criminality?

SURVIVING K6G: COLLECTIVE POSSIBILITIES FOR LIFE BEYOND

Never fully understanding the label of "scholar-activist," I spent most of 2014–15 deciding to slowly cycle off collective work in social justice organizing spaces, particularly queer and transgender of color, prison-abolitionist and labor organizations, actions, rallies, endless meetings, collective strategy sessions, dinner table dreaming and scheming, in order to complete a dissertation. I believed that by unplugging with these communities, this sacrifice would ascend my chances to steal away university resources for redistribution, as "the only possible relationship to the university today is a criminal one."[29] Little did I know, in transitioning to what I considered doing just "interpersonal community jail support," I would come to understand the importance of tracing the challenges and lessons learned in working, in the most mundane ways, both outside and within practical state-controlled justice channels as sometimes an extremely faulty but necessary means to meet people's livelihoods and self-determined requests. This section will offer some of those moments in pieces.

Los Angeles is often championed as a model city for its history of lesbian, gay, bisexual, and transgender (LGBT)–friendly social services, and particularly for the largest service-providing LGBT center in the world, the Los Angeles Gay and Lesbian Center (LAGLC). LAGLC is known for its partnership in modeling and educating the Los Angeles Police Department (LAPD), West Hollywood Police Department (WHPD), and Los Angeles Sheriff's Department (LASD) with more gay-friendly and transgender-sensitive reforms in policing and imprisonment. Not only is Los Angeles County Men's Central (MCJ) jail the largest jailer in the United States and the world, but the jail has provided much-lauded "gender reform" over the last three decades, offering a self-segregated gender jailing unit for incarcerated gay men and transgender women (named K6G, formerly K11).[30] K6G has been operative since 1985. These units were intended, like the current $2 billion contested plans to rebuild the MCJ jail and build an additional women's prison, to make existing jails and prisons "better and safer." The advent of K6G stemmed from a 1982 ACLU lawsuit brought upon the jail on behalf of "homosexual inmates" due to threat of sexual and physical violence faced when placed in the general population of the jail. Russell Robinson describes the policing of gender norms inside prisons as a part of the structural problem that incites interpersonal sexual violence on top of structural gendered and sexual violence, noting that

> the Jail's screening policy constructs gay and transgender identity in a narrow, stereotypical fashion and excludes some of the most vulnerable inmates. . . . The targeting of transgender and gay inmates for sexual assault emerges from a broader regime that valorizes an idealized form of masculinity and polices the gender performance of all people.[31]

Robinson centralizes the damage that postracial, white gay conceptions of homosexuality can reinforce and normalize through the process of entry into K6G. Not only must those incarcerated perform particular white-centric conceptions of homosexuality and masculinity, defining who truly deserves to belong in K6G, but these logics actually create situations in which sexual violence outside these assumptive roles of heterosexual "predator" and homosexual or transgender "victim" will then be elided. Research expert and advocate of K6G Sharon Dolovich writes, "I recognize that this enterprise [advocating for K6G] may expose me to the charge that, by seeking the means to improve carceral conditions, I may only be further entrenching a fundamentally illegitimate penal system."[32] Victoria Law describes such "pinkwashing" prison reform as "carceral feminism" that erases "the ways in which race, class, gender identity, and immigration status leave certain women more vulnerable to violence and that greater criminalization often places these same women at risk of state violence."[33] Such gender-responsive and restorative reforms fail to strategize against the penal institution to redirect power to those to whom the very reforms claim to be most indebted.

Further, the conditions of overcrowding, confinement, noise, light and air pollution, micro to aggressive health pollutants, and a state of constant hostile surveillance and authority—whether one enters with notable mental health issues or not—in MCJ, like in all jails and prisons in general, only provoke an intensification and exacerbation of one's state of vulnerable mental health. The unit of K6G is not impervious to the exact same damning conditions. The self-segregated gay and transgender unit not only mirror conditions of the larger jail, but celebratory coverage of K6G's "safety," for example in LA Weekly's 2014 digital video and article, "In the Gay Wing of L.A. Men's Central Jail, It's Not Shanks and Muggings but Hand-Sewn Gowns and Tears," overshadows issues of sheriff abuse, mental health negligence, and lack of access to transgender health resources, programming, a law library, and basic health care.[34]

I usually associate the area code 713 (Houston, Texas) with my mom or Taiwanese family who immigrated to Houston in the early 1990s to do restaurant importing in the wholesale district of Harwin Drive. This community of mostly East Asian wholesalers invited both Black patrons and small business owners but also openly surveilled and feared any Black social life in excess of familiar trusted patronage. A recent, missed 713 call, however, was not family but another call brokered by Global Tel*Link (GTL), the telecommunications "corrections innovations leader" for the last quarter century in North America, which manages an annual $1.5 billion "inmate calling service" (ICS) industry.[35] One of GTL's main sites for data backup is located in Houston, Texas—hence the dispatched 713 area code.[36] These 713 calls are a reminder of the messy entanglements of my own privilege accumulated from relationships of racial capital; here I was on the receiving end of the call, safely outside the jail. A phone call to the outside is sometimes a lifeline for those inside, an assurance that there is a world outside the cages that still witnesses and remembers the life of the people inside who are told repeatedly they do not matter.[37] When those incarcerated are placed in solitary confinement resulting from an "altercation" with a "peace officer," privileges are almost always revoked or restricted. Phone calls act as an imperfect but necessary tool, a means to report abuse, violence, mistreatment, and pressure for accountability, and almost exclusively require external actors and agencies. With risks of phone calls being audio recorded, manipulated as "self-incriminating" evidence, or possibly provoking officer retaliation, the only other existing legal channels to pursue sheriff accountability are "in-house complaint forms." Such in-house internal processes offer only as much uncertainty as those incarcerated permanently inhabit a place of "guilt," a debt that is always to be paid while in jail.

As a collective support team of friends, family, and community members in Los Angeles, the shared goal of the team has been to support several transgender and queer of color community members inside K6G. Identifying too as mostly all queer, transgender, and gender-nonconforming people of color with different sets of privileges, this small support collective of about ten people organized around teams of core coordination, legal support, spiritual/ mental health, fundraising, and a larger community support network. Identifying as well as community organizers, abolitionists, artists, mothers, siblings, queer poly family, and comrades, our roles fluctuated greatly over the course of 2014–16, depending on drastically shifting demands resulting from the extreme precarity of those inside. The collective team primarily worked on legal support and research, raising legal fees, scheduling consistent visitations, appearing for court support, writing letters and holiday cards, sending in jail-permissible books, alleviating attempts at self-harm and suicide, raising money weekly for commissary, depositing money in person, trying our best to receive phone calls, building strategies around their safety inside against staff hostility, abuse, and mental health negligence, alleviating more attempts at self-harm and suicide, advocating for proper hormone replacement therapy, and countering all levels of violence faced in being locked in a cage and/or desolate solitary confinement. The collective team, in an effort to counter reported abuse, sought whatever assistance was at our disposal, resources like the Los Angeles County (LAC) Office of Inspector General (OIG), a body said to offer "independent and comprehensive oversight, monitoring and reporting" over the Los Angeles Sheriff's Department (LASD).[38] The OIG was created as a department under the county board of supervisors, primarily overseeing the Men's Central Jail (MCJ) and Twin Towers, one of the largest de facto mental health facilities in the United States and the world.[39] The OIG is limited in its power to interrupt the "investigative function" of the LASD. Further, the issue of investigating "peace officers," the official euphemism for sheriffs and deputies inside the jail, is further protected by clauses safeguarding employee personnel files as privileged and confidential information. In other words, even if an officer is reported, most likely to a "civilian" outside the jail about an experience of abuse, both the OIG and community advocates are left with very little power to even *look into* the reported abuse.

In K6G and MCJ, if someone is being harassed by a "peace officer" and is forced to defend themselves verbally or physically, or performs any inaction or action that does not register as complicity or complete submission at the discretion of the officer, the individual can be penalized for belligerence. In other words, physical force, however excessive, is a legitimate means to force submission of those whom peace officers judge as "resisting" or in noncompliance. If the incarcerated person resists or defends themselves because they believe what the officer is doing is unfair or excessive, or if they are simply reacting instinctually to being violated, from the moment of violation through disciplinary hearing to the discipline itself, a testimony of an incarcerated person is never considered more valuable, more technically accountable to justice, than one of a "sworn officer." Accountability in the case of violence inside the jails and prisons cannot ever be won by those already seen as having been in violation to, discredited from, and committing an injustice in the system of justice ("criminals," "perpetrators," "inmates," and "prisoners" as less than "human"). When such disciplinary actions are taken, the incarcerated individual is likely thrown into solitary confinement and has all privileges revoked. This is an example of very typical "order" and "discipline" by officers asserting their authority and masculinity—not to mention the outright sexual abuse, violence, and verbal degradation that occurs between law enforcement and, most frequently, those policed at the intersections of gender, race, sexuality, class, and citizen-status. Over the course of ninety days, our collective team attempted to get the Los Angeles Office of Inspector General involved in overseeing what could only be described as excessive force on our community members inside. Not only did this form of internal accountability fail to offer any possibilities for relief of harm done, but it also became clear that every oversight process correctively tracking policy and procedure is first and foremost produced and controlled by the LASD. Tracing the paperwork, officer reports, and review board report assessing the "alleged" abuse was an orchestrated production fully overseen by the sheriff's department, thus any potential investigation by the OIG required the timely cooperation from LASD that they simply would not receive. We learned that if the LASD decided to be accountable to disciplining an officer for use of excessive force, the case would be referred to their office of Internal Affairs and, as outlined in their police union contract, would become a fully confidential issue between employee and employer. As the Los Angeles County Sheriff's Department and jail is under federal investigation by the U.S. Department of Justice, all internal attempts so far to address issues such as overcrowding have only resulted in proposals and plans for more jail construction and expansion. Attempts to account for injustices through extensions of the criminal system present only a side shuffle, a horizontal mutual exchange of power. Not only does the role of the OIG fail to enact even an inexact performance of justice, but current external oversight of the LASD simply has no interest in moving power away from itself; rather, such institutions seek only to have their self-circulating power be harnessed and or brokered more efficiently (with less visible friction). Accountability via the OIG would only ensure that the LASD perform more productively according to the rules and policies already in place, none of which have any interest in defining safety beyond degrees of more or less punitive discretion (excessive force or just regular force). The OIG is accountable most directly to its underwriters, the county board of supervisors, and to its ability to have as little or no interference on the LASD to investigate itself (its staff, officers, and inmates).

In an ongoing fight to shuffle power from the bottom up, the Los Angeles grassroots community organization Dignity and Power Now (DPN), formerly the Coalition to End Sheriff Violence in LA Jails (C2ESV), which has been consistently building coalitions and campaigns through research, reporting, organizing, and working groups led by formerly incarcerated staff and organization members, has over the last three years fought for the implementation of a law enforcement–free civilian review board (civilian oversight commission) with legal subpoena power. Demanding an oversight body constituted by exclusively formerly incarcerated individuals and family members, DPN has been willing to play "by the books" of the criminal justice system in order to attempt to reduce the violence inflicted upon those incarcerated. Their overall strategy has been to shift the discourse and channels in which power and resources are located—from the state to those in communities most directly impacted—quite literally through a refusal of the civilian review board to have representation from any former or current law enforcement officers. Further, DPN's work continues to center a structural analysis of the material conditions that produce "criminality" as poverty or mental illness. DPN's strategies, aimed to reform the criminal justice system, refuse to allow reform to be only performative, demanding instead redistribution of power to those most impacted and providing an example of abolitionist reform within a transformative justice framework.[40] Mark-Anthony Johnson, the current director of health and wellness at DPN, spoke out at a recent board of supervisors meeting in which the board went forward with permitting former law enforcement presence. He stated:

> Why would we consider and even entertain former law enforcement being on this commission?? That is a dangerously problematic proposition. We spent *six* months in the working group process, where the ALADS [Association of Los Angeles Deputy Sheriffs] representatives said to us that discriminating against law enforcement is *the same thing* as discriminating against Black people! Why would these supervisors align themselves with that analysis?[41]

This logic of inverted discrimination against the police, as a veritable embodiment of personhood and not a social role of state-funded public service, has gained much traction to the effect of #PoliceLivesMatter and #BlueLivesMatter against the assertion and movement of #BlackLivesMatter. Such logic discourages evaluation or even critical thought, opinion, or any level of even modest criticism of law enforcement as anything less than support-ing the enforcement of justice. Anything less, by this very popular logic, ought to be simply unthinkable on our part. The county board of super-visors indeed aligned itself with this logic because it is there, shamelessly, to serve the interests of its body, to reproduce, if not seek expansion of, state power. The civilian review board, in other words, could never *actually* exist, as long as the county board of supervisors was positioned above to oversee it. "Community," in other words, was just as flexible a term as "oversight" or accountability. What "community" could not mean was a legitimate avenue to expand power for those most directly impacted by jailing; instead, it could only offer flexible self-regulating performances of accountability.

Humaneness within a jail, or humanity through jailing, is an accounting for what can be added and what must be reduced for a population deemed less than human. You can add more public funding for the expansion of the jail, but the exchange is that you must reduce overcrowding. This type of infallible and inexact math tells us nothing about improved conditions or conditional improvement, and only promises to improve the penal system's ability to continue jailing. A different formula and transformative account-ing might instead insist that one can add more community-based resources such as education programming inside the jail but must promise to offer even more housing and living wage programming for those on parole or probation. Like the term "harm reduction," the analysis of what can be done in the *meantime* is a quick cost-benefit analysis, where suffering now must be addressed and other sufferings, perhaps those unregistered, unwitnessed, or unaccounted for, simply are not a part of the equation. Short of the full belief that redirecting all current funds used to sustain K6G could be placed into community-based services such as housing, healthcare, and livable wages would be possible in our lifetimes, knowing the failures and violence of the criminal justice system is sometimes not enough to rock the faith for those who remain loyal to its constant state of (dis)repair.

ORGANIZING LOVE, ACCOUNTING FOR ONE ANOTHER

Affective labor, trauma, grief, loss, and also love make up some of the non-things that cannot ever be sufficiently accounted for by way of state-based justice. Even the most illustrious and holistic forms of justice cannot fully witness such life matters. Most of us in our entire lives—the 2.2 million in prison, jails, and detention centers not included—will never have to account for the feeling of sitting in a cage for twenty-three hours of the day, for years, awaiting trial, and a lifetime without parole. Justice as a process and/or objective will continue to perform "truth" and naturalize *the state* as *being*, and such a justice will continue, however modified in intensity, to require punishment and debt to the state. Such carceral debt offers intergenerational trauma and life insecurity toward premature death (e.g., capital punishment, life without parole, carceral time), particularly for Black, Indigenous, Latinx, immigrant, jobless, houseless, gender nonconforming, and undocumented communities. State and police accountability, even as it is criticized and reformed, remains a means to address corruption or inequity of such systems, and at best to promote and restore performance productivity. Reform measures aimed to ensure a penal system's ability to do a better job can only do just that: penalize better.[42] When we think of what *works* for people inside jails to get free or to get care, it is almost always family members, friends, loved ones, and other community members who assist in their survival, their ability to get out, remain out, heal, and be—what have largely been called "community-based solutions and resources." Solutions through punitive legislation only fetishize and recriminalize unsafety on the inside as hot button issues mandating further state protection for some while doubling state criminalization for others. Such criminal expansive reforms only reproduce structuring logics of what is and is not classified as sexual violence to state violence. Such logics create a dangerous cleave between state violence and sexual violence, as if the former does not mediate the latter. Gender reform in prison does not offer a means to more correctly restore life; rather, it models the possibility for the carceral state to expand both its institutional and material power and authority.

Advocating for any unit of jailing, even if segregated, and not simultaneously advocating for the abolishment of the entire system leaves room for further seduction into the expansive prowess and more postracial skin of the criminal justice system. These contradictions must exist conterminously if we are to account for any degree of destruction such a penal system has had, not only on those most directly impacted but on our imaginations for a world beyond justifying death as collateral to an "objective" justice. Restorative justice practices continue to hinge on processes of discovering objective truth, offering a conceptual closure for the victim in order to restore the loss done against person(s) and community. Even at its best, a reformative restorative justice might reduce some kind of harm done, with the participation of the voluntary sector shadow state, but can only replace it with another harm—albeit in different capacity, tonality, and intensity. Jin Haritaworn writes, "Besides understanding the close relationship between criminalisation and pathologisation, across multiple formal and institutional sites, an abolitionist imagination might also involve attending to the way punitive and pathologising logics undergird informal sites, including those who identify as alternative, radical or progressive."[43] These are the abolitionist sentiments many neoliberal NGOs, nonprofit organizations, social science, and even social justice researchers are unwilling to tow, or at least to critically imagine, in real time and in real practice. We do in fact reduce the harm for those inside through abolitionist reform strategies paired with everyday uplift of the labor and community resources it takes to dislodge one prison brick at a time. The family and loved ones of those inside imagine and practice this harm reduction creatively and collectively, and in supporting this work they can regenerate power elsewhere away from material, ideological, and discursive expansion of a shadow state. Gender-sensitive and sexuality-based recommendations, like the ones brokered from the ACLU, LAGLC, and entities like the Transgender Law Center, are, in proposal and intention, aimed at serving, first and foremost, the community most impacted by policing and prisons. However, such partnerships do not always achieve a redistribution of power from state concentration. However, this does not abolish the need for critically engaging such reforms; instead, with intent to serve the survivors, like restorative justice, how might this service transform into a remedy against logics that measure more and less worthy victims "to reinforce our tenuous right to exist by undermining someone else's"?[44]

When the survivor became exclusively the victim, particularly in a duality of victim to perpetrator/offender/criminal, restorative justice became, as Joseph describes, a focus on social relations and not structural ones. Transformative justice is largely principled on social relations as grounded and conditioned by its structural relations of dominance, what Joseph describes in terms of alternative modes of accounting for injustices, "tracing dialectics of abstractions and particularities."[45] This can be understood as, similarly, a dialect between the interpersonal and the structural. Restorative justice, against a narrative of ruthless individualism, largely focuses on interpersonal wrong that has harmed a relationship within community, a wrong that can be restored.[46] What transformative justice reminds us is that the interpersonal is always conditioned by structural violence, often violences that are perpetually inchoate, normalized, reforming, and embodied as a choice between "worst or even worse options." Transformative justice allows us to imagine a world beyond accounting and repairing order through the likes of broken windows, a world not yet here but yet here.[47] Transformative justice, like restorative justice, can also become a tool enclosed to service the criminal justice system: at the end of the day any idea can be abstracted, proffering only illusions of life as *made* possible, a life unbecoming. However, it is by remembering collectively that we are still, against odds, learning, pushing, and transforming the language and sensations of life *as* possibility. Whether "deserving to live" or "deserving the death penalty," no one deserves anything and everything all at the same time. This life, unaccountable, is already here; however, we can know new ways to hold onto it more fully, together and not apart.

REN-YO HWANG is a PhD candidate in ethnic studies at the University of California at Riverside writing their dissertation on the complex political history of Los Angeles law enforcement partnerships with community organizations through the production of hate crimes and antiviolence organizing efforts, particularly its impact on queer and transgender of color communities. Ren-yo received their master's degree in Asian American studies at UCLA and a bachelor's in political philosophy at Bryn Mawr College. Ren-yo has recently worked collectively with Gender Justice Los Angeles and Dignity and Power Now (formerly the Coalition to End Sheriff Violence in LA Jails), and served on the editorial board for the Dignity and Power Now zine. Ren-yo served on the statewide executive board for their graduate union UAW 2865 and its Anti-Oppression Committee, and the L.A./Chino team for California Coalition for Women Prisoners. Ren-yo is interested in transformative justice frameworks of collaborative and community-based research as a means to popularize and map knowledge-making practices and alternative archives.

NOTES

1. *Online Etymology Dictionary,* s.v. "justice (n.)," http://www.etymonline.com/index.php?term=justice.

2. Lauren Berlant, "National Brands/National Body: Imitation of Life," in *The Phantom Public Sphere* (Minneapolis: University of Minnesota Press, 1993), 112–13.

3. Samuel Paul, "Accountability in Public Services: Exit, Voice and Control," *World Development* 20, no. 7 (1992): 1047.

4. Edward P. Weber, *Bringing Society Back In: Grassroots Ecosystem Management, Accountability, and Sustainable Communities* (Cambridge, Mass.: MIT Press, 2003), 30–31. Weber maps accountability "elements of the accountability framework," formal institutional structure, formal institutional processes or procedures, informal institutions or spaces, systems of management or bureaucracy, performance, and results.

5. Public accountability, however, calls into question the constituents or those opposing the interests of such institutional bodies, demanding more than simply the performance and effectiveness of policy and procedures within a system. Weber, *Bringing Society Back In*, 101.

6. Carol A. Chetkovich and Frances Kunreuther, *From the Ground Up: Grassroots Organizations Making Social Change* (Ithaca, N.Y.: ILR Press/Cornell University Press, 2006), 184.

7. Candace McCoy, *Holding Police Accountable* (Washington, D.C.: Urban Institute Press, 2010), xiii. McCoy describes the field as instead shifting toward discourses of police professionalism and community policing, even amid the highly publicized police scandals and corruptions of the 1990s and the first decade of the twenty-first century.

8. "Implicit bias" has been most famously attributed to the work of the Implicit Association Test (IAT) at Harvard University. Project Implicit was founded in 1998 by a team of research scientists, Tony Greenwald (University of Washington), Mahzarin Banaji (Harvard University), and Brian Nosek (University of Virginia). For more information, see http://www.projectimplicit.net/about.html.

9. The United Nations Office on Drug and Crime, *Handbook on Police Accountability, Oversight and Integrity* (New York: United Nations, 2011).

10. Beyond accounting for the performance of rules, policies, procedures, and regulations, police forces at their base only seek accountability unto themselves and the state.

11. Michel Foucault, *Discipline and Punish: The Birth of the Prison* (New York: Vintage Books, 1977).

12. See Dean Spade, *Normal Life: Administrative Violence, Critical Trans Politics, and the Limits of Law* (Brooklyn, N.Y.: South End Press, 2011).

13. Alicia Garza states, "Trayvon Martin was post-humously placed on trial for his own murder and the killer, George Zimmerman, was not held accountable for the crime he committed." Alicia Garza, "A Herstory of the #BlackLivesMatter Movement," *Feminist Wire*, October 7, 2014, http://www.thefeministwire.com/2014/10/blacklivesmatter-2/. The U.S and international grassroots movement of Black Lives Matter was born in a hashtag in 2013, in social media exchanges between longtime friends and organizers Alicia Garza, Patrisse Cullors, and Opal Tometi. A short list of the more prominent cases followed by the movement includes Oscar Grant, Michael Brown Jr., Ezell Ford, Akai Gurley, Freddie Gray, Walter Scott, John Crawford III, Tamir Rice, Eric Garner, Mya Hall, Tanisha Anderson, Sandra Bland, and Mario Woods.

14. "Do Black Lives Matter? Robin D. G. Kelley and Fred Moten in Conversation," video, December 13, 2014, https://vimeo.com/116111740.

15. For instance, proposals for passing legislation to enforce the use of police body cameras have critiqued what actual regulatory power body-cam footage has when written policy and legislation still leave interpretative gray areas for police discretion in manipulation, deletion, and retention of footage and in determining what footage is made available to the public based on issues of "civilian privacy protection." See Jay Stanley, "Police Body-Mounted Cameras: With Right Policies

in Place, a Win For All," *ACLU*, October 2013, https://www.aclu.org/police-body -mounted-cameras-right-policies-place-win-all. Body cameras for law enforcement are a means of portraying more public and internal accountability; however, even so, the power of the cop is only re-formed and re-fortified through such efforts. Frantz Fanon describes this extensively as a naturalization of violence in mind and home for the nonsettler, where agents of government train to openly practice a "language of pure force" and domination, and where centering the issue of body cameras does little to actually remove power from such agents. Frantz Fanon, *The Wretched of the Earth,* trans. Constance Farrington (New York: Grove Press, 1963), 29. We Charge Genocide Chicago organizer Monica Trinidad states, "This disregard for Black lives is systemic and cannot be solved by officers wearing cameras, as we clearly saw today. . . . Body cameras will not stop Black people from being tragically killed by police officers, and will sadly only give us more horrific footage to view, and more evidence that power needs to be taken away from them." Joseph Erbentraut, "Some Critics Aren't So Sure Body Cameras Are the Solution to Police Abuse in Chicago," *Huffington Post,* December 4, 2014, http://www.huffingtonpost .com/2014/12/04/chicago-police-body-cameras_n_6264826.html?ir=Chicago&utm _hp_ref=chicago.

16. For more information, see "Police Union Contract Project," http://www.check thepolice.org/#project.

17. Miranda Joseph, *Debt to Society: Accounting for Life under Capitalism* (Minneapolis: University of Minnesota Press, 2014), 29–31.

18. As Dean Spade explains, "Law reform work that merely tinkers with systems to make them look more inclusive while leaving their most violent operations intact must be a concern to many social movements today." Spade, *Normal Life,* 91.

19. Jennifer Wolch, *The Shadow State: Government and Voluntary Sector in Transition* (New York: Foundation Center, 1990); Treva Ellison, "Towards a Politics of Perfect Disorder: Carceral Geographies, Queer Criminality, and Other Ways to Be" (PhD diss., University of Southern California, 2015).

20. Lauren Berlant, "Slow Death: Sovereignty, Obesity and Lateral Agency," *Critical Inquiry* 33 (Summer 2007): 761. See also Lauren Berlant, "The Epistemology of State Emotion," in *Dissent in Dangerous Times,* ed. Austin Sarat (Ann Arbor: University of Michigan Press, 2005), 46–78.

21. Audre Lorde challenged such carving up of identity as a dangerous "hierarchy of oppression (an oppression Olympics)" that simply does not exist when inhabiting the reality of intersectional and complex identities. Audre Lorde, "There Is No Hierarchy of Oppressions," *Bulletin: Homophobia/Education* 14, no. 3/4 (1983): 9.

22. This is an allopathic social services approach of suppressing the symptom and ignoring the whole body.

23. Michel Foucault, *"Society Must Be Defended""* Lectures at the Collège de France, 1975–1976, trans. David Macey (New York: Picador, 2003); Michel Foucault, *The History of Sexuality,* vol. 1, *The Will to Knowledge,* trans. Robert Hurley (London: Penguin Books, 1976).

24. "The universal was invented as exclusion. Period." Robin D. G. Kelley, in conversation with Moten in the video "Do Black Lives Matter?"

25. Dylan Rodriguez challenges us to consider the use of "mass" incarceration as a mode of falsely distinguishing incarceration as a problem of the masses. He suggests that we consider how the carceral state acts as a particularizing settler-colonial project that has targeted functions of anti-Black racial and gendered control. Dylan Rodriguez, "Racial Genocide and the U.S. Carceral State: A History of the Present" (roundtable, Annual Meeting of American Studies Association, Toronto, Canada, October 10, 2015), https://asa.press.jhu.edu/program15/saturday.html.

26. Joseph, *Debt to Society*, 38. This debt is largely ideological yet material in time and captured life, as the government cost to incarcerate an individual is more than forty thousand dollars in California, more than four times the cost of providing public education. For a graph across U.S. states, see "Education vs. Prison Costs," CNN, May 8 2013, http://money.cnn.com/infographic/economy/education -vs-prison-costs/.

27. Stefano Harney and Fred Moten, *The Undercommons: Fugitive Planning & Black Study* (Wivenhoe, N.Y.: Minor Compositions, 2013), 155.

28. Sylvia Wynter, "No Humans Involved: An Open Letter to My Colleagues," *Forum N.H.I.: Knowledge for the 21st Century* 1, no. 1 (1994): 70.

29. Harney and Moten, *The Undercommons*, 26.

30. The general population at MCJ has averaged in the last few years from seventeen thousand to twenty-two thousand people on any given day, and K6G, as the only self-segregated gay men and transgender women's jail in the United States, is reported as housing the largest population of gay men and transgender women nationally.

31. Russell K. Robinson, "Masculinity as Prison: Sexual Identity, Race, and Incarceration," *California Law Review* 99, no. 5/3 (2011): 1313, 1354, doi:10.15779/Z381H6J.

32. Sharon Dolovich, "Two Models of the Prison: Accidental Humanity and Hypermasculinity in the L.A. County Jail," *Journal of Criminal Law and Criminology* 102, no. 965 (2013): 978.

33. Victoria Law, "Against Carceral Feminism: Relying on State Violence to Curb Domestic Violence Only Ends Up Harming the Most Marginalized Women," *Jacobin*, October, 17, 2014, https://www.jacobinmag.com/2014/10/against-carceral -feminism. See also Jai Dulani, Chen Ching-In, and Leah Lakshmi Piepzna-Samarasinha, eds., *The Revolution Starts at Home: Confronting Intimate Violence within Activist Communities* (Brooklyn, N.Y.: South End Press, 2011).

34. Ani Ucar, "In the Gay Wing of L.A. Men's Central Jail, It's Not Shanks and Muggings but Hand-Sewn Gowns and Tears," *LA Weekly*, November 18, 2014.

35. Founded in Mobile, Alabama, in the 1980s, GTL serves over 1.3 million people incarcerated whom, with imposed irregular access to phone use, attempt to reach their loved ones, support systems, someone outside the jail, the prison, the precinct, the detention facility, and so on. GTL, a private company, holds over 650 ICS public contracts with the government.

36. Missed calls lead to automated messages in the voice-mail inbox that read: ". . . phone call from [name], an inmate in the Men's Central Jail. To accept this call press zero, to refuse this call, hang up or press one. . . . Your call was not accepted. Please try again later."

37. GTL wants the public to believe it is providing an extraordinary service and that it wants inmates to stay connected at all costs, costs that even the Federal Communication Commission has had to reform via rate caps per minute (from highs of fourteen dollars per minute to eleven cents per minute).

38. For the Ordinance 2014-0034 that created the OIG as a department of the board of supervisors in Los Angeles County, see https://oig.lacounty.gov/Portals/OIG/Reports/Certified%20OIG%20Ordinance.pdf. For more on the criticism to go beyond an OIG, see reports published by Dignity and Power Now (DPN), particularly the Coalition to End Sheriff Violence in Los Angeles Jails (former name for DPN), "A Civilian Review Board for the Los Angeles County Sheriff's Department," May 2014, http://dignityandpowernow.org/wp-content/uploads/2014/11/CRBreport 2014.1.pdf. This report notes, "The OIG cannot, alone, keep a bright spotlight on the implementation of needed reforms of the LASD. On its own, the OIG will not provide a forum for visible public hearings, which can be an invaluable tool for exposing problems and engaging LASD leadership in a dialogue about the status of reform."

39. For more info on Twin Towers, see Dignity and Power Now, "Impact of Disproportionate Incarceration of and Violence against Black People with Mental Health Conditions in the World's Largest Jail System: A Supplementary Submission for the August 2014 CERD Committee Review of the United States," August 2014, http://dignityandpowernow.org/wp-content/uploads/2014/11/CERD_Report_2014.8.pdf.

40. "Severe overcrowding in LA County Jails has harshly impacted prisoners with mental health conditions subjected to what a recent U.S. Department of Justice (DOJ) investigation described as 'dimly lit, vermin infested, noisy, unsanitary, cramped and crowded' conditions. Due to lack of capacity and overcrowding, over a third of the 3,200 people identified as having a debilitating mental health condition are housed in the general jail population rather than in a dedicated mental health facility." Dignity and Power Now, "Impact of Disproportionate Incarceration," 3.

41. Mark-Anthony Johnson, director of health and wellness, Dignity and Power Now, speaking at L.A. County Board of Supervisors meeting, January 12, 2016.

42. Prison reform addresses and redresses the system in different skin. Mumia Abu Jamal warns, "We must be mindful of the old snakes in new skin." Mumia Abu Jamal, "If This Is a War, Then Black Lives Matter Is Losing," *Counterpunch,* October 16, 2015, http://www.counterpunch.org/2015/10/16/if-this-is-a-war-then-black-lives-matter-is-losing/.

43. Jin Haritaworn, *Queer Lovers and Hateful Others: Regenerating Violent Times and Places* (London: Pluto Press, 2015).

44. Morgan Bassichis, Alexander Lee, and Dean Spade, "Building an Abolitionist Trans and Queer Movement," in *Captive Genders: Trans Embodiment and the Prison Industrial Complex,* ed. Eric A. Stanley and Nat Smith (Oakland, Calif.: AK Press, 2014).

45. Joseph, *Debt to Society,* 60.

46. Over time, restorative justice has become integrated into juvenile court systems and K-12 public schools in order to reduce the structural impact of the aggressive policing of youth of color in large metropolitan cities. Restorative justice in

these cases, for instance, has replaced police officers in schools with community patrols or peace officers. For transformative justice alternatives, see Project NIA, "Transformative Justice: A Curriculum Guide," Fall 2013, https://niastories.files .wordpress.com/2013/08/tjcurriculum_design_small-finalrev.pdf.

47. Fred Moten, in a dialogue with Robin D. G. Kelly and Maisha Quint ("Do Black Lives Matter?"), concludes: "To fix a broken window is to fix another way of imagining the world, to literally fix it, destroy it, to regulate it, to exclude it, to incarcerate it, but also at the same time to incorporate it, to capitalize upon it, to exploit it, to accumulate it. This state can't live with us [Black life] and it can't live without us. . . . The broken window, the alternative unfixed window through which we see the world, is not just the way in which we see something that doesn't exist, but it's also the way we see and imagine that which does exist. It's important to imagine how things might be otherwise, but it's also *really really* important to understand and see *who* and *what* are right now."

Unjust Attachments

Mourning as Antagonism in Gauri Gill's "1984"

BALBIR K. SINGH

The year 2014 marked the thirtieth anniversary of Operation Blue Star and the Sikh genocide on the Indian subcontinent. Operation Blue Star was an attack on the Harmander Sahib complex (also known as Darbar Sahib or the Golden Temple), the holiest shrine for Sikhs, which includes the Akal Takht, the highest seat of earthly political and judicial power. This operation took place in early June 1984 and was an attempt to seize the Golden Temple, as the government feared the threat of supposed Sikh terrorism, militancy, and separatism in the form of an independent homeland called Khalistan. Organized by Prime Minister Indira Gandhi, the attack left the Golden Temple complex destroyed and five hundred to five thousand dead. It was confirmed in late 2014 by both the BBC and British Prime Minister David Cameron that the then prime minister Margaret Thatcher and her government had an integral role in organizing the attack on the Golden Temple.[1] Recently declassified documents reveal that Thatcher's regime had Special Air Services work closely with the Indian government in planning the attack. The state actions of June 1984 had left the Sikh religious minority in India both bereaved and enraged. On October 31 of the same year, two of Gandhi's bodyguards, both Sikh, assassinated the prime minister in what is widely regarded as an act of revenge. The assassination took place in the morning, and when it was announced in the afternoon via radio that two Sikh men were responsible for the attack, that evening saw the beginnings of mass violence against Sikhs, particularly heavy in the capital of Delhi. With the cooperation of the police and the national army, mobs were given voter lists and were able to locate Sikh homes. Recognized as an ethnoreligious minority in India, racially visible by the donning of turbans and full beards for men, Sikh men and some Sikh women were burned alive and attacked with state distributed weapons, and women were gang-raped; Sikh homes, *gurdwaras,* and businesses were ransacked and burned; buses and trains were pulled over by armed mobs in order to find Sikhs and kill them. These riots continued through November 3 and resulted in three thousand deaths in Delhi alone and eight thousand deaths in total across India.

Since 1984, many of those who survived and remained in India sought justice despite threats of intimidation and harm. In working to name and identify those responsible, especially powerful figures within the nation's bureaucratic structures who not only allowed but encouraged and made possible the murders of Sikhs, many widows of the Sikh men targeted and killed comprised the majority of those seeking justice in the wake of mass violence and death. The most significant result of their efforts toward justice and reconciliation occurred in 2000. The Justice G. T. Nanavati Commission was established by the Indian government in 2000 to investigate the 1984 Sikh genocide. The probe panel was given five orders: to look into the sparks that led to the attacks targeting members of the Sikh community; to examine the sequence of events; to determine whether these crimes could have possibly been averted and whether there were any lapses on the part of the authorities; to inquire into the usefulness of the administrative measures taken to stop and deal with the violence; and to recommend solutions to be adopted to serve justice. The commission submitted its final report, producing the 185-page Nanavati Commission Report, in February 2005 detailing accusations and evidence against senior members of the Delhi wing of the then-ruling Congress Party, the Indian National Congress, including Jagdish Tytler, later a cabinet minister, MP Sajjan Kumar, and late minister H. K. L. Bhagat. They were accused of instigating mobs to avenge the assassination of Indira Gandhi by killing Sikhs in their constituencies. The report also held the then lieutenant governor PG Gavai responsible for failure in his duty and late orders for controlling of the riots. The commission also held the then Delhi police commissioner S. C. Tandon directly responsible for the riots. There was widespread protest against the report as it did not clearly mention the role of Tytler and other members of the Congress Party in the 1984 anti-Sikh riots. The report led to the resignation of Jagdish Tytler from the Union Cabinet. A few days after the report was tabled in Parliament, the then Indian prime minister Manmohan Singh apologized to the Sikh community for Operation Blue Star and the riots that followed. The report stated that Jagdish Tytler "very probably" had a hand in the riots.

First published in 2013, and then republished in 2014 to mark three decades of injustice, including and highlighting the Nanavati Commission Report's aftermath, Gauri Gill shared an artistic notebook, "1984," on the 1984 Sikh genocide as an artist's testament to the defining moment of contemporary Sikh history. Made publically available for digital download on her official site, "1984" approaches the aesthetics and politics of post-1984 crises on the Indian subcontinent and its expansive diaspora.[2] Using the medium of photography, while creating the collective artistic endeavor of responding to photographic images, Gill, an acclaimed artist and member of the Sikh diaspora, along with her artist and writer colleagues, evoke the haunting of the events of 1984 on Sikhs and non-Sikhs alike. Many of the writings in the notebook come from members of Sikh and Indian diasporas broadly, most of whom were in Delhi, India. Gill does not define this work around the twin moments of early June 1984's Operation Blue Star and early November's Sikh genocide but rather focuses on November's genocidal attacks.[3]

In "1984," Gill has composed a collected notebook with a plethora of affectively charged images and writings that render its subjects as both victims and survivors. These are witnesses to the horrors of one of India's most bloody attacks on its own civilian population in the recent past. Gill captures the dynamics of the event as both then and as it is, here and now. The audience of this work is supposed to have some knowledge of the event: in this way, it is a work that demands intimacy and curiosity, cuts off the unfamiliar, as it reads and views history as living memory; as art, it is memory-work. For the uninitiated, it is nearly incomprehensible. There are scribbled notes that cover the front and back of the notebook, and throughout the work, the events are not ever detailed or accounted for in the mode of history-writing or official documentation. Rather, "1984" captures those who are familiar and intimate with and affected by the events it evocatively renders.[4]

There is no easy mode of inquiry with Gill's various images and written contributions; the messages vary from image to image, prose to prose, and poem to poem. Still, overwhelmingly, what is represented indicates the ways in which there has been little attempt to resolve the injustices wrought upon Sikhs in 1984. Furthermore, there is the fact that the Indian nation-state would reject naming as a humanitarian crisis the various forms of crises that have plagued Sikhs throughout India and in diaspora since '84. Nevertheless, there is ample evidence of the various ways the events of '84 have had disastrous short- and long-term effects on Sikhs globally and especially on the subcontinent. In this article, I argue that in merging aesthetics with politics, Gill's artwork articulates alternate visions of justice for Sikhs globally in the wake of 1984. I further assert that mourning enables political models

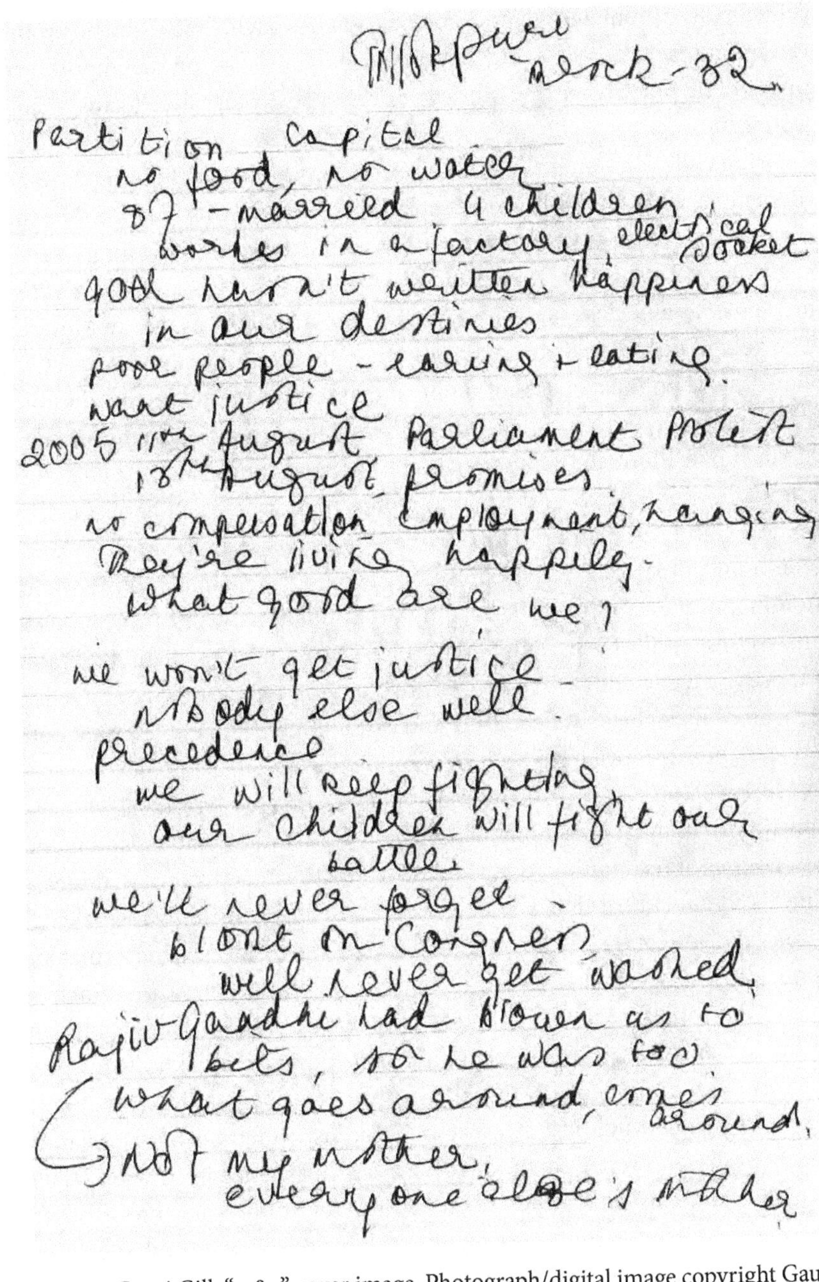

Rishpuri
Block-32.

Partition   Capital
   no food, no water
      87 -married 4 children
         works in a factory   electrical socket
god hasn't written happiness
   in our destinies
poor people - earning + eating.
want justice
2005 11th august Parliament Protest
   18th August promises
no compensation employment, hanging
they're living happily.
   what good are we?

we won't get justice.
   nobody else will.
precedence
   we will keep fighting
      our children will fight our
         battle.
we'll never forget.
   blot on Congress
      will never get washed.
Rajiv Gandhi had blown us to
   bits, so he was too.
(what goes around, comes
                        around.
) not my mother,
         everyone else's mother

Figure 1. Gauri Gill, "1984," cover image. Photograph/digital image copyright Gauri Gill, 2014. Courtesy of Gauri Gill, gaurigill.com.

for resistance and militancy by attending to Gill's emphasis on gendered dimensions of remaining and remembering. As such, "1984" opens up the terrain of justice as it is defined by the state by insisting on the importance of aesthetic practices as modalities of protest and alternative forms of collective knowledge.

Using Gill's work on the 1984 Sikh genocide as a mode of thinking through mourning, violence, and desires for justice, I situate this piece within the contemporary work being done within queer studies of mourning—especially David L. Eng and David Kazanjian's 2002 anthology *Loss: The Politics of Mourning*, as well as work by Gayatri Gopinath and José Esteban Muñoz.[5] The field of queer studies, specifically when thinking through the affective, violent, and political effects of mourning, offers an immense and rigorous examination of death and mourning through and against normative models of kinship. It allows for the nonrelational care and concern for the dead that often gets lost in studies and accounts of mourning where emphasis is placed on how tightly akin and proximate one is to the dead, be it familial, racial, communal, or spatial. In light of this, melancholia becomes another useful framing, as it accompanies mourning in foundational work from psychoanalysis, especially by Sigmund Freud and anticolonial psychoanalyst Frantz Fanon.[6] By using Gill's work as a way of studying 1984's anti-Sikh violence, with all of its inclusion of multiple and distant perspectives, I employ both a queer and a minoritarian politics of mourning and melancholia.

Moreover, on a historical and material level, this piece reckons with and contributes to the intersecting fields of genocide studies, trauma and memory, politics of recognition, truth and reconciliation, and historical amnesia. The Sikh genocide of 1984 is not necessarily included within widely recognized genocides of the modern period—such as the Holocaust, the Armenian genocide, the Cambodian genocide, and the killings in Darfur—primarily due to the contested nature of the label "genocide," and the unwillingness of the Indian nation-state to recognize the magnitude of Sikh deaths during this time. I argue for its inclusion within genocide studies, as not only a crucial juridico-political strategy but also as a method of articulating and honing in on renewed and incessant calls for justice in its wake.[7] This modality contains radical potential not just for studies of Sikh or South Asian diaspora but in multiple geopolitical locations seeking and imagining worlds full of just, equitable, and reparative futures—be it for Ferguson, Missouri; Gaza and the West Bank in Israel/Palestine; or those recently seeking renewed life through migration across Europe.

RETHINKING MOURNING

The mourning that I speak of is one that exists in the wake of unjust death. These deaths are unjust for the ways in which they occur and the ways in which they occur prematurely, are often targeted and violent, and go under- or unrecognized by the state. Perhaps apparent, those targeted in the event of unjust death are those who are considered members of disposable populations, usually minority communities and populations denied basic rights and legitimacy in the eyes of the nation-state.[8] As such, this form of mourning in the wake of unjust death works to enable and enact justice on the terms of mourners. It is with this assemblage of unjust death and the state's disavowal of said death that the work of mourning emerges; in its emergence, mourning becomes something outside the parameters of individualized grief as it transforms into something communal, collective, and intentional. In that intentionality, mourning serves a larger function of the necessary dwelling on death and its attendant affective strategies of pain, anger, sorrow, and indignation.

To live within the tension of having to dwell on the dead forces true and conscious reckoning with the forces and contingencies that made such death possible. In many ways, dwelling on death can be individual or on a group or collective scale, and becomes a point of rupture for those who understand the death or deaths as circumstantial and those who see it as part of a large, ongoing, systemic problem. For many, it becomes paramount to read and understand these bodily losses as unjust death, and as constituting genocide due to the mass scale of murder. For these same people, death is real and symbolic, at once personal and representative; the grief in the wake of unjust death is an affective strategy to work against the mass and institutional injustice that has enabled and perpetuated these attempts at annihilation.

Centrally, I locate in Gill's project that inherent to the work of mourning is the condition of antagonism. That is to say that mourning exists as a form of antagonism to various political, social, and cultural forms and agents. Specifically, in the case of Gill's "1984," the audience is presented with a compendium of Sikh suffering in the wake of the events of 1984, when, in contradistinction, the Indian nation-state perpetuates and prefers collective amnesia and disavowal. Disavowal then operates in opposition to mourning as the state's construction of narratives that rationalize their monopoly on violence, as well as through multicultural narratives that domesticate histories of radical opposition to incorporate them within national ideologies. In disavowal, there can be no mourning or care for the other, and more often than not, disavowal often reveals the contempt for the other. Disavowal is the state response to minoritarian mourning, demonstrating the disdain for the dwelling on unjust death and its accompanying calls for justice.

Gill's "1984" therefore not only represents the work of the artist and the notebook's contributors but also stands against statist attempts at disavowal and disinterest. It works as a way to imagine narrative construction outside state reports and official documentation. In presenting new forms of articulation, Gill ably compiles a series of images that produces modes of witnessing heretofore unavailable to those previously and newly engaged in remembering the lost histories of '84. The images are particularly visionary in that they elicit insight and affective response without ever revealing an excess of information or lengthy testimony from the subjects of the images. In their stead, many of the written contributions provide varied forms of witnessing and narrative accounts that are often wayward or distant in their relation to survivors of '84. The distance might also be understood in terms of how Gill forces many of the writers to directly respond to her images, lending a speculative quality to many of the written pieces. In many ways, the very fact of its artistic sensibility makes it illegitimate or unrecognizable to official historical records; never mind the fact that official historical records more often than not represent the state and its interests. Its very form, or formlessness, arrives as an exact form of narrative antagonism to official historical records.[9]

That is not to say that it does not produce or affect the historical narrative of '84, as it is very much the opposite: Gill's work comprises the very kind of minoritarian cultural production that is deeply invested in historical memory and politically engaged, future-oriented calls for justice. It is subversive for its synesthetic quality as an artist's notebook; it is readily available for wide, mass consumption in its digital composition. In choosing to make this work available digitally, Gill recognizes the need for the already established Sikh diasporic commons to consume and engage with the multinarrative and visual components of her work. While "1984" exists as a world unto itself, it is engaged in a much longer, larger historical narrative arc. The audience viscerally feels the antagonism that the notebook presupposes. As it exists digitally, this antagonism presents to the Sikh diasporic commons a form of virtual solidarity. The future orientation of Sikh calls for justice in the wake of '84 and its ongoing production of Sikh political prisoners makes digital availability of "1984" all the more crucial. It participates in the network culture of contemporary Sikh diaspora insofar as it positions itself as part of, and unique from, other forms of minoritarian cultural production that engage and reckon with the events of '84.

THE SUBJECTS OF "1984"

Gill's work notably focuses on older women and younger men, as she rightly represents the survivors as widows and children of the Sikh genocide. The focus on two of Delhi's "widow colonies" in the districts of Trilokpuri and Tilak Vihar highlights the living conditions of the widows, their children, and any other remaining survivors.[10] The gendered dimensions of the events of '84 come into very clear focus here. The targeting of Sikh males for torment, assault, and death gives this particular event of genocide, however unofficial, nods to genocidal conventions of "sparing" women and children as well as pointing to the framing of this mob violence as a form of national and collective revenge on Sikh males, as Indira Gandhi's two Sikh bodyguards were responsible for her assassination.

The collective revenge was then primarily taken out on Sikh males: husbands, fathers, sons, and grandfathers. The brutality as described is unfathomable and disgusting, there being something simultaneously primal and calculated about the violence. In fact, the violence was heavily organized and calculated, as some in Gill's notebook recount. This, of course, is not to discount the violence done to women during the genocidal attacks. Women were assaulted, primarily through sexual violence, and many women were killed.[11] However, what marks Gill's work is how women suffer through their survival and living on or beyond. In bearing witness to violence and death of male kin as well as the death of a community made up of Sikh brothers and sons, women are portrayed as having been given the burden of existence in the wake of mass personal and collective death. Survival for these women appears to be animated by the effects of grief and ongoing mourning; specifically, these women are *haunted* by the absence of sons, fathers, and husbands.

The collectivity of women and children in the widow colony areas of Tilak Vihar and Trilokpuri in Delhi are reminders of the events of '84 and the ways in which the violence cut off nuclear and extended families. The figure of the widow is most apparently put into view. The widow stands apart from other survivors as a kind of sole bearer of the effects of genocide. The death of the husband is thus produced centrally, as a way of marking a primary fissure in the Sikh family. Under normal circumstances, the status of the widow could be understood as pathetic, as one who is regarded with pity. However, the widow colony creates a very different kind of widow, one who evokes different reactions. She is the wronged, she is the bereaved, she lives under the unjust conditions of the state—and outside the colony, all know this. Further, we might read this prolonged collectivity in two ways: first, as a way of marking the erasure of violence against women in the genocide; and second, as a way of thinking through how the preservation of this form of togetherness forms a queer or nonnormative kinship structure. Expanding on this second notion, the widow colony might represent a default feminist collectivity, unintentional and ambivalent as it may have manifested. Their continued linkage through extended proximity demonstrates an ongoing commitment to their livelihood as widows living in memory. Their lack of relation, or abstract relation, makes for a complex community of Sikh women and children. Such collective life reflects the ways in which the targeting of Sikh men in 1984 was not symbolic revenge for Gandhi's assassination but rather a way to cut off the reproduction of Sikh life for generations of future Sikhs.[12] The widow colony thus appears as a result of the genocidal pogroms, enabling a queer domestic space that both provides alternative forms of care and enlivens the shared work of historical memory.

In one example, Gill's photograph from August 2005, sixteen widows are posed for a portrait outside of one of Trilokpuri's blocks (see Figure 2). The

Figure 2. Gauri Gill, "1984," 15. Photograph/digital image copyright Gauri Gill, 2014. Courtesy of Gauri Gill, gaurigill.com.

women are either sitting or standing in their salwaar kameez with white dupatta, their arms on their sides or resting on their laps.[13] The foreground is of dust and rubble; the background is of a nondescript building, with openings for windows and a dark, unlit courtyard, as well as a tree enclosed within the compound by a tall iron fence. There is a sign on the building with unreadable Punjabi, adorned by a Sikh khanda—the symbol of the Sikh religion—and sandwiched by likenesses of both the founding Sikh Guru, Guru Nanak, and the tenth Sikh Guru, Guru Gobind Singh. Gill's caption reads: "The widows of Block 32, Trilokpuri, on the morning after the Nanavati Report was released."[14]

The women in the image appear despondent; they are not actively upset. They appear as a collective, but each face tells a different story. The caption cuts off the quotidian nature of the image by historicizing this portrait as a frozen moment in time, fraught with meaning and weight. Gill captures the day after the possibility of justice for these women was again denied. The Nanavati Report had the potential to condemn particular agents and agitators in the violence and genocide of Sikhs in 1984. Many of these women bore witness to these agents and agitators, inciters of violence against their kin and Sikh brothers and sisters alike. The women are portrayed as a collective after what might have been a historic moment, placed together to note that they were all present and alive for another day of injustice.

The image resolves for viewers nothing, much in the way that only so little resolutions, reparations, and reconciliations have been achieved before and after this image. As much as the events of '84 haunt the women of the widow colony, it is the active diminishment of these events on the national level that truly juxtaposes the women's traumatic survival. That is, the women of the widow colony, insofar as they embody living memories of '84, comprise an active opposition to the will of the state and its desire for collective amnesia or forgetting, if not outright collective disavowal. That is not to say that all women, as portrayed in Gill's work, are equally committed to the stringent upholding of traumatic memory. Some wish and hope to lose the imagery of those days from their minds.

An example of this attempt at traumatic memory loss is Gill's image from August 2005 (see Figure 3). It portrays a woman in shadow, only lit as a silhouette from the sun pouring in from a small balcony. Beyond in the sun are an adjacent apartment complex and a steel water tower, shrouded by trees. The woman, placed in the foreground, clad in her dupatta, with her ear poking out of the left side, is standing left of center, with a curtain and clothes strewn on the balcony's rail on her right. Gill's caption reads:

The woman in the picture was one of the witnesses to the presence of Jagdish Tytler at the scene of the killings in 1984. More than ten members of her family were killed before her eyes. A son rescued by her neighbours and the grandchildren survived hidden in a nearby house. She was among the three women from her neighbourhood who filed an affidavit naming Tytler. At the very first hearing her lawyer was shot at; the bullet was meant for her. She withdrew the case. Today, age has erased memories, or perhaps, she prefers to forget. She says she cannot even recall who Tytler is, "How do I know who the killers were, the violence left me numb."

The individual refusal, the enunciated disavowal in this moment, is meant to invoke the imperative of knowing who is guilty while at the same time making clear that to know is to suffer. The sentiments she expresses reflect the level of numbness that is both voluntary and involuntary. The numbness is voluntary in that her previous knowledge and ability to testify against Tytler proves to only serve as an assurance of her targeting for death; and the numbness is involuntary in that this unnamed woman unconsciously submits to the state imperative to forget the massive violence and horror that she witnessed in '84.

Figure 3. Gauri Gill, "1984," 57. Photograph/digital image copyright Gauri Gill, 2014. Courtesy of Gauri Gill, gaurigill.com.

To forget is to ensure survival, whereas to remember carries the potential harm of accounting, of acknowledgment, of an ethical will toward justice. Rather than let her memory serve her correctly, she distances herself from her memory in order not to simply put herself out of harms way but to surrender to the overwhelming and overpowering will of the state. Preferring to forget, as Gill puts it, is a means of dulling memories that will never be legitimated in the eyes of the state. The knowledge of her memories' illegitimacy on the national level evokes a pained resistance to the kind of work that Gill is doing in "1984"—the memory-work, the labor of remembrance in this history of violence.

Meenal Baghel, editor of the *Mumbai Mirror,* reflects on this image in Gill's notebook.[15] She notes that in the image itself, "she, this woman of no name, stands at the doorway between light and dark. . . . She is looking not outside but inside, into dark deep recesses: a silhouette and no more." Acutely, Baghel captures how Gill's silhouetted female figure's looking inside is an inward glance. In the silhouette, the facing toward the viewer is unnecessary and provokes an audible *why?* Later Baghel remarks on the woman's tilt of her head: "There is resignation in the tilt of her head, but also the merest hint of something else. . . . The merest hint of contempt in the tilt of the head and the half raised shoulder belies her amnesia." In evoking Gill's caption and the woman's tilt of her head, Baghel actively recognizes how the woman bluffs her purported forgetting. Even in this minor moment of Gill inviting the woman to name the agents of the '84 violence, I read the woman as instead choosing to exhibit a strategic indifference: she is not indifferent in an authentic way but rather exhibits indifference as a maneuver to dismiss (and perhaps delay) the inevitable follow-up questions.

Aware that Gill's work invites her to share and remember against the will of the state's urging to forget, she distances herself from her memories in three modes: (1) as a form of contempt, in Baghel's words; (2) as a form of weariness; and (3) as a form of self-preservation. Note that these three aspects are not mutually exclusive. First, in contempt, the audience ascertains the ways in which the role of the witness, especially the female witness, is recognized as nuisance. She places herself at the center, as victim-witness, one who remembers when urged to forget; she is viewed with overwhelming contempt by those who hear her narrative accounts of things past as a hindrance on the present and future of the state. In turn, she wills herself to forget and move on, superficially. The surface of this forgetting is bubbling underneath with the absolute contempt for the despicable and unfathomable injustice that occurred, occurs, and will occur to her and her people.

Second, in weariness, the audience reads the woman's forgetting as world-weariness, as a fatigue in the face of mass injustice. She is justifiably exhausted from how the state drains her and others like her, and the state in turn relies on time-consumption to age and wear down even the most steadfast seekers of truth, justice, and reconciliation. Weariness is not weakness; rather, it articulates the unbreaking of will, of exhaustion that may pass, and is not yet rupture. Third, in self-preservation, the audience understands that to seek justice often means to put oneself in harm's way. This is especially true for the women seeking justice and redress in the wake of the events of '84. Thus, forgetting serves the powerful purpose of survival. By ignorance and disavowal, one claims no stakes in battles large or small. The method of forgetting, or feigning ignorance, as it may be, is inevitably fraught with how one justifies the will to forget within oneself.

Ultimately, these three modes underscore that the will of memory persists. To distance oneself from the memory or memories is not true forgetting. Even in these examples of supposed forgetting, Gill's "1984" is the work and revelation of memory. The revelatory aspect of the work reaches farther into the recesses of the minds of survivors; they elicit agitated responses, as the triggering of memories in relation to '84 produces frequently painful and strained images. However, Gill's work should not be noted for the way it forces these survivors and witnesses to reckon with '84. Instead, Gill's work reveals that these survivors and witnesses confront and deal with these moments of past trauma regularly, daily. As much historical recuperation as "1984" provides, it is a story of haunting. By existing as impacted bodies, forever attached to the memory of the dead, these women live among ghosts insofar as their existence is daily evidence of and testament to the horrors of the past. The material reality of the widow colony is one of living in memory, and therefore one of haunting.

Invariably, the audience receives Gill's account of how the ghosts of '84 are regular visitors to the women and children of the widow colony. This narrative is at the heart of the work. In many ways, the centrality of this narrative rightly places the gendered dimensions of the Sikh genocide in clear perspective. Coping with the tethering of Sikhi (or Sikh religiosity) to masculinity and visible devout identity (donning of turban and beard), Gill skillfully presents how the loss of Sikh men in the events of '84, and the widows left in their wake, serves as a longer arc of Sikh minoritarian identity. By placing members of Delhi's widow colony in sharp focus, "1984" is especially revelatory for its comment on the gendered dimensions of this genocide.

Hartosh Bal, political editor of *Caravan* magazine, recounts how the 2005 Nanavati Commission report characterized Kishori Lal, a prime inciter of violence in November '84:

> We may notice that the acts attributed to the mob of which the appellant was a member at the relevant time cannot be stated to be a result of any organized systematic activity leading to genocide. Perhaps, we can visualize that to the extent there was unlawful assembly and to the extent that the mob wanted to teach stern lesson to the Sikhs there was some organization; *but in that design that they did not consider that women and children should not be annihilated which is a redeeming feature.*[16]

This passage from the Nanavati Commission Report emphasizes the ways in which the logics of war and genocide unfolded in the events of '84. The contestation of the courts to ever state outright that the days of organized, vengeful, mass Sikh death constituted or constitutes genocide would implicate state officials and subject the Indian government to international scrutiny and to the judicial conventions of the United Nations. Rather, only minor concessions are made. The Nanavati Commission refuses to read this history as the history of war or genocide. The logic is that of the nation at war with its citizens, the civil war of Hindu majoritarian violence against Sikh minoritarian bodies.

Furthermore, Bal rightly finds richness in Nanavati's language here, for it grasps how the sparing of women and children was the pivotal reason the events of '84 were not ruled to be called genocide. The primary harm and annihilation of Sikh men in these days can be read in two ways. First, the targeting of Sikh men for death can be read as an act of war. War becomes a frame in which to better understand the purported exclusion of women and children, but it also functions as a mode in which to form a new rubric for specific violence.[17] Of course, this is not a formal war, as it is not a war of equals, prepared and armed to battle one another. This form of war is one wherein members of the national majority become agents of the state, soldiers and warriors in the name of the assassinated prime minister. The call to avenge Gandhi's death is then a call to arms, a call to war. Sikh men thus represented enemies of the state, slated for annihilation by the state. This form of state-sanctioned violence militarized majoritarian male citizens, armed however poorly but armed nonetheless. Women and children were primarily excluded because they were not representations of those responsible for Gandhi's death, while Sikh men were read as terrorist threats before and after Operation Blue Star in June.

Second, the targeting of Sikh men for death can be read as a form of racial genocide. This form of genocide is also coded as masculine, and, as I previously explained, Sikh masculinity was and is indexed by the Indian nation-state as a primary enemy of the state, forever a threat to the cohesion of a Hindu majoritarian state. In many ways the gendered dimensions of mourning 1984 have affected and necessarily tinged how Indira Gandhi has been immortalized, both conflicting and converging with the nationalist mourning for the feminine immortalized figure of Gandhi. Of course, Gandhi's political power undermines any tangible connection to the widows of '84. Nevertheless, in thinking through genocide as racial and gendered, it is beneficial to draw out some key distinctions.

By its very nature, genocide is about the killing of a specific kind of people, usually an ethnic group or nation. At its very root, *genos* from the Greek translates to race, and *cide* from the Latin translates to an act of killing. Thus, at its very core, genocide is racial death.[18] The modern interpretation and legal codes of genocide have made the official definitions and parameters of the term quite fraught. A major focus of the constitution of genocide is the deliberate nature and structure of killing. This factor is especially important in the logic of the Indian nation-state's refusal to deem the events of 1984 as a genocide. Time and again, Gill's notebook includes various contributors citing "mob violence" as the official terminology; however, just as often, the contributors are citing this term in order to undermine its significance, demonstrating exactly how the killing of Sikhs was targeted and organized. In an important example from the notebook, Indian journalist, novelist, and literary critic Nilanjana Roy provides in her entry, "Voter's Lists, Trilokpuri," a critical examination of the official, national narrative of '84. She writes:

> You can call them up on the internet today: names laid out in a clean innocuous grid. . . . In 1984, someone took the lists and had them photocopied . . . and waited while the machine whirred, and this person demanded unsmudged copies, because the work was of some importance. Ink was used, and then there would be a need for chalk, to mark "S" on the houses of Sikhs.
>
> If you lived through 1984, you cannot forget. . . . S for Sikh and the other S in invisible ink for Safe. Overnight, they had made for us a new alphabet, borrowing the old one from Partition, from Krystallnacht, from a thousand other pogroms.

They had time to create their spontaneous massacre. Time to buy chalk, to cyclostyle voter's lists, to organize the necessary supplies. Block 32 alone took massive concrete pipes, cleavers, scythes, kitchen knives, scissors, lathis, machetes, kerosene.

The end product of all this organization, this careful, unspontaneous massacre, was bodies and blood and then, decades of amnesia and an unspooling list of things left undone.[19]

Roy rightly points out how organization was key to identifying Sikh households. In using voter lists, precisely the kind of official documentation that categorizes and easily records the demography of its locale, there exists a trail pointing to the high level of state involvement in the killing of Sikhs. As such, this is state-sanctioned violence, not the narrative of random and sporadic mob violence. To sift through copies of voter lists, to mark households with an "S": these are not the markings of spontaneous and public spectacles of violence and death. Rather, we have the systematic and organized entrance into the domestic space of Sikh homes and systematic and organized murder of Sikh men. The nation-state's classification regime enabled such "random" genocidal practices and this both constituted and covered up such practices as they took place outside the purview of the state, despite using its resources; hence, the state remains innocent of wrongdoing, thus refusing to use the same regime of knowledge to hunt down the killers. Through Roy's language, there is a distinct emphasis on how this organization mirrors other historic massacres, and how time and effort were spent to target and annihilate these supposed new enemies. Where she states, "They had time to create their spontaneous massacre," Roy swiftly and critically undermines the notion of "spontaneous massacre" while implicating the state and its civilian agents in the mass death of Sikhs.

Furthermore, in the final paragraph, Roy underscores in plain terms that this massacre—composed of time, effort, and resources—left bodily remains and "decades of amnesia." In this notation there is a clear contempt for how little has been done to address these events. Roy articulates, through reiteration, how collective, national amnesia has been the default mode for the Indian nation-state. The disavowal of the events of '84 marks the very terrain of memory for those who witnessed and survived. Roy, like so many others in and out of Gill's notebook, is preserving the memory of Sikh genocide and anti-Sikh violence en masse. In many ways, the notes of Gill's work are the filling in and fleshing out of a narrative that has been refused recognition on a collective scale. Roy's notes might then be understood as a form of historical retrieval that mirrors witnesses and survivors, instead of the official national narratives including the Nanavati Commission Report.

The tone in Roy's entry is specifically antagonistic. She uses irony and is righteously critical of the government and national narrative of the events of '84. The antagonism that Roy presents plays a major role in how the audience must confront the disavowal of Sikh genocide. Specifically, in focusing on the women, children, and descendants of the widow colony—the survivors, those who have lived beyond—their lives, stories, accounts, and testimonies exist as a counterpoint to the making of an absent narrative, a history of disavowal, "collective amnesia," as Roy puts it. As such, we must understand Gill's work as the work of mourning, for it operates as such in a few ways: as an artistic piece, as historical memory, and as part of the process of collective grief. In every way, the work of mourning is *work*; it is a labor borne of pain, remembrance, rage, and the imperative for preservation.

When I express mourning as a form of work, this is intended as a gesture that recognizes that in the event of unjust death, mourning enables the search for justice. That is, those in mourning or extended periods of mourning are very well those who actively seek justice for their proximity and visceral experience of unjust loss. This seeking of justice, as a form of resistance and laborious struggle, is the unintended consequence of loss. Still, this is not to say that state-sanctioned forgetting is not a form of work, a hard effort on behalf of those working to disavow and disregard those seeking justice; on the contrary, both mourning, as antagonism, and disavowal constitute the two poles constantly battling and working toward opposite ends. Nevertheless, in mourning's functioning antagonism toward the state, the struggle is real—difficult, impossible, and never complete. Of course, mourning is a process intended to be completed, to get through, making ongoing or perpetual mourning a frustrating and irritating presence for the state and its culpability in the event of unjust death; therefore, large-scale collective mourning becomes, and exists as, sheer antagonism in the eyes of the state.

REFUSING RESILIENCE

Following her monograph *The Gift of Freedom*, transnational feminist studies scholar Mimi Thi Nguyen theorizes how the category of what she names "humanitarian aesthetics" is currently experiencing transformation in "the politics of self-determination in an age of liberal empire."[20] *The Gift of Freedom* rigorously focuses on the figure of the refugee, specifically the Vietnamese refugees during and following the Vietnam War; Nguyen's critical and fundamentally feminist approach to the refugee body is incredibly generative for the ways in which it opens up the nature of war and its inherent genocidal drive. In her recent theorizing on humanitarian aesthetics, she articulates how crises are those points at which the collective will toward being in the world can be either recuperated or repudiated. In one sense, recuperation acts as a mode in which to transform those affected by violence or conditions of violence from, as Nguyen puts it, "victim to survivor, misery to resilience, suffering to empowerment."[21] Repudiation, on the other hand, is about the rejection of a neoliberal politics of self-determination, and therefore a rejection of a transformative, progressive narrative shift in the wake of crisis and violence. Rather than practice resilience, there are those who collectively repudiate participation in the values that humanitarian intervention so steadfastly attempts to instill— survival and empowerment, in addition to resilience. This rejection is the negative space of humanitarian aesthetics and politics, wherein worldviews are not shaped by the individualist logic of making the most of one's circumstances. Resilience as the positive, affirming space of humanitarian aesthetics and politics is constituted by receiving crisis and conditions of violence with apparent virtues of grace and hope. Nguyen's ideas further the notion that in scenes of violence, crisis, and catastrophe, the appearance of resilience by those made victim of the event is vital to the functioning of liberal empires and democratic civil society. The aesthetics of crisis and postcrisis make significant the ways in which whole peoples come to represent crisis itself and subsequent rebuilding efforts. In melding how visual representations of crisis and disaster, including photographic images, interactive graphics, witness and documentary footage—all genres that constitute the category of "disaster porn"[22]— Nguyen highlights the relation between aesthetic and political fields.

Highlighting the lingering injustice that has especially affected women and descendants of those killed, Gill's "1984" functions as memory-work, thirty years on. Overwhelmingly, this work might then be framed in terms of a repudiation of the terms of neoliberal practices of individual self-determination that Nguyen has characterized as one option in the wake of disaster. Gill's work suggests that by simply living beyond the dead and surviving the crisis, these are not acts of resilience, nor are they attempting acts of affirmation to provide unbridled hope in the wake of their personal tragedy. Notably, many women dwell in this space of mourning and remembrance. The predominant disinterest in cultivating and molding narratives that endeavor to create portraits of women and children who are resilient— that is, living life, preferably working, accepting and moving on from the traumatic event—is clear in Gill's work. Neither the images nor the language of the notebook speak to a buoyant spirit that emerges after decades of injustice. Rather, what remains, and both haunts and animates "1984," is what queer poet Jackie Wang names "a political fidelity to wounds."[23] Wang, in describing the work of Black literary and cultural studies scholar Saidiya Hartman, employs this phrase as a mode in which to express debt and gratitude to Hartman's allegiance to centering trauma in her studies of racial enslavement.[24] This phrasing is particularly useful in the study of Gill's work. In identifying the sometimes latent and sometimes manifest disinterest or contempt for resilience in these images, their captions, and the various writings, the audience is held captive by the clear meeting of aesthetics with politics here.

In Wang's phrasing, fidelity connotes calls for loyalty and trust, with more stringent requests for necessary affiliation and obedience. Wounds suggest the sites or sources of pain and trauma, ones that live forever on the body, individual and collective, and are incapable of erasure. Therefore, "a political fidelity to wounds" might then suggest at once loyalty and trust in wounds—or the source of pain and trauma—and an affiliation and submission to said wounds. Such an interpretation might be read as dogma, as an ideological formation—and it may well be; it is certainly a political formation. However, this reading of this phrase is meant to suggest the modes in which wounds can be generative and useful for those unwilling to prescribe to the neoliberal ideologies of resilience, survival, and empowerment that Nguyen critiques. In their rejection of resilience and in their allegiance and obedience to the wound, they carve out a political gesture that forms a new register of resistance. Politics emerging from the wound provides a model that dwells in the space of pain and grief as a way not only to remember but to enliven commitment to the historical processes of injustice that made such pain and grief possible. Dwelling on or lingering in the space of the wound is a way to inhabit and acknowledge the depth of the injury, the grievousness and severity of pain, and the breadth of loss.

By inhabiting and acknowledging the injury, a creative and antagonistic politics must emerge, though the force of the rhetoric of resilience is ever-present. The urge to present those who have witnessed mass violence and death as survivors—resilient only in their simple act of living on—is deeply embedded in a neoliberal logic that perpetuates the illusion of self-determination under regimes of state-sanctioned violence.[25] Under neoliberalism, resilience appears as a mode of representation that projects the victim, survivor, or witness as one who has overcome the "event" of violence or death and has completed the process of mourning. In this overcoming and completion, the event is over, as is the process of getting over said event. This now commonplace depiction is one that evidences how self-determination has come to overrule the event as the primary form of narrative in the wake of events of unjust violence and death. By having those affected by the events of violence and death move on through narratives of resilience and recovery, said individuals or communities can be read as having transcended the event. Beyond that, these same people can be read as possessing the individual will to resume life, if not life as it was prior to the event. The emphasis then remains on having the will to transcend the anguish, sorrow, and grief of the event, in order to rid the state of its participation and attachment to the event. Thus, in this scheme, the state sanctions violence and death on its members of excess or disposable populations—those rendered minority and threatening—and wills those who survive to transcend the very pain and grief that the state inflicted. Beyond this, the state additionally desires that the unjust targeting and murder of these populations go un- or underrecognized as a cause for social or political concern. This process demonstrates how easily and exacting collective disavowal or amnesia occurs, as it undermines the event and those affected at each stage of suffering.

Alternatively, living in the space of unjust violence and death, the dwelling on grief, enables an antagonism to the collective disavowal or amnesia the state not only enables but forcibly impresses upon its citizens. In Nguyen's phrasing, this antagonism might be interpreted as a repudiation of being in the world; in Wang's phrasing, this antagonism might be interpreted as a "political fidelity to wounds." This grammar is distinct but still related: in Nguyen's formulation, the rejection of the world is the rejection of the status quo, the abandonment of the world as is, in all of its flawed, violent, and uncaring ways; in Wang's formulation, there exists the ideological imperative to keep the historical memory of the wound alive as a means of creating an alternative politics and, alongside that, new ways of being in the world with others. Together, in the negative space of rejection and the alternative space of political possibility, there exists a modality that desires little to no affirmation of life in the world as it exists. For Wang's formulation in particular, there exists a bodily and collective attachment to the wound that can only affirm life in the abstract: wounds may fester or heal, but they define one as living in the present while honoring the past. Rather, what remains is a form of life that honors and remains loyal to the wound and seeks justice in the wake of, and in spite of, world-shaping violence.[26]

For those calling for justice in the wake of '84, the abstract notion of justice itself is made quite concrete. What the Nanavati Commission Report overwhelmingly demonstrates is how justice is constituted by using the accounts of Sikhs who witnessed the horrific violence of '84, and holding those perpetrators accountable for both their inciting of violence and their violent acts. Justice appears to ask only for the very little, but always already asks for too much. The demand for more appears impossible: there is no revolutionary justice possible, as it exists outside any such enabling modality. Without such possibility comes the narrowing of a political horizon, and the aggrieved possession of wounds becomes a necessary and powerful tool. To counteract the degradation of blatant and ongoing injustice, a steadfast "political fidelity to wounds" imagines and creates an urgent sense of collectivity for those whose political horizon remains set on revolutionary justice. In many ways, the contributions of Gill's notebook are not simply individual modes of remembrance; in their collation, they accumulate to something much grander. In "1984," there exists uneven affective modes of agitation, ambivalence, hope and hopelessness, anger and rage, despair and despondency, in addition to utter disbelief. The possibilities that such affective rage enables ensure a larger, even global sense of Sikh collectivity.

BALBIR K. SINGH is a postdoctoral research associate in the Department of Asian American Studies at the University of Illinois, Urbana–Champaign. Her research focuses on Sikh and Muslim racialization, theories of terror and policing, gender and sexual politics, and histories of resistance. She is currently preparing her first manuscript, "Militant Bodies: Policing Race and Gender in Sikh Diasporic Memory."

NOTES

This article is drawn from "Militant Bodies: Policing Race, Religion, and Violence in the U.S. Sikh Diaspora" (PhD diss., University of Washington, 2016), chapter 4, "Minoritarian Mourning: 1984 and Sikh Sovereignty in the Wake."

1. This information was only declassified by WikiLeaks and the Guardian in late 2014. Rajeev Syal and Phil Miller, "Margaret Thatcher Gave Full Support over Golden Temple Raid, Letter Shows," Guardian, January 15, 2014.

2. Gauri Gill, "1984." This eighty-four-page notebook with forty-two black-and-white photos was released on www.kafila.org in April 2013 and rereleased in November 2014. Free to download, print out, staple, and distribute, it is available at the author's website, http://www.gaurigill.com/works.html.

3. This deliberate focus is crucial in understanding how, while these two events are, at the core, connected, their disconnection here is politically charged. Part of my argument in this article is to show how Gill's focus remains on the widows of '84, and what happened to Sikhs and non-Sikhs alike during this time, especially in Delhi.

4. Certainly, Gill's "1984" is not the only piece to artistically or creatively approach the subject of anti-Sikh violence in 1984. Gill's website links to a bibliography for "1984," which includes a variety of cultural works, including those by writers Amitav Ghosh, Khushwant Singh, and Jaspreet Singh; film directors Harjant Gill and Shonali Bose; and visual artists the Singh twins, among various others. To access this bibliography, see http://www.gaurigill.com/works.html.

5. David L. Eng and David Kazanjian, eds., *Loss: The Politics of Mourning* (Berkeley: University of California Press, 2002); Gayatri Gopinath, "Archive, Affect, and the Everyday: Queer Diasporic Re-visions," in *Political Emotions: New Agendas in Communication,* ed. Janet Staiger, Ann Cvetkovich, and Ann Reynolds (New York: Routledge, 2010); José Esteban Muñoz, "Photographies of Mourning," in *Disidentifications: Queers of Color and the Performance of Politics* (Minneapolis: University of Minnesota Press, 1997); David L. Eng, *The Feeling of Kinship: Queer Liberalism and the Racialization of Intimacy* (Durham, N.C.: Duke University Press, 2010).

6. See Freud's work on mourning and melancholia and Fanon's work on racial-colonial melancholia. Sigmund Freud, "Mourning and Melancholia," trans. James Strachey, *International Journal for Medical Psychoanalysis* 2, no. 6 (1917): 288–301; Frantz Fanon, *Black Skin, White Masks,* trans. Richard Philcox (New York: Grove Press, 2008). Studies on racial melancholia, specifically by Anne Cheng and David Eng, have been formative. Anne Cheng, *The Melancholy of Race: Psychoanalysis, Assimilation, and Hidden Grief* (New York: Oxford University Press, 2001); David L. Eng and Shinhee Han, "A Dialogue on Racial Melancholia," *Psychoanalytic Dialogues* 10 (2000): 667–700.

7. For contemporary studies within the fields of genocide studies, trauma and memory, politics of recognition, truth and reconciliation, and historical amnesia, see Alex Alvarez, *Governments, Citizens, and Genocide: A Comparative and Interdisciplinary Approach* (Bloomington: Indiana University Press, 2001); George J. Andreopoulos, ed., *Genocide: Conceptual and Historical Dimensions* (Philadelphia: University of Pennsylvania Press, 1994); Omer Bartov, Anita Grossmann, and Mary Nolan, eds., *Crimes of War: Guilt and Denial in the Twentieth Century* (New York: New Press, 2002); Kenneth J. Campbell, *Genocide and the Global Village* (New York: Palgrave, 2001); Frank Chalk and Kurt Jonassohn, *The History and Sociology of Genocide* (New Haven, Conn.: Yale University Press, 1990); Israel W. Charny, ed., *The Encyclopedia of Genocide,* 2 vols. (Santa Barbara, Calif.: ABC-CLIO, 1999); Levon Chorbajian and George Shirinian, eds., *Studies in Comparative Genocide* (New York: St. Martin's Press, 1999); Robert Gellately and Ben Kiernan, eds., *The Specter of Genocide: Mass Murder in Historical Perspective* (Cambridge: Cambridge University Press, 2003); Adam Jones, ed., *Genocide, War Crimes & the West: History and Complicity* (London: Zed Books, 2004); Leo Kuper, *Genocide: Its Political Use in the Twentieth Century* (Harmondsworth: Penguin, 1981); Raphael Lemkin, "Key

Writings of Raphael Lemkin on Genocide," compiled by Prevent Genocide International, http://www.preventgenocide.org/lemkin; Manus I. Midlarsky, *The Killing Trap: Genocide in the Twentieth Century* (Cambridge: Cambridge University Press, 2005); Patricia Marchak, *Reigns of Terror* (Montreal: McGill-Queen's University Press, 2003); Nicolaus Mills and Kira Brunner, eds., *The New Killing Fields: Massacre and the Politics of Intervention* (New York: Basic Books, 2002); Samantha Power, *"A Problem from Hell": America and the Age of Genocide* (New York: Basic Books, 2002); Samuel Totten, William S. Parsons, and Israel W. Charny, eds., *Century of Genocide: Eyewitness Accounts and Critical Views* (New York: Garland, 1997); Samuel Totten and Steven Leonard Jacobs, eds., *Pioneers of Genocide Studies* (New Brunswick, N.J.: Transaction, 2002).

8. As a social and political category, disposability is best elucidated by feminist political theorist Neferti Tadiar, who characterizes disposability within biopolitical terms: "the expended, surplused populations figured as forms of bare life, at-risk populations, warehoused, disposable people, urban excess (planet of the slums), out of which is to be gleaned new political subjects and potentials for resistance already convertible to the ruling political currencies of the day." Neferti Tadiar, "Life Times of Disposability within Global Neoliberalism," *Social Text* 31, no. 2 115 (2013): 24, doi:10.1215/01642472-2081112.

9. "Formlessness" here is meant to connote the ways in which Gill purposely subverts artistic, narrative, and testimonial genre-based tropes. There are various expectations of what work dealing with historical trauma and violence should be or appear as, as it is widely considered well tread in historico-cultural terrains.

10. In 1984 Tilak Vihar and Trilokpuri existed only as a tiny extension of Tilak Nagar, a largely Sikh colony in West Delhi, and it was counted as firmly on the outskirts of Delhi. In the early 1980s the Delhi government had constructed close to one thousand one- and two-room flats here, intended to serve as quarters for doctors and other medical staff employed with the Delhi government. All the homes in C-Block as well as some in B-Block were allotted to women left widowed by the 1984 riots. Altogether, 944 families affected by the 1984 riots are reported to live in Tilak Vihar and Trilokpuri now. Important scholarly research on Delhi's widow colony is being done by Kamal Arora, who provides a brief synopsis of her work in the podcast recording "The Widow Colony in Delhi: Female Bodies as Vessels for Remembrance," *Archipelago*, May 26, 2014. For another important work on the violence of 1984 and the production of the widow colony, see Veena Das, *Life and Words: Violence and the Descent into the Ordinary* (Berkeley: University of California Press, 2006).

11. For thorough historical accounts of the violence of 1984, and the underdocumented violence against women at the time, see Harpreet Kaur, *The Widow Colony* (Ellicott City, Md.: Sach Productions, 2006), film; "Conference Report: *After 1984?* A Workshop Held at the University of California, Berkeley," *Sikh Formations: Religion, Culture, Theory* 5, no. 2 (2009): 115–41; Cynthia Keppley Mahmood, *A Sea Of Orange: Writings on the Sikhs and India* (Bloomington, Ind.: Xlibris, 2001); Hartosh S. Bal, "Sins of Commission," *Caravan*, October 1, 2014; Jarnail Singh, *I Accuse . . . : The Anti-Sikh Violence of 1984* (New Delhi: Penguin Books India, 2009); Barbara

Crossette, "Foreword," in *Twenty Years of Impunity: The November 1984 Pogroms of Sikhs in India*, 2nd ed., by Jasakaran Kaur (Portland, Ore.: Ensaaf, 2006); Veena Das, *Mirrors of Violence, Communities, Riots and Survivors in South Asia* (New Delhi, India: Oxford University Press, 1990); Yasmeen Arif, "The Delhi Carnage of 1984: Afterlives of Loss and Grief," *International Journal for Ethnic Studies* 3 (2007): 17–40.

12. This idea of genocide, race, and reproduction being linked is explored in detail in Amy E. Randall, *Genocide and Gender in the Twentieth Century: A Comparative Survey* (London: Bloomsbury, 2015). For a more specific reference to the race-reproduction bind in the context of the nation-state, see Alys Weinbaum, *Wayward Reproduction: Genealogies of Race and Nation in Transatlantic Modern Thought* (Durham, N.C.: Duke University Press, 2004).

13. Salwaar kameez is a traditional outfit originating in South Asia and is a generic term used to describe different styles of dress. The salwar kameez can be worn by both men and women, although styles differ by gender. They are often worn by women with a dupatta, a long, multipurpose scarf or shawl-like garment that is essential to many South Asian women's suits and matches the women's garments. The dupatta is most commonly worn with salwaar kameez. White dupattas are common for Sikh widows to wear, as white symbolizes loss and death, especially of the husband figure.

14. Justice Nanavati Commission of Inquiry, "1984 Anti-Sikh Riots," vol. 1, http://www.mha.nic.in/hindi/sites/upload_files/mhahindi/files/pdf/Nanavati-I_eng.pdf.

15. Meenal Baghel, in Gill, "1984." 55.

16. Hartosh Bal, in Gill, "1984," 6, emphasis added.

17. See Mimi Thi Nguyen, *The Gift of Freedom: War, Debt, and Other Refugee Passages* (Durham, N.C.: Duke University Press, 2012); and the below section "Refusing Resilience," which opens up this argument on war as a rubric for specific kinds of violence, including the racially charged category of genocide.

18. Although the concept of "genocide" is bound up in juridical, criminal justice, and supranationalist discourses, it is a useful analytic through which to understand the conditions under which racialized and gendered communities survive and organize throughout the world. Critical ethnic studies scholar Dylan Rodríguez argues that genocide is not a discrete moment of the past but part and parcel of the "historical and racial present tense." This argument employs an expansive definition of genocide that does not fetishize body counts but rather attends to the normalization of the social, cultural, and biological death and confinement of racialized and gendered communities. Dylan Rodríguez, "Inhabiting the Impasse: Racial/Racial-Colonial Power, Genocide Poetics, and the Logic of Evisceration" *Social Text* 33, no. 3 (2015): 24.

19. Nilanjana Roy, in Gill, "1984," 58, emphasis added.

20. Mimi Thi Nguyen, "Formulating Outrage: The Language of Political Struggle," *Archipelago*, podcast, July 26, 2014. The mode in which Nguyen engages the category of self-determination is critical, one that is not concerned with mid-twentieth-century notions of liberation and decolonization but rather takes up how self-determination has been individuated by neoliberal social practices.

21. Nguyen, "Formulating Outrage."

22. "Disaster porn" was a phrase that gained momentum online around 2010 as a mode in which to describe the increased technologization of global news media and the digital and televisual intake of visual images of disaster. The phrase is a particularly crude term that implies the pleasure gained from viewing such images of natural disaster, war, poverty, and other forms of human suffering. Direct and significant critiques of the phrase include Carolyn J. Dean, "Empathy, Pornography, and Suffering," *differences: A Journal of Feminist Cultural Studies* 14, no. 1 (2003): 88–124; Karen Halttunen, "Humanitarianism and the Pornography of Pain in Anglo-American Culture," *American Historical Review* 100, no. 2 (1995): 303–34.

23. "T Clutch Fleischmann and Jackie Wang on Queer Essays," *Essay Daily,* January 19, 2015, http://www.essaydaily.org/2015/01/t-clutch-fleischmann-and-jackie-wang -on.html.

24. Saidiya Hartman, *Scenes of Subjection: Terror, Slavery, and Self-Making in Nineteenth-Century America* (New York: Oxford University Press, 1997); Saidiya Hartman, *Lose Your Mother: A Journey along the Atlantic Slave Route* (New York: Farrar, Straus and Giroux, 2008).

25. Nguyen, "Formulating Outrage."

26. Both Nguyen's and Wang's formulations, though particularly Wang's, are antithetical to early critiques of identity politics. Specifically, these theorizations are at best disinterested if not antagonistic to Wendy Brown's critique of "wounded attachments" as a modality in which to politicize aggrieved minority communities and populations. See Wendy Brown, "Wounded Attachments," *Political Theory* 21, no. 3 (1993): 390–410.

Not Enough Human

At the Scenes of Indigenous and Black Dispossession

STEPHANIE LATTY AND MEGAN SCRIBE,
WITH ALENA PETERS AND ANTHONY MORGAN

The politicians—sharks eating fishes
it's big business, big business
they don't think seven generations ahead
they got the knowledge to stop it, they feed they pockets instead
see they make the laws then throw you in they prisons
all this white supremacy, environmental racism
welcome to America leave your hope at the door
cuz Snyder like a sniper with his focus on the poor
this don't happen in the burbs or where the politicians live
wouldn't give that same water to the politician's kid

— Soufy, *Pay to Be Poisoned*

He said, I don't know what the water wanted. It wanted to show you no one could come. He said, I don't know what the water wanted. As if then and now were not the same moment.

— Claudia Rankine, *Citizen: An American Lyric*

TIMING/PLACING

On December 10, 2015, the Department of Social Justice Education at the University of Toronto hosted "Who Is the Human?," an event to both observe Human Rights Day and also celebrate the launch of Sherene Razack's book *Dying from Improvement: Inquests and Inquiries into Indigenous Deaths in Custody*. The event addressed racism within the Canadian justice system and featured speakers who worked through formal legal processes and community-based organizing and education to confront settler colonialism and antiblackness.[1] In this article, we pick up from where the event left off. Our intent in discussing the "Who Is the Human?" event is not to retell the panel or presentation but to elaborate upon the theories and ideas the discussions put forth. We then turn to a discussion of the joint inquiry into the deaths of seven Indigenous youth in Thunder Bay, Ontario.[2] We discuss the delay of the inquest, its terms and practices, and the circumstances of one of the Indigenous girls in order to detail the specificities of the sociohistorical logic of exclusion of Indigenous peoples from the category of human in the settler state of Canada.[3] Then, we turn to a discussion of the necropolitical governance at play surrounding the state-sanctioned poisoning of the water supply in Flint, Michigan, and the spatial-racial logics through which the conditions of the Flint water crisis were engineered. We provide a summary of the Flint water crisis and analyze a briefing document on the crisis provided by the Michigan Department of Environmental Quality in correspondence with the Office of the Governor of Michigan. Both the inquest and the Flint water crisis are events that continue to unfold as we write, and will perhaps still be unfolding as you read this. In this way, this article embarks upon an analysis that understands events that cordon off who is and is not human as they continue to take shape and space, even as we consider the utility of the category of "human" toward more justice.

Before we pick up where the event left off, we need to say more about our collaboration. Writing about collaborations between Indigenous and Black people, Eve Tuck, Mistinguette Smith, Allison M. Guess, Tavia Benjamin, and Brian K. Jones emphasize the importance of contingency. Contingent collaborations, along with providing a "counterpoint to how others have theorized solidarity and allies," are guided by an ethic of incommensurability.[4] Elsewhere, Tuck, Guess, and Hannah Sultan view their collaboration as contingent because of how they are "differently implicated and invested, differently coded, by settler colonialism, Indigenous erasure, and antiblackness."[5]

In this article, we remain keenly and viscerally aware of the ways in which our experiences, histories, oppressions, and future trajectories are entangled and in tension. Stephanie Latty, a Black woman of Caribbean descent, and Megan Scribe, an Ininiw iskwew (Cree woman) from Norway House Cree Nation, Manitoba, met at an orientation event for the doctoral program in which we are currently enrolled. Both of us were drawn to the program by a sense of urgency to theorize antiblackness and settler colonialism, respectively. Over time and through holding space for one another, intellectual, emotional, or otherwise, we were both heartened and horrified when the parallels between our respective fields began to reveal themselves in our work. Soon, we found ourselves working together as colleagues, alongside Sherene

Razack, on a project investigating the deaths of Black and Indigenous people in state custody. We could not ignore the ways in which antiblackness and settler colonialism were operating in conjunction with one another to enact violence on Black and Indigenous bodies. We recognized that our pursuits for justice and accountability may not have had the same future ends, but we also knew, on what seemed like a cellular level, that to do our work in isolation also had its own very real, material dangers. Our collaborative work acknowledges that all violence, including anti-Black racism in all its multifarious forms, is situated on a colonial landscape. Accounting for these complexities meant more than being sympathetic friends to one another, but further, meant interrogating these connections and tensions in our work and using this as the starting place, the groundwork, on which to map out all of our future independent and collaborative work. As Mary Louise Fellows and Razack advise, "It is ultimately futile to attempt to disrupt one system [of oppression] without simultaneously disrupting others."[6] Similarly, we are guided by Tiffany Lethabo King's critical methodological consideration that adequately captures the tensions that underpin our collaborative work: "How have and how do our respective struggles to survive the horrors of genocide and anti-Black racism fuck one another up?"[7]

The pronouns "we" and "our" are used throughout this article not to indicate a union or symbiosis of thought or experience but instead to indicate the contingently collaborative juncture at which we find ourselves. The pronoun "we" is used to identify the voices of Latty and Scribe. The contributions of the coauthors (Alena Peters and Anthony Morgan) and contributor (Razack) appear as block text and are attributed to them directly. So, with all of this said, we come to this work as colleagues, collaborators, and friends. We come as scholars and researchers engaged in a project (directed by Razack) in which we painstakingly document the deaths of hundreds of racialized and Indigenous people in state custody. We come to this work in the wake of the non-indictment rulings in the cases of Tamir Rice and Sandra Bland, the initiation of a federal inquiry into the more than 1,200 missing and murdered Indigenous women and girls in Canada, and the ruling that James Forcillo is guilty not of second degree murder but of attempted murder in the shooting death of Sammy Yatim.

These events never leave me. The nature of my work and lived experience as a young Black man don't afford me the luxury of those events ever leaving my conscious reality.

—Anthony Morgan

This is the timing and placing of this article. Staying in the wake and wading through these problems help to situate our work. All of this uneasiness, this dis/array, and this dis/order is what makes our collaboration and all of our future collaborations contingent.

WHO IS THE HUMAN? THE ELUSIVENESS OF JUSTICE

When Razack approached us to assist with planning the "Who Is the Human?" event, she revealed that one of the underlying objectives was to generate discussions, connections, and strategies of thinking about long-established concepts, theories, and praxis relating to Indigenous and racialized deaths in custody. As we further conceptualized the event, it became apparent that broader discussions linking Indigenous deaths in custody to Black and racialized peoples' experience with custodial deaths within the context of ongoing settler colonialism in Canada were absolutely necessary. The question then became how to frame such an event, one that strives to acknowledge previously unrecognized connections while respecting the specificity of Indigenous, Black, and other racialized peoples' experiences and structural location. Part of the goal of the event, as well as in our work around racialized and Indigenous deaths in state custody, involved a deliberate broadening of the term "custody." While deaths in custody are often discussed in terms of deaths at the hands of police or other penal sites, we take an expanded view of custody that recognizes the historical and contemporary role of the state in enacting violence of many kinds and at many sites. Indeed, the very condition of being a colonized subject is in itself a form of custody. The process of trying to capture all of these complexities into one event involved proposing and rejecting many possible event "themes" before selecting a question that resonated with everyone on the planning committee: "who is the human?" If the innumerable examples of so-called human rights violations suggest anything, perhaps it is that Indigenous, Black, and other racialized peoples are not regarded as human by the state.

When we decided to launch *Dying from Improvement* on International Human Rights Day, and Stephanie proposed that the book launch be organized around the question "Who is the Human?," these decisions affirmed for me that, in fact, conceptions of the human underpin my research on racial violence. As Denise Ferreira da Silva, among others, has put it, the human is always already a racial project.[8] In modernity, all humans are placed on a scale of development defined as their gradual emergence from a state of nature. Becoming human entails domination over nature and over body. In this framework Indigenous and racialized peoples are unable to emerge from the state of nature and thus never manage to emerge as fully human. Owing to their assumed incapacity to be rational beings, self-determining beings, Indigenous and racialized peoples are evicted from the category "human," and evicted from the modern.

—Sherene Razack

Razack's decision to schedule the event to coincide with Human Rights Day invited all those present to complicate their understanding of the "human" by locating it in the heart of the modern racial project and, further, to question current approaches to addressing racial injustice.

I think the significance of holding the event on Human Rights Day is that it encourages a much-needed move away from "the human" as being overly determined by narrow Western nation-state conceptualizations and constructions of human rights doctrine.

—Anthony Morgan

Given the diverse personal and professional backgrounds from which the coauthors enter this discussion, it makes sense that while our conversation on justice at times harmonized, many times these discussions on justice were fraught and in fact revealed differing conceptualizations and approaches. It was clear that much like the concept of the human, there is little consensus around what justice means for Black and Indigenous peoples. Justice has many faces and sometimes appears couched in appeals to state recognition or situated in the realm of the Western juridical system.

Dominant conceptualizations of the human within human rights law prioritize and elevate the human-as-individual as being the singularly most important unit within society. The unbalanced overprivileging of the individual human within the dominant human rights regime is largely responsible for persistent systemic disproportionalities and disparities that plague Black communities in various areas of Canadian social life.

—Anthony Morgan

Morgan goes on to describe the role that the human rights lawyer has in upholding a Western concept of the human.

An honest reflection on our Western European conception of human rights requires a recognition of the fact that the human rights lawyer upholds a concept of the human who is a white, Anglo-Saxon, Protestant, wealthy capitalist, able-bodied, middle-aged, English-speaking, heterosexual, cis-gender male with full citizenship rights. I would suggest that a critical legal studies analysis offers too limited a frame for assessing and interrogating the relation of anti-Black racism–focused human rights work to conceptualizations of the human.

—Anthony Morgan

In the context of our respective histories of antiblackness and settler colonialism, justice remains slippery and elusive. It seems that often our dialogues about justice are actually about injustice—that is, fleshing out the enormity of the violence done to our bodies in an anti-Black settler-colonial state. When we are not focused on the multitude of injustices, then our stories tend to frame justice in the juridico-empirical sense. We might feel that justice is served when a perpetrator is criminally convicted or when some type of punishment is administered. In other instances, justice is taken up in the context of social justice. As two doctoral students housed in the Department of Social Justice Education, we are keenly aware of the emergent difficulties with this concept and the myriad ways that this term is invoked, not all of them with attentiveness to antiracism or decolonization. Tuck and C. Ree write:

> Social justice is a term that gets thrown around like some destination, a resolution, a fixing. "No justice, no peace," and all of that. But justice and peace don't exactly cohabitate. The promise of social justice sometimes rings false, smells consumptive, like another manifest destiny. Like you can get there, but only if you climb over me.[9]

If we know nothing else about justice, we know with certainty that the landscape of justice is as fraught as it is mutable. For instance, what does justice look like for Black people who live at once in the wake of the trans-Atlantic slave trade and simultaneously on occupied Indigenous land?

Yet, whether harmonious or competing, conceptualizations of justice do not typically include African Canadians.

—Anthony Morgan

Justice is not a concept that is extended freely to all, and this is made particularly clear in the juridico-empirical sense of the term, as Alena Peters observes in her telling of Cece McDonald's story.

> Black trans women experience racialized transmisogyny that at once denies their womanhood and attempts to justify any and all of the violence they face by enforcing myths about criminality and deception. Cece McDonald, a Black trans woman from Minneapolis, was sentenced to forty-one months in prison for manslaughter after defending herself from a racist, sexist, transphobic attacker. She was held in two men's facilities for the duration of her sentence. Activists worked to petition prison officials to move Cece and ensure she had the appropriate hormone treatments. While I do want to point to the specific gendered and transphobic ways the justice system dehumanized Cece and does other trans women of color, I am reminded of the sentiment that Cece conveyed upon her release. She wanted folks to know that whether she was imprisoned with men or women had little bearing on her safety, because she recognized prisons as inherently violent institutions.
>
> —Alena Peters

Alena captures an important point here through Cece's story—that justice has a limit. Indeed, the contours and limits of justice are structured by the limits of Western ways of knowing.[10] Any analysis of the limits of justice, da Silva writes, "demands an engagement with what is taken for granted in explanations."[11] Thus, da Silva shows us that our conceptions of justice are ultimately tethered to our conceptions of the human, and if there is indeed justice to be claimed, it will not be found within our current frame of knowing—a frame that itself produces injustice.

In the remainder of this article, we take up a discussion of two ongoing events: the inquest into seven Indigenous youth who died over a span of ten years after relocating to Thunder Bay, Ontario, to attend high school and the ongoing water crisis in Flint, Michigan, where mostly Black and poor residents are being (at times fatally) poisoned by lead-contaminated water. If upon first glance these two crises seem dissimilar, that is because they are. What these crises do have in common is the striking way in which they expand notions of custodial death by exposing the role of the state in the production of the crises. We resist theorization that treats Black and Indigenous peoples' experiences with anti-Black racism and settler colonialism as interchangeable phenomena, and our decision to investigate these distinct scenes of dispossession reflects this commitment. By "scenes of dispossession," we allude to Saidiya Hartman's *Scenes of Subjection: Terror, Slavery, and Self-Making in Nineteenth-Century America*, a formative text that informs our analysis.[12] Furthermore, "scenes of dispossession," as outlined by Audra Simpson, refers to the settler-colonial context in which these examples of racial violence occur. Simpson further contends: "In situations in which sovereignties are nested and embedded, one proliferates at the other's expense; the United States and Canada can only come into political being because of Indigenous dispossession."[13] As our analysis will reveal, the flourishing of these two settler states has indeed been made possible by the structured dispossession of Indigenous land and life and, crucially, Black life. In each case, we attend to emerging themes that are demonstrative of settler-state injustice and anti-Black racism. It is not our intent to expose some hidden violence enacted by these two settler states. We are not interested in taking a tally of the total lives lost, nor are we attempting to reinstate the racialized body within the realm of humanity. Rather, we take up an analysis that seeks to understand *how* it becomes possible to disregard the loss of life. As da Silva argues, "Instead of the question of who or what we are, we need to go deeper into the investigation of how we come up with answers to these questions."[14] As indicated above, we are writing amid the ongoing inquest proceedings and lead poisoning of the residents of Flint. This is just another way of saying that we do not yet know what the outcome (if such a thing is possible) of each event will reveal. Nevertheless, we proceed with an examination of the production and management of Indigenous and Black bodies by two settler states as part of our endeavor to find what justice wants.

SCENE OF DISPOSSESSION: THUNDER BAY, ONTARIO, CANADA

On October 5, 2015, a joint inquest into the deaths of seven Indigenous youth attending high school in Thunder Bay commenced. Between 2000 and 2011, all seven youth died under violent and suspicious circumstances while attending high school away from their respective remote First Nations communities in Nishnawbe Aski Nation (NAN) territory. Initially, the Office of the Chief Coroner called an inquest into the death of just one youth in 2009; however, NAN advocated for a larger discretionary hearing to investigate the deaths of six additional youth who died under similar circumstances. On May 31, 2012, three years following the initial announcement, the chief coroner called an inquest into the deaths of seven Indigenous youth, including fifteen-year-old Jethro Anderson of Kasabonika Lake First Nation, eighteen-year-old Curran Strang of Pikangikum First Nation, twenty-one-year-old Paul Panacheese of Mishkeegogamang First Nation, nineteen-year-old Robyn Harper of Keewaywin First Nation, seventeen-year-old Kyle Morrisseau of Keewaywin First Nation, fifteen-year-old Reggie Bushie of Poplar Hill First Nation, and fifteen-year-old Jordan Wabasse of Webequie First Nation.[15] The inquest experienced yet another delay when the chief coroner of Ontario, Dr. Dirk Huyer, postponed the inquest, citing questions around Aboriginal representation within Ontario's jury roll system.[16] The morning the long-awaited inquest was scheduled, many family and community members were dismayed to find that one of the largest discretionary inquests ever held in Ontario would be held in one of the smallest courtrooms in Thunder Bay Courthouse. NAN Grand Chief Alvin Fiddler observed, "We have lots of room for First Nations peoples in jails. . . . But when it comes to access to the courtroom, there's no room at all."[17] Fiddler's evocative statement draws attention to both the disproportionate rate of Indigenous and Black peoples who are held in state custody in Canada, including carceral and child welfare spaces, and, significantly, the failure of the Canadian legal system to provide these people with access to justice.

As we write, the inquest into the deaths of the seven youth is ongoing. We are still awaiting the outcome. Here, we pause to reflect on the "deferral of justice" that seems to characterize the inquest proceedings and, more generally, the experience of being Indigenous, Black, or racialized in Canada. We are concerned that the preoccupation with inclusion obfuscates the manner in which interlocking systems of oppression, such as settler colonialism, white supremacy, and anti-Black racism, defer justice. We proceed cautiously so as not to dismiss the critiques and concerns of the families and communities. Indeed, the significance of Indigenous peoples' efforts to address immediate experiences of injustice within the criminal justice system through the rhetoric of inclusion must not be immediately dismissed, as demands for inclusion often signal a deeper awareness of underlying structures of violence. With that stated, the analysis of the ongoing inquest will reorient the focus of discussion from a sociologics of exclusion toward the interlocking structures of oppression that sustain processes of dehumanization in this white settler society.

When the state declares, as it often does in inquests and inquiries, that Indigenous peoples are uniquely vulnerable (and on the path to extinction),

and announces its duty to care for such damaged beings, it renders Indigenous people as impossible to harm. They are dying anyway and all we can
do is to be compassionate.

—Sherene Razack

While the matter of underrepresentation of Indigenous peoples on Canadian juries has been raised as a systemic barrier for many years, the issue
reemerged when counsel for Clifford Kokopenace, an Indigenous man who
was convicted of manslaughter by a non-Indigenous jury, challenged the
decision on the grounds that Kokopenace's right to a representative jury had
been violated.[18] The delay of the inquest into the deaths of the seven youth
(along with twelve other cases), Huyer claimed, was in an effort to resolve
the question of Indigenous inclusion within Canadian legal processes to
ensure a fair inquest.[19] Huyer's decision to postpone the inquest proceeding
originally scheduled for the spring of 2013 was met with widespread criticism by family and community members of the youth, legal experts, and
politicians. In response to this announcement, one of the lawyers for six of
the seven families of the deceased youth, Jonathan Rudin, expressed feeling
"very disappointed."[20] Christa Big Canoe, another lawyer representing the
family, added, "Some of the families said they're not surprised, given the
number of times we've had to inform them the inquest has been delayed."[21]
One media outlet suggested that the postponement has "prolonged [the]
grief" of the families.[22] Ontario's advocate for children and youth, Irwin
Elman, argued that there were alternative routes in place that would allow
Ontario to address the issues around the jury roll without causing the delay,
such as a public inquiry.[23]

Contrary to Huyer's concern regarding the question of Indigenous representation on jury rolls, we argue that justice for the seven Indigenous youth
and, more generally, Indigenous peoples is not realized through Indigenous
inclusion within the criminal justice system. Indeed, Patricia Monture has
argued that Canadian law does not have the capacity to address systemic
forms of oppression inflicted upon Indigenous peoples by the Canadian
state. She further suggests that while reforms to the Canadian legal system
can ameliorate individual conditions, reforms cannot adequately address
Indigenous peoples' collective oppression.[24] Da Silva's critical discussion on
the sociohistorical logic of exclusion yields further insight into questions
of "inclusion" within the legal system.[25] She extends Monture's views on the
limitations of seeking inclusion within the criminal justice system by elabo-
rating on the practice of attempting to situate racialized subjects into the

category of the universalized human. Da Silva argues that critical race scholars informed by sociohistorical logics of exclusion fail to appreciate that the production of particular bodies as racialized makes the universal human subject position possible. She maintains that seeking inclusion is thus a futile pursuit that further entrenches the system producing this hierarchy. Rather than pursue "projects of inclusion," da Silva suggests that it is far more effective "to turn the transparency thesis on its head."[26] In other words, interrogating dominant conceptions of the human is likely to yield a more nuanced and in-depth understanding of racialized hierarchies of oppression.

In considering da Silva's instructions, we cannot help but call to mind the sunrise ceremony commencing the inquest.[27] Without diminishing the significance that this traditional ceremony holds for Indigenous peoples, we complicate the state's incorporation of Indigenous traditions into legal proceedings by reflecting on the manner in which ongoing settler colonialism interferes with Indigenous peoples' ability to engage in land-based systems and structures such as ceremony. The state's inclusion of the sunrise ceremony is best regarded as a "settler move to innocence," a phrase introduced by Tuck and K. Wayne Yang to describe strategies undertaken by settlers to relieve responsibility without relinquishing "land or power or privilege, without having to change much at all."[28] Monture has argued that it is far more effective to interrogate the Canadian criminal justice system than to seek cultural inclusion.[29] She offers a persuasive critique of "culturally appropriate" reforms and initiatives:

> In Canada much has been made of the many initiatives taken "for" Aboriginal people in the justice system. . . . All of these programs are mere "add-ons" to the mainstream justice system. . . . This should be recognized for what it is: a misappropriation of culture. The programs are really based on the notion of Aboriginal inferiority, and if we Aboriginal people just become more knowledgeable about the Canadian system, the problem is solved. Culture has been used to obscure the structural racism in the Canadian criminal justice system.[30]

The state's inclusion of a sunrise ceremony is a tactic intended to advance the national narrative that Canada is "both (post)colonial and multicultural."[31] Moreover, such nominal inclusions obscure the disproportionate rates of Indigenous peoples in the custody of prisons or foster care. Given that many Indigenous ceremonies are land based, we are disturbed by the state's appropriation of Indigenous spirituality that many Indigenous peoples themselves are unable to engage because of incarceration and ongoing land theft. The Canadian state's understanding of Indigenous cultures and spiritual paradigms is remarkably different than those of the Indigenous nations from which these systems and structures emerge.[32] Glen Sean Coulthard observes that Indigenous nations interpret culture "as the interconnected social totality of distinct *mode of life* encompassing the economic, political, spiritual, and social."[33] The Canadian state, on the other hand, deploys a depoliticized and dematerialized notion of culture. Coulthard further contends that the state is only willing to accommodate (or appropriate) culture to the extent that it would not interfere with colonial sovereignty or economic systems.[34] Thus, cultural inclusions are less about goodwill than advancing the settler state.

Throughout the proceedings, an Anishinabe interpreter has been made available for witnesses providing testimony in Anishinabemowin. As an Indigenous person who belongs to the ever-unfurling legacy of the Canadian residential school system, I (Megan) am heartened to hear Anishinabemowin, yet I am aware that many Indigenous peoples lack fluency in their respective Indigenous languages because of Canadian educational policies. The Canadian state's systematized attack upon Indigenous languages is one tactic among many deployed to secure Canada's overall objective to eliminate and assimilate Indigenous peoples through the education system and its myriad iterations.

It is important to situate the deaths of these seven youth within the broader context of violent colonial educational policies in Canada. The circumstances compelling each youth to leave home to attend high school bears striking similarities to those of Helen Betty Osborne, a Cree girl who shortly after leaving her community, Norway House Cree Nation, to attend high school in The Pas, Manitoba, was murdered by four white men in 1971. The Aboriginal Justice Inquiry into Osborne's death established critical links between her life circumstances and ongoing settler colonialism that have relevance to the seven youth.[35] The commissioners argued, "The very reason that Betty Osborne was compelled to leave her home and move to The Pas also was rooted in racism. Like so many other Aboriginal young people, she was forced by long-standing government policy to move to a strange and hostile environment to continue her schooling."[36] The commissioners establish crucial links between contemporary policies and practices compelling Indigenous youth to leave home to attend secondary school and the Canadian residential school system. Following the height of the residential school era, settler-colonial objectives to assimilate, eliminate, and dispossess Indigenous peoples through educational policies continued unabated, albeit more insidiously. As part of the state's necropolitical governance of First Nations communities, Indigenous children are deprived of life-giving services, such as water, food, and shelter, in addition to schools.[37] The commissioners argue that policies compelling Indigenous children to relocate for secondary education as opposed to building schools in their communities are informed assimilatory logics that regard these spaces as "neither viable nor desirable."[38] Notwithstanding the commissioner's reflections that remain true twenty-five years later, the softly stated condemnation of the federal government does not address Indigenous peoples' desire to have meaningful control over the education of their children and adequate funding.[39]

As the inquest proceedings have thus far revealed, the startling lack of concern for the safety and well-being of the youth gestures to processes of dehumanization. Regrettably, the scope of this article prevents a close engagement with each youth. With this in mind, we lay the focus on the lack of care afforded to Robyn Harper, the only girl among the youth. Just days after arriving in Thunder Bay, Harper was found dead on the floor of the downstairs hallway of her boarding home after a night of heavy drinking. It was reported that Harper was intoxicated to the extent that she could not stand, let alone walk home. In fact, as one media outlet reveals, Harper was dragged by her ankles through the snow by friends to a city bus terminal on the night of January 12, 2007. Security footage shows at least one passerby and a security guard approaching Harper before a staff member of the Northern Nishnawbe Education Council drove Harper to her residence. A former roommate testified that the reason Harper was left lying in the hallway was supposedly because she was too drunk to be assisted to her bedroom.[40] In the descriptions of the night of Harper's death there is a notable absence of legal or assigned caregivers, guardians, or parents attending to or caring for her. The responsibility of care is placed squarely on the shoulders of Harper's peers, other youths. This failure is particularly unsettling in light of long-standing concerns over Indigenous students' living arrangements. The commissioners condemn the state's failure to provide Indigenous students with adequate support services and "safe and culturally appropriate" boarding homes. Furthermore, they maintain that cases of physical and sexual abuse, mistreatment, and neglect are directly attributable to Indian Affairs policies.[41] As Razack has shown, the eviction of Indigenous peoples from the realm of humanity is a settler ritual that must be repeatedly enacted to consolidate white settler society.[42] Indigenous peoples' eviction from humanity coincides with their eviction from law. Through the eviction from law, it is possible to take the life of an Indigenous person without committing a crime.[43] Harper's final interactions, or lack thereof, with people charged with the responsibility of ensuring her well-being and safety are telling. These encounters confirm her eviction from humanity, thus diminishing the culpability of her assigned guardians. Otherwise, how does it become possible to witness an unconscious girl being dragged by her ankles through the snow or to leave her slumped in a hallway to be stepped over like a stack of mail with little more than fleeting interest?

Attending to processes of dehumanization in the lives of Indigenous peoples such as Robyn Harper and the other six youth provides a critical entry point from which to interrogate Canada's regime of strategic inclusion. So-called initiatives launched by the state do not address underlying structural oppression. Discussions preoccupied with inclusion fail to consider that the legal system, along with the state itself, cannot accommodate Indigenous bodies quite simply because the integrity of these structures depend upon the subjugation of Indigenous peoples. Ultimately, strategic inclusion does more to obfuscate ongoing settler colonialism and, furthermore, reinforces the national narrative of Canada as a multicultural and friendly country. By linking existing laws and policies that compel Indigenous youth to leave their communities for school to Canada's ongoing effort to assimilate, eliminate, and dispossess Indigenous peoples of land and life, the violent character underlying the state's friendly visage becomes apparent. In the following section, we take up a discussion of the necropolitical governance of the mostly Black residents of Flint, Michigan, that has resulted in the lead poisoning of the town's water source. As emphasized from the outset, we avoid making convenient connections that suggest this could have happened to anyone anywhere. We resist a simple comparison of the Flint water crisis to the 92 First Nations communities in Canada (excluding British Columbia) with 136 drinking water advisories as of November 30, 2015, that fails to account for the nuances of anti-Black racism and settler colonialism. As we shed light on the necropolitical governance that is deeply informed by anti-Black racism of this community within the context of ongoing U.S. settler colonialism, the distinctness of this crisis will become evident.

SCENE OF DISPOSSESSION: FLINT, MICHIGAN, UNITED STATES

In January 2015 a state of emergency was declared by Michigan Governor Rick Snyder after nine residents of the city of Flint died as a result of drinking water that was contaminated with lead and Legionnaire's disease–causing bacteria. For more than one year, residents of Flint complained on several platforms that their tap water was brown and foul-smelling and that they and their children were being made ill, but seemingly, their concerns failed to be addressed with any urgency. In October 2015, one week after the State of Michigan released an action plan to address solutions to the water crisis, three schools were found to have toxic levels of lead in their water. One in particular, a Flint elementary school, was found to have water lead levels seven times higher than the level at which action is required under the United States Environmental Protection Agency's (EPA) Safe Drinking Water Act.[44] Health care providers were seeing increased numbers of children experiencing rashes, skin lesions, and hair loss, and one year after these complaints began, a local hospital in Flint released several blood test results that showed intolerably high levels of lead in residents' blood. Flint was in the throes of a deadly water crisis. In what follows, we articulate our concern with what we assert is a form of necropolitical governance at play in Flint and the spatial-racial logics through which the conditions of the Flint water crisis were engineered. We begin with a brief summary of the Flint water crisis and with an awareness that the events in Flint continue to unfold as we write this, perhaps even as you read this. We then turn our attention to a briefing document about the Flint crisis provided by the Michigan Department of Environmental Quality in correspondence with the office of the governor. Our analysis of this document and the broader Flint water crisis reveals the ways in which necropolitical racial-spatial logics operated in Flint to situate the largely Black and poor residents of Flint as outside the limits of the human. We situate the deaths in Flint as deaths in custody in recognition of the direct role of the state in the engineering of the crisis and the historical context of colonization that made a crisis of this magnitude possible.

Flint, Michigan, is a city of 99,000 residents located seventy miles northwest of what is now the city of Detroit. Flint exists on occupied Indigenous land along what settlers call the Saginaw Trail, an Anishnaabeg route between what is now Detroit and Saginaw.[45] According to Michigan census data from 2010, 40 percent of the residents of Flint live below the poverty line, 60 percent of the residents are Black, and about 1 percent of the population is Indigenous.[46] The water poisoning began in April 2014 when Flint's water source was temporarily switched from Lake Huron to the Flint River after officials were unable to negotiate a financially attractive enough deal to continue feeding water to Flint from Lake Huron. Almost immediately following the switch, residents of Flint began to complain about the water quality, claiming that it was brown, bad tasting, and foul smelling. In August 2014 a boil-water advisory was issued for Flint after the water tested positive for E. coli, and again in September when coliform bacteria was found in the water, indicating the possible presence of fecal matter. Flint residents knew that something was wrong with the water, yet state officials repeatedly assured residents that the water was safe to drink and that their concerns were merely aesthetically based—that is, officials were saying that the water simply looked odd because of rust and oxidization but maintained that it was perfectly safe to consume. Eventually it was revealed that the water being drawn from the Flint River was so corrosive that over time it had eaten away at the pipes, causing lead to leach into the water supply of Flint residents. This was ultimately found to be preventable had the water been appropriately treated with a suitable anticorrosion agent. Yet the questions remain in full view, floating right at the surface: Why did it take one year for these concerns to be addressed by government officials? What were the conditions that made a crisis of this severity possible?

In January 2016 Governor Snyder publically released several e-mail correspondences between himself and other state employees related to the Flint water crisis, in response to increased pressure and a public demand for governmental transparency. In a briefing document compiled by the Michigan Department of Environmental Quality (DEQ) in February 2015, three particularly disturbing comments emerged regarding what the state viewed as the "aesthetic values" of the water. Noting first that the "Safe Drinking Water Act does *not regulate* the aesthetic values of water," the briefing note goes on to make three points about the ongoing complaints of Flint residents: "1) It's the Flint River. . . . With hard water, you get a different flavor and feel. It's why General Motors suspended use of Flint Water—it was rusting their parts. Also, there's the 'organics' factor." It goes on to say: "2) The system is old. Flint has more than 500 miles of water pipes. More than half of those pipe miles are more than 75 years old. Much of it is cast iron. Hard water can react with cast iron and exacerbate the rusty factor, which creates that brown water that angry residents were holding up in jugs for the media cameras last week." Finally, the third point included in the briefing document states: "3) Flint is old. Many of the homes served by the system are old. . . . Again, discoloration is not an indicator of water quality or water safety, but we recognize that nobody likes it."[47] It would seem reasonable to conclude that Flint officials knew very well that the water was far from ideal, even if they gesture only to the aesthetics: the "flavor and feel" of it. Yet, of note to some is that in January 2015, in the midst of the crisis, government offices in Flint were fitted with filtered water coolers. This occurred one year before the mainstream media would even begin to take up the issue of the ongoing water crisis that residents were experiencing.

If having access to clean water is a fundamental and inalienable human right, then how does the Flint water crisis force us to shift our understanding of the boundaries of humanness? How are these boundaries materialized through spatial violence? We contend that the spatiality of the Flint water crisis provides a map/blueprint of the human. Achille Mbembe's conceptualization of necropolitics provides inroads for investigating ways in which racial-spatial logics are operant in Flint. For Mbembe, sovereign power resides in "the capacity to determine who may live and who must die."[48] Through a necropolitical regime, as distinguished from a biopolitical one, "the sovereign might kill at any time or in any manner."[49] It is a form of governance that permits the sovereign to determine "who is 'disposable' and who is not."[50] Further, Mbembe argues that necropolitical governance entails the maximum destruction of a person, a suffering that biopolitics cannot account for.[51] Mbembe goes on to articulate the centrality of "territorialisation" to necropolitical governance, which refers to the "seizing, delimiting, and asserting control over physical geographical area" and "the writing of new spatial relations."[52] Writing of the effect of necropolitics, Razack notes that "infrastructural warfare—control of water, air, and space—performs a kind of 'invisible killing.'"[53] Necropolitical governance, in the case of the Flint water crisis, is a territorial violence that we see enacted first through the violent dispossession and reconfiguration of Indigenous spatial arrangements and, eventually, through the enactment of anti-Black structural violence. In Flint, this "invisible killing" enacted through spatial violence has played out in the sense that it is categorically the Black and poor areas of Flint that water lead levels are highest and most toxic.[54] Further, anti-Black racial issues in Flint have been long standing. In 1930 the Home Owners Lending Corporation (HOLC), a governmentally backed agency, created what was called "residential security maps" for several American cities including Flint. These maps ranked certain parts of the city based on several criteria on a color-coded scale of desirability. Areas of the city that were considered too "heterogeneous" or that featured "undesirable populations" were denoted on the maps in the color red and colloquially deemed "red districts."[55] Mortgage brokers would then use these maps to determine who would be eligible for mortgages. This process effectively barred racialized people from accessing mortgages and homes that appreciated in value and thus generated intergenerational wealth.[56] This denial of access was a deliberate segregating action by the state that would have long-lingering and devastating effects on Black and poor residents of Flint.[57] This history makes apparent the ways in which the water crisis in Flint is the product of a series of racial-spatial conditions that have been engineered over time. In this context, the DEQ's deeply apathetic stance that "it's the Flint River" serves not only to shirk state accountability but, going further, it also naturalizes that which is the product of long-standing and ongoing state violence against Black bodies. In conjunction, the statement "The system is old. . . . Flint is old" similarly works to naturalize enduring violence but also establishes a temporality where Flint residents are cast into a perpetual past and their condition is produced as that of an inherent susceptibility to this type of crisis.[58] It follows then that the poisoned water is produced as a natural outcome of residents' refusal to progress with modernity. That is, the lead-lined pipes of Flint are old and ultimately satisfactory for a not-quite-human population from a primordial past.

Lisa Marie Cacho writes, "Certain populations' very humanity is represented as something that one becomes or achieves, that one must earn because it just cannot be."[59] That residents of Flint are majority Black and poor and living with poisoned water is not innocuous. Their blackness means that their bodies are always already evicted from the category of human, and it is, in part, through the violence of state-sanctioned lead poisoning that power is rendered readable on their bodies.[60] Indeed, what use would a nonliving, nonhuman thing have with clean, unpoisoned, drinkable water? Da Silva holds that the Western subject "comes into being as a self-determined thing" by existing in opposition to "the affectable other."[61] She defines affectability as "the condition of being subjected to both natural (in the scientific and lay sense) conditions and to others' power."[62] Thus, it is only against the backdrop of affectable nonhumanness that the Western subject comes to understand itself as human. What is more, it is through this enactment of power, often in the form of spectacular violence, that the boundaries of justice and the human are drawn along racial lines.

In this context of antiblackness, non/humanness, and space, what is of note to some is the particularity of lead being the major contaminating agent in Flint. In the midst of responsibility for the crisis being passed between municipal and state governments, pediatrician and advocate Mona Hannah-Attisha observed:

If you were to put something in a population to keep them down for generations and generations to come, it would be lead. . . . It's a well-known, potent neurotoxin. There's tons of evidence on what lead does to a child, and it is one of the most damning things that you can do to a population. It drops your IQ, it affects your behavior, it's been linked to criminality. It has multigenerational impacts. There is no safe level of lead in a child.[63]

Taking up Sylvia Wynter's essay "1492: A New Worldview" in the context of a post-Katrina New Orleans, Bench Ansfield asks the questions "Are black bodies and spaces really vulnerable to toxins? Can a black body—the raw material for dysgenic narratives of racial apocalypse—be further contaminated?"[64] As a necropolitical site, Flint residents too are considered always already toxic and thus impossible to further poison. Indeed, the impossibility of being further poisoned is already imagined as a condition of nonhuman existence: it is impossible to poison a nonhuman thing. This point is reflected clearly in the DEQ briefing note where a momentary mention is made of General Motors' December 2014 decision to cease using the Flint River as the water supply for their factory because it was corroding their machines and car parts. To be clear, water deemed unfit for use on corporate machinery was deemed suitable for the largely Black and poor residents of Flint. It is disturbing to consider that while every consideration was given to how Flint's corrosive water was eating away at metal car parts, so little was given to what this water was doing to human parts. Or, perhaps there was indeed consideration given to what the poisoned water was doing to human parts, leading to the installation of filtered water coolers in Flint government office buildings, while residents were encouraged to continue consuming the poisonous water from their taps. Looking at Flint through these lenses allows us to see Flint not as an unfortunate confluence of un/natural forces unmoored from questions of antiblackness and the human but instead as the material product of a set of conditions that have been engineered over time and space through racial-spatial violence, marked by the ready and unimpeded flow of poisoned water through the city pipes. Flint, as a site of necropolitical governance, reveals the boundaries of the human.

It bears repeating that the events in Flint, Michigan, are still unfolding. What is frequently omitted from public dialogues about the Flint crisis is an attentiveness to colonization and the simultaneous abjection of Indigenous peoples from the category of the human. Our goal here and elsewhere has been to foreground the links between antiblackness and settler colonialism. As interlocking forms of oppression, antiblackness and settler colonialism operate together to enact violence on both Black and Indigenous bodies, working to relegate both, in particular ways, to the domain of the nonhuman. If we consider the events unfolding in Flint only as events located in a specific moment in history, in the present, and not as a site of spatial violence, then we obscure and erase the materiality of historical ongoing settler-colonial violence in this space.

UNTETHERING MAN:
THE HUMAN AS AN OBJECT OF INQUIRY

On Human Rights Day 1992, the General Assembly of the United Nations (UN) declared 1993 as the International Year of the World's Indigenous People (IYWIP). According to UN Secretary General Boutros Boutros-Ghali, the decision was made in recognition of the systemic forms of violence and oppression Indigenous peoples experienced globally.[65] In Canada, the white settler society from which we write, various grassroots and international campaigns and movements have generated increased awareness of settler violence, but in the near twenty-three years that have followed the IYWIP, everyday, extraordinary forms of violence inflicted upon Indigenous peoples continue apace. Perhaps the reason that human rights violations are enacted with impunity is because Indigenous peoples are not considered human in a white settler society. After all, it was only in 2008, fifteen years after the IYWIP, that section 67 of the Canadian Human Rights Act was repealed. Through section 67, those registered under the Indian Act or members of a First Nations Band and other individuals residing on a reserve could not file a complaint of discrimination to the Canadian Human Rights Commission on matters relating to the Government of Canada's application of the Indian Act. In other words, prior to 2008, the Canadian Human Rights Act did not fully apply to Indians.

Alongside the legal eviction of Indigenous peoples from humanity, Black people are removed entirely from Canadian consciousness which, in effect, contributes to their dehumanization.

> How can folks appreciate the nature, meaning, and significance of Black experiences of state violence in a state they imagine as void of a black presence? If there are no Black people within the public imaginary of Canada, how can there be Black suffering in Canada? What do the sufferings and struggles of an absent(ed) people look and feel like? How do you even imagine such a thing? . . . Humanity is empty when excised from social context. It cannot be valued when conceived within a social vacuum. Yet this is how blackness in Canada is imagined today: bodies without real context,

without history, legacy, contribution, and so of course, without conceivable humanity.

—Anthony Morgan

Indigenous, Black, and racialized peoples' claims to humanity seem to have little effect when attempting to redress so-called human rights violations committed by the state. While some activists and scholars have observed the way in which humanity is organized along a hierarchy in Western society, these discussions tend to be oriented around exclusion.[66] Concomitant to this concern is a preoccupation with statistical figures.

> Those outside of the official national narrative not only have no legitimate claim to equal or equitable treatment from the institutions that govern that state, but they also have no right to recognition of their full humanity. They are regarded as shadows, not people. This is why when speaking about Black deaths in custody of the Canadian state, it is numbers and statistics that capture the public's attention: "Mr. Morgan, tell me of numbers, percentages, proportions, and of piles of bodies please, because here, we do not talk or know of Black humanity."
>
> —Anthony Morgan

More recently, scholars have begun to question whether Indigenous, Black, or other racialized peoples' inclusion into humanity is possible. Indeed, such scholars have argued that conceptions of the modern human are inextricable from modern liberal thought, which depends upon the subordination of the non-European subject. For Lisa Lowe, the emergence of the "human" as a universalized concept coincides with the emergence of modern liberalism.[67] Through liberalism, ideas such as political emancipation, individualism, and capitalism flourished; however, such developments resulted from the dispossession and subordination of colonized subjects through colonial expansion.[68] The process in which liberalist thought defined the human is unavoidably violent. Lowe elaborates that "while violence characterizes the exclusion from the universality of the human, it also accompanies inclusion or assimilation into it."[69] The deployment of modern race through the inscription of racial difference on colonized subjects assists in delineating the boundaries of humanity. In other words, through the process of racialization, colonized others come to form the constitutive outside of humanity, thus "creating the conditions of possibility for that freedom" for modern liberal subjects.[70] Razack elaborates upon the production of the modern human and its subhuman counterparts:

[The human is] a single project but there are multiple aspects to this governance. There is, after all, a typology of the human, with groups placed differently on it. We must trace the links between racial forms of governance and different racial logics, exploring how different racial subjects are connected historically.

—Sherene Razack

The development and deployment of modern race and racial difference became further entrenched through the advancement of race as an object of scientific inquiry. Da Silva describes this politicized knowledge project, in which "strategies of intervention deployed in the initial moment of the *analytics of raciality* required the manipulation, measurement, and classification of bodies to produce the racial soul. In that, they produced the *racial subject* (the *raced consciousness*) as a fundamentally mediated, determined, spatial, condition."[71] Ultimately, race as a category of scientific inquiry supported the claim that "while the human body could be found across the surface of the globe, man existed within the limits of the modern European space."[72]

Upon establishing that racialized others cannot enter the realm of universal humanity, as it is their difference that creates the conditions of the human, scholars might ask, "Where does this leave us?" Alexander Weheliye proposes that we reconfigure the human as a relational concept and as an object of inquiry. Indeed, when we untether the human from nature, we can come to understand it as a frame from which to ask questions rather than answer them.[73] Meyda Yeğenoğlu contends that it is necessary to deconstruct the binary structure that produces the modern human and racialized other.[74] This involves a revaluing of the devalued (racialized other), and the subsequent locating of the subordinate term within the core of the dominant one, thus revealing the dependence of the subject on the other.[75] Once more, Yeğenoğlu reveals that any question of a subject's humanity is already weighed down by the frame of the question itself. Yeğenoğlu dismisses the criticisms that arise as a result of deconstructing the subject without producing an alternative framework.[76] She contends, "This widespread criticism misses the point, not so much because it insists on the necessity of agency but rather because it risks leaving the very structure of the subject intact. The dangerous result of this attitude is to reverse the structure and to enact the same subject, to repeat the same desire for a sovereign, autonomous position on the side of the subordinate, hegemonized, second term."[77] Morgan identifies a similar risk:

I am left thinking about the extreme dangers of Black inclusion and recognition in a national narrative of a colonial, fundamentally anti-Indigenous state. This thought reminds me that Canadian-brand white supremacy sets state acknowledgement, respect, and protection of Black humanity up as a challenge that contests Indigenous sovereignty, a zero-sum colonial equation.

—Anthony Morgan

DISENTANGLING JUSTICE FROM THE HUMAN

Some readers might be unsettled by our insistence on abandoning the concept of the human without offering a new framework. We want to first address this concern by turning to the powerful visionings of our coauthors who imagine a just future.

Is it possible for those of us being offered some humanity to humanize another? I do not believe that is possible if humanity is still a gift to be given, if the human makers are simply working to "empower" those who are being made to be subhuman.

—Alena Peters

These visionings challenge the ascendency of the individual secured through the modern human over communal relations. Peters reminds us of the importance of recognizing the communal work that is being done in the face of ongoing violence and the repeated eviction of Indigenous and Black people from humanity:

The initiation of the inquiry into missing and murdered Indigenous women first and foremost deepened my strength and love for the Indigenous women who are at the forefront of a movement to reclaim the dignity and honor of their daughters, sisters, and elders. Often my work involves having difficult conversations about real violence and pain. It would be jaded of me not to state how encouraging it has been to see the real progress being made toward justice for Indigenous women and their communities.

—Alena Peters

Morgan envisions a just future with an attentiveness to interlocking forms of oppression:

I envision justice as the realization and maintenance of sustainable and equitable balance between people, animals, and Earth. By this I mean nurturing and facilitating anti-exploitative and anti-oppressive access to what each of these categories of beings need to remain in healthy, equitable co-dependent, cooperative, and harmonious co-relation. My conceptualization of justice includes African Canadians' collective and individual freedom from systemic oppression without frustrating any other peoples' ability to experience the same. Further, it involves supporting the freedom of other peoples from oppression, especially Turtle Island's Indigenous peoples.

—Anthony Morgan

What remains troublingly consistent across both scenes of structured dispossession that we have described is the conviction that since Indigenous and Black people are already on the brink of death, it is not worth the inconvenience of dispensing lifesaving services and care. As a close analysis of the circumstances surrounding Robyn Harper's death reveals, processes of dehumanization are enacted in law. Necropolicies upheld by the Indian Act, including the ongoing practice of denying Indigenous communities water, food, shelter, and schools (lifesaving services guaranteed within treaty agreements), confirm that Indigenous peoples, including Harper, are not human enough for essential services and care afforded to white settlers. So-called cultural accommodations do not address racism embedded within the legal system. Rather, these tactics mask racial violence. In Flint, necro-political racial violence as seen through the poisoning of mostly Black and poor residents through lead-contaminated water is both sanctioned and obscured by law. Claims such as "it's the Flint River" or the old pipes or the old houses make it possible for the state to ignore underlying anti-Black and settler colonial violence in the manufacturing of the crisis. It is through these statements and others like them that Flint residents are positioned as not-quite-human things that are impossible to further poison and thus unworthy of the lifesaving intervention needed. In both cases, these so-called crises are not aberrational but the products of structured dispossessions that situate Black and Indigenous peoples outside the realm of humanity and, thus, beyond the reaches of justice. Confirming that the anti-Black and settler-colonial violence taking place within these scenes work in and through each other, Simpson reminds us that these "'events' and 'crises' are of apiece with each other."[78]

To return to the question of who is the human, first posed on Human Rights Day, what we really wanted to know was to whom is humanity afforded in contexts where it is a requisite for accessing rights and justice? Indeed, the conversations that emerged from the Human Rights Day event have made it clear that describing state violence inflicted upon Indigenous and Black peoples as human rights violations is something of an oxymoron. To redress pervasive systemic injustice, some activist movements have attempted to demonstrate Indigenous and Black peoples' humanity, as if processes of dehumanization are a mistake resulting from lack of knowledge. Drawing from da Silva and Lowe, this article has interrogated these approaches and, instead, reveals the human to be a racial project emerging from modern liberalism. It needs to be said again that racialized peoples will not secure justice by gaining entrance into humanity because the human as a frame is always already violent. In order to understand more about the limits of the human as the pathway to justice, we want our work also to help expand what is understood as "custody" when we go about documenting deaths in custody. Pushing the definition of "in custody" to include more than only deaths at penal sites, such as in jail cells and police cruisers, means taking into account the multifarious ways in which the state facilitates death. In taking a broad view of state custody, it becomes possible to examine the state's role in producing structured scenes of dispossession, which has resulted in the deaths of the Indigenous youth who were compelled to leave home to attend high school and the deaths in Flint, Michigan. Looking to the future, we call for further critical interrogation that recognizes the impossibility of justice for Indigenous, Black, and other racialized peoples in white settler societies and, moreover, is committed to disentangling justice from the grasp of the modern human.

STEPHANIE LATTY, a Black woman of Caribbean descent, is a scholar, writer, and educator. Her doctoral research focuses on visuality and the gendered particularities of anti-Black racism. Her other research interests include Afrofuturism, critical race theory, Black feminism, Indigenous feminism, and settler colonialism. She is also a published poet and an activist.

MEGAN SCRIBE is a 2Spirit Ininiw iskwew from Norway House Cree Nation, Manitoba. She is a family- and community-oriented scholar who is actively involved in both Toronto and Norway House. She returns home twice a year for extended visits with her family, community, ceremony, language, and the land. In 2012 she became a youth leader for Native Youth Sexual Health Network (NYSHN). Since 2013 she has been a community council member for Aboriginal Legal Services of Toronto's (ALST) Diversion Program. From

2012 to 2015, she was a member of Tities Wîcinímintôwak Arts Collective. In 2015 she became the student co-chair for the Indigenous Education Network at the University of Toronto.

ALENA PETERS is an outspoken activist, educator, and arts facilitator born and raised "in the 6" (Toronto). A founding member of Black Lives Matter Toronto, she was instrumental in shaping the groups' early organizing. In addition to grassroots organizing, she has facilitated workshops and trainings on rape culture and colonialism, antiracism, and femmephobia. An advocate for community-based learning spaces, she left Carleton University in her third year studying international history. Since then, she has been working to create more educational spaces that encourage self-discovery and curiosity over authority and repetition.

ANTHONY MORGAN is a lawyer and frequent social and public affairs commentator on issues concerning race and racism, critical multiculturalism, and critical race theory in Canada. His comments on these issues have been featured in major news outlets such as the *Globe and Mail, National Post, Toronto Star,* and *Huffington Post Canada.* His practice focuses on human rights and state accountability litigation, with an emphasis on local, national, and international manifestations of anti-Black and anti-Indigenous racism, as well as race-based discrimination in general.

NOTES

We thank Sherene Razack for her generous and insightful contributions to the article.

1. Panelists who participated in the "Who Is the Human?" event included Sherene Razack, who provided a reading from her new book; Christa Big Canoe, Anishinaabekwe, mother, lawyer, Legal Advocacy Director of Aboriginal Legal Services of Toronto (ALST); Anthony Morgan, a human rights lawyer specializing in anti-Black racism in Canadian law and policy; and Alena Peters, an activist and community-based educator.

2. Throughout this article we predominantly use the term "Indigenous" to refer to the original peoples of the territories now known as Canada and the United States. At times, especially when making reference to legal documents, we use the terms "Aboriginal," "Indian," and "First Nations" to maintain consistency with official terminology.

3. Denise Ferreira da Silva, *Toward a Global Idea of Race* (Minneapolis: University of Minnesota Press, 2007), xxiv.

4. Eve Tuck, Mistinguette Smith, Allison M. Guess, Tavia Benjamin, and Brian K. Jones, "Geotheorizing Black/Land: Contestations and Contingent Collaborations,"

Departures in Critical Qualitative Research 3, no. 1 (2014): 57, doi:10.1525/dcqr.2014 .3.1.52.

5. Eve Tuck, Allison Guess, and Hannah Sultan, "Not Nowhere: Collaborating on Selfsame Land," *Decolonization: Indigeneity, Education & Society,* June 24, 2014, 1, https://decolonization.wordpress.com/2014/06/26/not-nowhere-collaborating-on -selfsame-land/.

6. Mary Louise Fellows and Sherene Razack, "The Race to Innocence: Confronting Hierarchical Relations among Women," *Gender, Race & Justice* 335 (1998): 336, http://scholarship.law.umn.edu/faculty_articles/274.

7. Tiffany Lethabo King, "Interview with Dr. Tiffany Lethabo King," *Feral Feminisms* 4 (2015): 67, http://feralfeminisms.com/wp-content/uploads/2015/12/ff_Inter view-with-Dr.-Tiffany-Lethabo-King_issue4.pdf.

8. da Silva, *Toward a Global Idea of Race,* 3.

9. Eve Tuck and C. Ree, "A Glossary of Haunting," in *Handbook of Autoethnography,* ed. Stacey Holman Jones, Tony E. Adams, and Carolyn Ellis (Walnut Creek, Calif.: Left Coast Press, 2013), 647.

10. da Silva, *Toward a Global Idea of Race,* 11.

11. Ibid., 527.

12. Saidiya Hartman, *Scenes of Subjection: Terror, Slavery, and Self-Making in Nineteenth-Century America* (: Oxford: Oxford University Press, 1997), 3.

13. Audra Simpson, *Mohawk Interruptus: Political Life across the Borders of Settler States* (Durham, N.C.: Duke University Press, 2014), 12.

14. Denise Ferreira da Silva, "Radical Praxis or Knowing (at) the Limits of Justice," in *At the Limits of Justice: Women of Colour on Terror,* ed. Suvendrini Perera and Sherene H. Razack (Toronto: University of Toronto Press, 2015), 104.

15. Office of the Chief Coroner for Ontario, "Chief Coroner Calls Joint Inquest into the Deaths of Seven Aboriginal Youth in Thunder Bay," *Ontario Newsroom,* May 31, 2012, https://news.ontario.ca/mcscs/en/2012/05/chief-coroner-calls-joint -inquest-into-the-deaths-of-seven-aboriginal-youth-in-thunder-bay.html.

16. Jody Porter, "First Nations Student Deaths Inquiry Faces Further Delay," *CBC News,* July 15, 2014, http://www.cbc.ca/news/canada/thunder-bay/first-nations -student-deaths-inquiry-faces-further-delay-1.2706771.

17. CBC News, "First Nations Student Deaths Inquest: 7 Youths Died in 10 Years," *CBC News,* October 3, 2015, http://www.cbc.ca/news/canada/thunder-bay/ first-nations-inquest-student-deaths-1.3255052.

18. *R. v. Kokopenace,* 2015 SCC 28, [2015] 2 SCR 398, https://scc-csc.lexum.com/ scc-csc/scc-csc/en/item/15373/index.do. The question of Aboriginal representation on jury rolls has notably been taken up in Alvin C. Hamilton and Murray C. Sinclair, commissioners, *Report of the Aboriginal Justice Inquiry of Manitoba,* 2 vols. (Winnipeg: Public Inquiry into the Administration of Justice and Aboriginal People, 1991); and in the Honourable Frank Iacobucci, *First Nations Representation on Ontario Juries: Report of the Independent Review* (Toronto: Ontario Ministry of the Attorney General, 2013).

19. Porter, "First Nations Student Deaths."

20. Ibid.

21. Donovan Vincent, "Inquest into Deaths of Young Natives Halted over Imbalance on Jury Rolls," *Toronto Star*, July 14, 2014.

22. Jen Mt. Pleasant, "Inquest into Deaths of 7 Native Youth Delayed Again," *Two Row Times*, July 23, 2014.

23. Porter, "First Nations Student Deaths."

24. Patricia Monture, "Standing against Canadian Law," in *Locating Law: Race, Class, Gender, Sexuality Connections*, ed. Elizabeth Comack (Halifax: Fernwood, 2006), 77.

25. da Silva, *Toward a Global Idea of Race*, 50.

26. Ibid., 7.

27. Colin Perkel, "Long-Awaited Inquest into Deaths of Aboriginal Youth Begins in Thunder Bay, Ont.," *Huffington Post*, October 5, 2015, http://www.huffingtonpost .ca/2015/10/05/lengthy-inquest-into-deaths-of-young-aboriginals-starts-in-thunder -bay-ont_n_8245766.html.

28. Eve Tuck and K. Wayne Yang, "Decolonization Is Not a Metaphor," *Decolonization: Indigeneity, Education & Society* 1, no. 1 (2012): 10.

29. Monture, "Standing against Canadian Law," 77.

30. Ibid.

31. Renisa Mawani, "From Colonialism to Multiculturalism? Totem Poles, Tourism and National Identity in Vancouver's Stanley Park," *ARIEL: A Review of International English Literature* 35, nos. 1–2 (2004): 34.

32. Glen Sean Coulthard, *Red Skin, White Masks: Rejecting the Colonial Politics of Recognition* (Minneapolis: University of Minnesota Press, 2014), 66.

33. Ibid., 65.

34. Ibid., 66.

35. Hamilton and Sinclair, *Report of the Aboriginal Justice Inquiry of Manitoba*, vol. 2, *The Deaths of Helen Betty Osborne and John Joseph Harper*, 92.

36. Ibid., 91.

37. Pamela Palmater, *Indigenous Nationhood: Empowering Grassroots Citizens* (Halifax: Fernwood, 2015), 64.

38. Hamilton and Sinclair, *Report of the Aboriginal Justice Inquiry*, 2:92.

39. Palmater, *Indigenous Nationhood*, 171.

40. Matt Vis, "Hospital Never Considered on Night of Robyn Harper's Death, Inquest Hears," *tbnewswatch.com*, October 29, 2015, http://www.tbnewswatch.com/ News/376768/Hospital_never_considered_on_night_of_Robyn_Harper's_death,_ inquest_hears.

41. Hamilton and Sinclair, *Report of the Aboriginal Justice Inquiry*, 2:32.

42. Sherene Razack, *Dying from Improvement: Inquests and Inquiries into Indigenous Deaths in Custody* (Toronto: University of Toronto Press, 2015), 60.

43. Ibid., 65.

44. Mona Hannah-Attisha, Jenny LaChance, Richard Casey Sadler, and Allison Champney Schnepp, "Elevated Blood Lead Levels in Children Associated with the Flint Drinking Water Crisis: A Spatial Analysis of Risk and Public Health Response," *American Journal of Public Health* 106, no. 2 (2016): 283–90, doi:10.2015/AJPH.2015 .303003.

45. Dylan T. Miner, *Tikibiing Booskikamigaag: An Indigenous History and Ecology of Flint, Michigan* (Grand Rapids, Mich.: Issue Press, 2013), 5.

46. United States Census Bureau, "Flint City, Michigan," http://www.census.gov/quickfacts/table/PST045215/2629000.

47. State of Michigan Executive Office, released e-mail correspondence, Lansing, Mich., 2016.

48. Achille Mbembe, "Necropolitics," trans. Libby Meintjes, *Public Culture* 15, no. 1 (2003): 11.

49. Ibid., 25.

50. Ibid., 27.

51. Ibid., 40.

52. Ibid., 25.

53. Razack, *Dying from Improvement,* 53.

54. Hannah-Attisha et al., "Elevated Blood Lead Levels," 287.

55. David Theo Goldberg and S. Hristova, "Blue Velvet: Re-dressing New Orleans in Katrina's Wake," *Vectors* 3, no. 1 (2007).

56. Ibid.

57. Nicholas Blomley, "Law, Property and the Geography of Violence: The Frontier, the Survey and the Grid," *Annals of the Association of American Geographers* 93, no. 1 (2003): 121–41.

58. Lisa Marie Cacho, *Social Death: Racialized Rightlessness and the Criminalization of the Unprotected* (New York: New York University Press, 2012), 6.

59. Ibid.

60. Christina Sharpe, *Monstrous Intimacies: Making Post-Slavery Subjects* (Durham, N.C.: Duke University Press, 2014), 3.

61. da Silva, *Toward a Global Idea of Race,* 199.

62. Ibid., xv.

63. Hannah-Attisha, quoted in Sara Ganim and Linh Tran, "How Tap Water Became Toxic in Flint, Michigan," *CNN,* January 13, 2016, http://www.cnn.com/2016/01/11/health/toxic-tap-water-flint-michigan.

64. Bench Ansfield, "Still Submerged: The Uninhabitability of Urban Redevelopment," in *Sylvia Wynter: On Being Human as Praxis,* ed. Katherine McKittrick (Durham, N.C.: Duke University Press, 2015), 126.

65. Boutros Boutros-Ghali, "Foreword," in *Voice of Indigenous Peoples: Native People Address the United Nations,* ed. Alexander Ewen (Santa Fe, N.Mex.: Clear Light, 1994), 9.

66. da Silva, *Toward a Global Idea of Race,* 10.

67. Lisa Lowe, *The Intimacies of Four Continents* (Durham, N.C.: Duke University Press, 2015), 6.

68. Ibid.

69. Ibid.

70. Ibid., 7.

71. Denise Ferreira da Silva, "Towards a Critique of the Socio-logos of Justice: The Analytics of Raciality and the Production of Universality," *Social Identities* 7, no. 3 (2001): 429.

72. Ibid., 430.

73. Alexander Weheliye, *Habeas Viscus: Racializing Assemblages, Biopolitics, and Black Feminist Theories of the Human* (Durham, N.C.: Duke University Press, 2014), 8.

74. Meyda Yeğenoğlu, *Colonial Fantasies: Towards a Feminist Reading of Orientalism* (Cambridge: Cambridge University Press, 1998), 8.

75. Ibid., 7.

76. Ibid., 8.

77. Ibid.

78. Simpson, *Mohawk Interruptus,* 34.

On Rocks and Hard Places

A Reflection on Antiblackness in
Organizing against Islamophobia

DÉLICE MUGABO

> I begin at a place where language ends and where new utterances must
> begin. I come to this project trying to find the language for my own
> presence in the New World. My name as slave, or Black female flesh, in
> the Western Hemisphere is well known by now. However, when I look for
> my name at the times when I am made to appear on the blood soaked
> "clearing," I am at a loss for words. At the clearing, the space of genocide
> and settlement is where I experience a form of aphasia. I do not have a
> location or a vantage point from which to orient and understand myself.
>
> —Tiffany Lethabo King, "In the Clearing"

This article focuses on the debate that occurred in 2013 and 2014 in
Quebec on the proposed "Quebec Charter of Values," which called for
the ban of religious symbols in the public sphere. The debate provides us
with insight into how this so-called distinct nation organizes its policies
and public discussions to construct itself in ways that continue to disappear
Black people. Quebec has its own particular ways of erasing its history of
slavery, while casting white French-speaking Quebecois in innocent historical roles. I will illustrate how both the detractors and defenders of the charter obscured or cast out the antiblackness that constituted their disparate
political projects. I come to this topic as a Muslim Black feminist raised
in Quebec, whose political trajectory started in various left-wing Quebec
nationalist institutions, leading to what Michel-Rolph Trouillot has called "a
legacy of intimacy and estrangement."[1] A primary objective of this research
has been to follow Denise Ferreira da Silva's invitation to "write blackness
back into the political."[2]

To do this, I begin with a personal anecdote as a case in point of how
Muslim Black people were ejected from the public debate on the Charter of

Values. I then explain how Afro-pessimism as a theory allows us to understand how Black subjects are evicted from reflections and discussions about social life, leading me to a critical reassessment of conventional scholarly understandings of Islamophobia that do not acknowledge the specific position of the Muslim Black subject. I then historicize the presence of Muslim Black subjects in North America in the context of enslavement and colonization, and show how my ontological understanding of antiblackness is rooted in that history. Tying together the scholarly work on Afro-pessimism and that on Islamophobia, I bring into focus the figure of the Muslim subject and how it is imagined in such a way that the possibility of a Muslim Black subject disappeared during the charter debate. I use the charter to look at how blackness was outside the relation between the religious and subjectivity. To reflect on this special issue's theme, I then offer my critique of the mobilization that occurred against the charter and how it played into the Quebec nation-building project. I end with a reflection on coalition politics and offer some questions that arose for me after observing how antiblackness was manifest in the anti-Islamophobia organizing that took place during the debate on the charter.

"THIS HAS NOTHING TO DO WITH BLACK PEOPLE": ANTI-ISLAMOPHOBIA AS ANTIBLACKNESS

The "Quebec Charter of Values" was the common name given to proposed legislation that was first announced in May 2013 by the newly elected Parti Québécois (PQ) government and eventually submitted to the National Assembly as Bill 60 in September of the same year. The PQ presented the charter as a solution to the debate that had started in 2006 around the "reasonable accommodation" of religious and cultural minorities in general, and religious symbols in the public sphere in particular. Arguing that these "minority" issues had yet to be resolved—*and* badly needed to be resolved— the PQ proposed a series of measures that it argued would create the frameworks needed to ensure the French-Quebecois majority was at ease with religious and cultural diversity. These frameworks included (a) amending the Charter of Rights and Liberties, (b) restricting state employees from wearing "conspicuous" religious symbols, and (c) making it mandatory for one to uncover their face in order to receive public services.

While much has been written about how racial politics played out during the debate on the charter and the racist discourses that its defenders employed,[3] this article argues that opponents of the bill developed their own anti-Black strategies. As an example of how antiblackness was manifest in the organizing against the charter, I offer an experience I had with a group that I was involved in at the time of the debate, Indépendantistes pour une laïcité inclusive (Sovereigntists for an inclusive secularism).[4] The group merits attention especially because of its composition of high-profile public figures and the discourses that it contributed to produce or propagate throughout Quebec, which ensured that its ideas played a key role in defining how people in Quebec understood the parameters of the public debate. The wider implications of their work points to how white radical and liberal activism often also serves to rehabilitate and preserve whiteness and white racial rule and order. My argument is that both the charter and its critics articulated a vision of a future society that retained key elements of the antiblackness of the present. The incapacity to imagine a future that is more than a perpetual repeat of the present—even among activists who define themselves as antiracist—should awaken us to some of the limits of coalition politics.

The Indépendantistes organization informally started to take shape in the summer of 2012 and was officially formed in early February 2013 in anticipation of the PQ's unveiling of the charter.[5] The group, composed of sovereigntists of various political affiliations, was meant to present an alternative vision of Quebec and Quebec nationhood to that proposed by the PQ through the charter. One of its immediate concerns when it was first conceptualized was to lobby the Bloc Québécois—a federal political party whose goal is to represent Quebec's sovereign interests—to adopt a position against Bill 60. Later it developed a wider goal of taking a position against the charter in order to avoid losing further political support for the sovereigntist project from racialized people. In their main public statement, the group argued that the charter was "a serious strategic mistake":

> A sovereigntist government must avoid adopting policies that systematically ensure that minorities who feel excluded and oppressed find refuge in the protections offered by the federal parliament, and thus, justify a belief that Canada is the last resort against abuse.[6]

The group included political activists from all three of the main sovereigntist parties in Quebec. I was invited to the group due to my active participation and membership in both the Quebec feminist movement and the province's social democratic political party, Québec Solidaire. Shortly after the events I describe below, I permanently left Quebec nationalist and white-led feminist organizing, due to the deep antiblackness at their core.

From the beginning, at each meeting of the group notable thinkers and activists would join in. At one meeting, a prominent white francophone academic known for his research on the Muslim North African community in Quebec joined the group. I will call him Professor C. As we always did when new members arrived, the group's existing members took turns introducing ourselves to the new arrivals. My turn was last but my introduction did not go as planned. Professor. C boldly interrupted me after I had said my name: "I don't understand why you're here. You're Black. The charter has nothing to do with Black people so why are you here?" I was speechless.

After my initial shock, I told him that I am Muslim. He sighed in exasperation and replied, "Okay okay, yes there are a few African people who are also Muslims but this is about Quebecers and Arab people; it has nothing to do with Black people." Still in disbelief, all I could say was that whether Black people are Muslim or not, living in Quebec meant that Black people can participate in any discussion or debate about life in this province. Nobody at the meeting interjected against Professor C's comments.

Noticing that I had mentally checked out of the conversation after my exchange with Professor C, a white woman cut the introductory part of the meeting short and explained to everyone around the table that I was part of the group due to my work in the feminist movement. It seemed at the time this was her way of reassuring Professor C that I was not there simply as a Black woman but as someone who had paid her dues in the white Quebec feminist movement. In any case, I did not read her comments as an expression of solidarity. To me her comments revealed how femininity and feminist activism continue to be imagined as the purview of white women, in a way that could not have been transferred to my Black female body in that moment, in that meeting, and certainly not in Professor C's eyes. So defending my presence in terms of my association to the Quebec white feminist movement could only fall flat. My race, gender, and religious identity converged in a very specific way in that moment. In many ways, because so much of the discourse on Islamophobia centers around the bodies of non-Black Muslim women, I could not be Muslim because I am Black, but also because I am a Black *woman*. The Arab, Asian, and Persian femininity that Islamophobes and their counterparts swear to defend and promote is the same femininity that black women have not possessed ever since slavery.

That meeting was the last one that I attended. It was also the last time I was involved in organizing against the charter since I learned that Muslim Black women were evidently not interpolated to participate in the debate as their other "sisters" in Islam were. After the humiliation and the rage, I decided to revisit that interaction with Professor C and reflect on the place(lessness) of the Muslim Black subject in Quebec.

ANTI-BLACK ISLAMOPHOBIA: TOWARD A THEORETICAL FRAMING

Afro-Pessimism: Theorizing the Position of the Unthought

Afro-pessimism offers fruitful grounds of analysis to examine how Muslim Black people were ejected from the debate and organizing around the charter. Afro-pessimism is a theoretical disposition developed in opposition to Marxist, liberal, and/or New Left perspectives on Black life. In a personal communication with the author on February 10, 2015, Black cultural critic Art McGee described Afro-pessimism as follows: "basically [Afro-pessimism is] the idea that western society is inherently antagonistic to Africanity and Black people, that it is anti-Black at its core, that it cannot be reformed in such a way that would give Black people or African descendant people full human rights, or that Black people [c]ould come to be recognized as being a part of the human family, without any qualifications or contextual requirements." The central claim here, that Black people are permanently expelled from the category of the human, is explored in the Afro-pessimist literature. In general, the claim rests on the observation that modern conceptions of the human were forged alongside and through relations of racial slavery that cast Black people as uniquely enslaveable. The characteristics ascribed to humanness were, not coincidently, those denied to Black people. These characteristics simultaneously protected non-Black people from enslavement and authorized Black enslavement around the world. Structured by an anti-Black ontology, racial slavery produced effects that have outlasted the institution of slavery itself. Conceptions of the human, Afro-pessimists argue, retain their original anti-Black foundations.[7] To be human is thus to be anything but Black.

As an approach that posits blackness as ontology and not identity, Afro-pessimism continuously reveals all the ways in which the specific position that Black people occupy in society cannot be analogized. In other words, blackness must be addressed in its specificity and singularity. I also find Afro-pessimism useful because it allows us to understand how antiblackness organizes social and political life in contexts where we may least expect it. In other words, antiblackness was present but obscured in the proposed charter and also manifested itself in the strategies developed by groups opposing the charter. Using an Afro-pessimist approach allows me to examine how antiblackness and Islamophobia serve to evict certain populations from the category of the human.

Antiblackness has become the subject of an extensive literature that seeks to disentangle anti-Black subjection from the ostensibly broader category of racialized.[8] In this article, antiblackness is conceived as a structure that is foundational to the modern world, a structure that was constituted through racial slavery and that endures into the present, in a period Saidiya Hartman calls "the afterlife of slavery."[9] Thinking through the constitution and consequences of this structure is the purpose of the emerging literature on Afro-pessimism. As Hartman, Frank Wilderson III, and Tiffany Lethabo King have stated, colonialism started with the Middle Passage and Black people continue this experience regardless of their origins.[10] As Quebec rewrites its founding myths to add secularism as one of its pillars, it is all the more important that we foreground the place and the role of slavery in the genealogy of these specific settler-colonial politics.

Afro-pessimist thinkers have been critiqued for overly prioritizing the American context in their analysis. Notable scholarship has since developed on antiblackness in Brazil and the Netherlands.[11] This article seeks to expand on the Afro-pessimist literature on antiblackness by offering a case study in which state policies organize ethnic and religious affiliations as a move to contest or negate blackness.

Islamophobia: On Being a Problem People

Sherman Jackson defines Islamophobia as the production of Muslims as "problem peoples."[12] He then explains that it can be manifested through misrepresentation, harassment, intimidation, physical violence, and continued suspicion from private citizens, government officials, and the many tentacles of the state apparatus. Some scholars identify the attacks of September 11, 2001, as a conjunctural moment that heightened and legitimized Islamophobic discourses and policies in the United States and in Western society more generally.[13] Others date the defining moment to the original Gulf War in 1990.[14] Either way, most scholars of and activists against Islamophobia ground their analysis in Edward Said's seminal work *Orientalism*.[15]

Some scholarship on Islamophobia has attended to Muslim Black populations specifically. Junaid Rana, for example, endeavors to explain how Islam in particular and religion in general came to be "racialized." An important part of the history she recounts is that the initial encounter with Islam in what is now the United States was through enslaved Africans who arrived in the Americas already practicing the Muslim faith, some with a knowledge of the Qur'an and even a mastery of Arabic. "Early on the concept of the

African Negro was placed into a logic that paired it with Moors, Indians, and Jews," Rana writes. "[Thus] in the context of the American colonies and then the formation of the United States, religion was not far from the construction of the logic of nation and race."[16] Rana's argument is useful in that she explains how religion did not supersede race through offering Muslim Black people an entry into citizenship. On the contrary, it became "part of that continuum that understood Black Muslims as Black" and, I would add, enslavable.[17] Despite Rana's efforts to specify the experiences of Black Muslims, she eventually falls into the trap of universalizing the racializing tendencies of Islamophobia later in her work. As per an Afro-pessimist understanding, without offering an analysis of the specificities of the Muslim Black experience, we risk enacting anti-Black modes of thinking.

In other similar work, the Muslim subject is not specified as Arab or South Asian but is nevertheless treated in a universalistic manner that forecloses any potential attention to the subject's racialization as Black. In Canada, for instance, Sherene Razack's work has analyzed how public discourses frame Muslim subjects as a risk to Western civilization and how this myth then serves to cast them out physically and even legally from the polity.[18] Razack focuses on an abstracted Muslim subject that one could assume applies to all Muslim subjects. Yet her analysis examines how Muslim subjects are "cast out" of the nation or placed in a "state of exception" to the usual state-based procedural and legal protections afforded to its citizens. These arguments do not account for the ways that Black people, Muslim or not, are always already cast outside the categories of the human and the citizen. The place of Muslim Blacks cannot be fully addressed in work that universalizes the Muslim subject.

In a promising contribution, Rinaldo Walcott provides us with the conceptual language to avoid such pitfalls through using the figure of the queer Muslim Black to question how the "Muslim" figure has been represented since 9/11. For him, "the limits of our imaginations have significant implications for our politics of liberation."[19] He offers an oppositional history of the Muslim presence in North America, one that challenges Rana's version:

> Kantian, modernist "Reason" could not make sense of an enslaved Muslim presence, especially its representativity in Arabic, and in the practice of Islam, which had to be vigilantly denied and invalidated for Christian doctrine to endorse slavery. Thus all enslaved Africans had to be reduced to the non-religious or the African practices of monotheism (in this case Islam) had to be ignored and denied since those practices troubled certain European reasons for African enslavement.[20]

What is especially useful in Walcott's argument is that it allows us to understand how Muslim Black people have never occupied the same category of humanity as their Arab co-religionists. Since religion is one key marker of the human, Arab Muslim subjects, however much they have been reviled in Western culture in the Saidian sense, remain intelligible as human. Black subjects, however, could not be read as properly Muslim, because doing so would make them human and thus un-slavable. Walcott insists that we read the Muslim presence in North America based on this centuries-old history, since it is "an intervention that blackens and thus complicates a number of histories, trajectories and politics."[21]

While it may seem that non-Black Muslims are also cast out of the human—there are certainly contexts where violence is inflicted on non-Black Muslim bodies as Muslim—that anti-Islamophobia political strategies that non-Black Muslims operationalize often rely on antiblackness reminds us of the differentiated position of Muslim Black subjects. As an example, in a February 2015 interview, Samah Jabbari, the spokeswoman of the Canadian Muslim Forum, vociferously argued against the charter. Near the end of her interview, her argument reached an apex when she said, "We [non-Black Muslim people] won't accept to be the slaves, nor the negroes of Quebec."[22]

Jabbari's statement ("we will not be the negroes of Quebec") betrays a profound conviction that Muslims are not Black and, therefore, will resist any attempt to be treated as Black people. The statement also reveals blackness to be the nothingness that stands in opposition to a beingness; it presents blackness as a cautionary tale. Such a fear in becoming Black can only be reality for those who *are not* Black. That fear also has a geography. The refusal to become the "negroes of Quebec" makes implicit that there are places where nonblackness is clear.[23] Arab, Persian, and South Asian Muslims declaring their humanity amid discourses that ever-increasingly conflate them with terrorism is part of a plight for recognition. Black people's experiences of Islamophobia are thus distinct. Attempting to capture this specificity, I use the concept "anti-Black Islamophobia" through the remainder of the article.

EVICTING BLACK SUBJECTS FROM THE RELIGIOUS

Situating Anti-Black Islamophobia in the "Afterlife of Slavery"

Although the case study that I analyze here took place in Quebec, it is rooted in the continued history of global antiblackness. How antiblackness structures not only Islamophobia but also activism against it is something to which we must continue to pay attention. My aim is to contribute to the broader reflection on anti-Black Islamophobia to which important thinkers such as Ndella Paye and Joao Gabriell in France, Egbert Martina in the Netherlands, Donna Auston and Muna Mire in the United States, and Hawa Mire in Canada have contributed.

Having described the impossibility of a Muslim Black subject in the minds of both the charter's supporters and some of its detractors, it is important that we take a step back here to think about the longer history of such an impossibility. I want to situate the impossibility of the Muslim Black subject in North America within a historical framework that takes the trans-Atlantic slave trade as a defining moment in the dehumanization of Black people and, notably, of Black people of Muslim faith. This historical perspective grounds my ontological conception of blackness and of Muslim Black (non) subjecthood. In so doing, I am suggesting that the erasure of Muslim Black subjects within Quebec's public discourse is no accident. Such work brings us to rethink not only the debate around the Charter of Values in Quebec but also what we may broadly refer to as secularism in relation to Black subjects.

To be clear, written, oral, and artistic records have shown that Black people were the first Muslims on this continent. Black scholars have long documented the resistance of Muslim enslaved Black people in Brazil and the United States,[24] yet we must further investigate the stories of enslaved Black people in Canada who were of the Muslim faith. For example, in my own preliminary research on Black slaves in Quebec, I have found a boy, Jacques Le Ber, who lived in Montreal and originated from Guinea, a largely Muslim territory at the time. His owner was Pierre Le Ber, a merchant. Jacques was baptized at thirty-six years old in 1694 and given the name of the owner's father.[25] According to some records, Olivier Le Jeune, who is said to have been the first Black slave in New France, also originated from Guinea. Antoine, Archange, Jacques, Jean Boyd, Louis, and Pierre-Joseph-César were all enslaved Black men and women in Quebec who originated from Muslim-majority societies.[26] Speaking at McGill University earlier this year, Frank Mackey, a white historian of slavery and Black life in Quebec, made the claim that a good example of white Quebecers' historical benevolence toward slaves is that they converted them to Christianity, baptized them, and gave them Christian names as a way to incorporate them into society. Mackey's words were typical of the type of anti-Black violence that is common in society, in that white society generally judges the unfreedom of Black people in relative terms—it could have been worse; we treated slaves well—in order to recenter the experiences of white people and to recast Black suffering outside the national narrative. Again, the impossibility of Black life, since it necessarily exposes antiblackness, is manifest, even in the very moment when slavery is acknowledged at all.

Jacques's probable situation may allow us to retrace the history of Islamophobia in Quebec and to recognize the falsity of the argument about Black inclusion in Quebec society: such inclusion has never brought freedom or promise to Black people but has in fact been central to our subjugation. Converting enslaved Black people in Quebec to Christianity only reinforced their unfreedom and served to mark their owner's "humanity." Jacques's case, along with Mackey's statement, reveals the extent to which Quebec uses Black bodies to cleanse itself and its history (to make Quebec look good and allow the French-Quebecois to feel better about themselves). The forced conversion of Muslim Black slaves in Quebec parallels political projects such as the charter that seek to regulate and "include" Muslim Black subjects into white society. This is the larger history of secularism in the province that Quebec must contend with. Again, these are forms of antiblackness masking themselves as a commitment to Black freedom.

The stories of Black people from Guinea who were enslaved in Quebec show us how being Muslim did not make them unslaveable, nor did their conversion to Christianity. No religious practice or affiliation propelled them into the category of the human; they always bore the marker of the slave. Secularism solidifies religion as a category that allows non-Black people of color to be categorized as human. Walcott explains that during slavery, enslaved African peoples who were Muslims were not recognized as such but instead were understood as practitioners of various African superstitious and antireligious beliefs and that the fact that the Western definition of the human has become secular does not translate into a recognition of various modes of Black religiosity or spirituality.

To further this point, Sylvia Wynter's work describes how race is invented in many ways not just to justify the enslavement of Black people but also to protect religious subjects from enslavement, which automatically placed Black people outside of the religious. In actuality, perhaps it is not so much that they are outside of the religious but rather that they are not taken seriously as religious subjects. Wynter does this by locating the shift from understanding the world as divided into believers and nonbelievers, as in the Middle Ages, to white versus nonwhite/Black, after 1492. The important thing about this shift is that though nonwhite, non-Black, nonbelievers were seen as nonhuman, they were not constructed as nonhuman enough to be dragged into trans-Atlantic slavery. Antiblackness had to be invented for that.

Wynter notably makes this argument in relation to Arabs (Moors).[27] In other words, secularism, for Wynter, has a very particular relationship to antiblackness. In her understanding, secularism is constitutive of antiblackness.

As secular as Quebec and Western societies proclaim to be, therefore, access to the category of the religious is a determination of political subjectivity. The charter illustrates how religion continues to be a descriptor of the human, and how political society convenes discussions among people admitted to this category. If we keep in mind that religiosity is a category reserved for the human, Black religious practices in Quebec remain unintelligible because of their impossibility.

This is why I suggest that secularism (or what is called *laïcité* in Quebec and in France) did not open up ways for Black people to be recognized as human. Much of the erasure of the Black subject during the debate on the charter actually served to negate religious or spiritual Black people's access to a category reserved to humans. The charter centers religious identity and practice as the main point of entry into a conversation on race and racism. That framing dismisses Black peoples from the conversation because we do not have a specifically recognized religious practice or identity. Religion continues to offer a door through which some people can enter humanity. This debate on religion reveals how religious identity is an identity only accessible to those already considered human.

The Quebec Charter of Values: Looking for My People

From the beginning, the Quebec Charter of Values received widespread support from the white French-speaking population,[28] which represents roughly 70 percent of Quebec. In other words, it did not break down along the familiar federalist and sovereigntist divide but appealed to French-speaking white people of both major political persuasions, a rare feat in post-1970s Quebec politics.[29] From artists to former premiers, a wide array of social actors seemed to have ideas on how to tweak the proposed charter in such a way as to ensure it would best defend and promote Quebec's "distinct nationhood."[30] Despite its broad support among white French-speaking Quebecois, the Charter of Values nevertheless sparked a wide-ranging debate and lively forms of contestation. The bill's major point of contention was the interdiction against public-sector employees wearing "ostentatious" religious symbols (viz. the hijab for Muslim women) at work. It was mainly this element of the charter upon which opposition groups formed.

While it was certainly premised on the idea that Quebec needed to be defended (in certain ways), the text of the bill is remarkable in that it does not explicitly call out any group in particular. No religious, ethnic, or racial group is referenced in the text of the charter. Instead, like much modern legislation, the text is written in a seemingly neutral, abstracted language. As such, the precise "threat" to Quebec remained opaque. "Quebec values" were repeatedly presented as being in danger, much as the French language has been over generations. Following its liberal pedigree, it is important to note that the charter implies we are all Quebecois, and that it aims to make Quebec better for everybody. At a partisan event called "a secular brunch," the then minister Bernard Drainville told the crowd: "We decided 40 years ago to make French our common language. With the Charter of Values, we are in continuity with Bill 101 [that made French the only public language in Quebec]. As a matter of fact, this Charter . . . *is* the Bill 101 of values."[31]

Behind the seemingly "color-blind" charter, however, was a specific racial project. The racial content of the project was revealed rather plainly in the poster that the PQ government published to help people understand exactly which religious symbols would be banned from the public sphere.[32] Among the banned symbols, the poster illustrated a drawing of a hijab, a niqab, a kippa, a pendant with a large cross, and a Sikh turban. Revealed here is the racism of the charter, or its operation as a vehicle through which white French-speaking Quebecois people regulate a series of brown and Black bodies who are Muslim, Sikh, or Jewish.

Before continuing with my specific analysis, it is important to situate the charter within a broader understanding of the relationship between blackness and Islam. I argue that the Muslim subject that was at the center of the charter debate and the organizing against Islamophobia was imagined as Arab, Persian, or South Asian, and at times as a white convert, but definitely not as Black. It is important to look more closely at that erasure and think about the political implications of such a negation as we consider how better to organize against Islamophobia.

Indeed, Black people were absent from any of the religious categories that the charter sought to regulate. Black people's religious practices appeared in the charter debate—when they appeared in the debate at all—in the form of "irrational" pre-Christian practices. The then minister of culture Maka Kotto, born in Cameroon, described himself at a press conference as a "Catholic with shaman tendencies." To the assembled crowd of journalists, Kotto said: "If my intention was to play Mystic, I would walk around with my panther skull on my chest. It's my family totem but I don't do it because I adhere to the values that we agreed to adopt in the host society."[33] His intervention was one that introduced illegitimate religious practices in the form of African religiosity. As a matter of fact, his words maintained a division between what constitutes an authentic religious expression in the first place. Indeed, the news headline that followed Kotto's press conference read: "Maka Kotto prefers to leave his panther skull in the closet," mentioning nothing about the religious significance such a practice may have. Instead, much as Kotto had intended, African religion and spirituality were cast aside as antireligion.

Haitian people compose the large majority of the Black community in Quebec, and how the media portrayed Maka Kotto's religious practice is very much in line with the way that Haitian voodoo often appears as spectacle in and for white Quebec imagination and consumption. Kotto is encouraged to make a caricature of what Black religiosity may look like: relegated to the absurd, unthinkable, or only thinkable in the space of a prehistoric sub-Saharan Africa. In this respect, although Bill 60 is anti-Muslim, in a sense Islam is still legible as a modern "threat." This relates to the violence of Professor C's insults in that he expressed not only the impossibility of Muslim Blacks but also the impossibility of Black religiosity within global modern politics. It is interesting how Muslim Blacks are not "true Muslims" because Kotto's comments also suggest that Catholic Blacks are not true Catholics. Rather, Muslim Blacks and Catholic Blacks are configured as almost-civilized Black people who are attempting to enter civilized religion, and thus exiting blackness and entering the category of human. As Zakiyya Jackson so poignantly argues, "There are no practices that an individual black person can take up that will settle once and for all the doubt that accompanies the assertion of a black humanity."[34] Here Jackson echoes the core argument in Calvin Warren's "Onticide."[35] In that important work, Warren writes that we cannot speak of identity, sexuality, gender, or even orientation as it applies to the Black subject because these are categories that belong to the human, one in which the Black subject does not belong. When state and white social power intervenes on their lives, it is because their blackness, and not their religiosity, embodies violence and terror.

While some may consider it to be positive that the bill did not explicitly target Black people, we need to be wary of these types of silences because there is no such thing as benevolence in white supremacy. These absences speak to the ways in which the charter sets a perimeter around those who are always already constituted as political subjects and those who may only become subjects if they follow the proper trajectory. Both the invisibility of the Muslim Black in the charter debate and the continued unthinkability of Black religious practice suggest that blackness is itself imagined as out-side the religious. Black people occupy a position that is rendered to some extent as a temporal/racial outside and antipolitical in the sense of being ontologically antisocial and anticivil.

Although race and racism were always the elephant in the room during the debate on the charter, blackness, antiblackness, or the Black experience never entered the public conversation. A popular reason for the general dis-regard of antiblackness in the debate was the small number of Muslim Black people in relation to either Arab or South Asian Muslims. The fact remains that Black lives do not matter, regardless of how numerous we are. As Jared Sexton writes, in a U.S. context where African Americans constitute a numerical majority in several important urban centers, "black suffering—especially in its gendered and sexual variations—is in no way visible, known, remembered, or properly told. . . . Such exposure is structurally foreclosed by the force of antiblackness."[36] And so it is in Quebec as well.

ORGANIZING IN AN ANTI-BLACK WORLD

I will now steer the discussion toward the aspects of coalition building that from the outset limited the scope of Black politics within the coalition: first, citizenship and democracy, and second, "unity." Both sides of the debate used as a starting point the notion that Quebec is not and never was racist. Among those who opposed the charter, the group that garnered the widest support and received the most attention in the media was Québec Inclusif, which was started by "academics and professionals from the legal, philo-sophical and journalistic fields."[37] Québec Inclusif's manifesto states that "with this draft Charter of Values, the PQ fulfills its shift from a civic or liberal nationalism towards an exclusionary one" and that it is "at great risk of weakening . . . Québécois identity rather than strengthening it."[38] Indeed, many opposed the charter because they saw it as a setback from the work that Quebec has done over the past three decades to acquire a respectable status among other Western nations (and also win over "immigrants" to the sovereigntist camp). Interestingly, both "sides" of the debate on the charter presented their arguments such that it was their shared long-term objective to make Quebec into a model postracial society. This excerpt is from the conclusion of the Québec Inclusif manifesto:

> The proposed Charter of Values would force minorities to choose between their conscience and their survival. Never in history has exclusion in this

form been a part of Québécois values. Québec has for long been a warm and welcoming land where each person could contribute to our great social tapestry. We believe that it's through greater social diversity, not by ostracizing certain individuals that we can continue to live in harmony. Québec identity is not built upon the rejection of the Other.[39]

Perfectly in synch with Québec Inclusif's framing of the issue, part of the discursive strategy that was mobilized by non-Black Muslims who were active during the debate on the charter was to appeal to the state as citizens. Every time they were heard in public during the debate, they would preface their statements with appeals to their Quebecois pedigree. In a radio interview in April 2013, Rachida Azdouz (a professor at Université de Montréal) became audibly irritated after being asked to speak as a Muslim. She explained that other (non-Black) Muslims like her consider themselves as citizens first:

> I hear a different discourse that is about associating oneself to a citizenship. What they say is that Islam is not a citizenship. They say that for them, Islamlandia is not a country, Muslimlandia doesn't exist. . . . And these people claim a dual citizenship. They are Canadian and Algerian, Canadian and Tunisian, Canadian and Moroccan, Canadian and Afghan, but don't want to be considered Canadian and Muslim because Muslimlandia doesn't exist. Islam is not a country and not a citizenship and that's what I hear from them.[40]

This type of discourse on rights and citizenship is not one that corresponds to the position of the Black subject, nor does it address the project of Black freedom. Saidiya Hartman signals the fallacy of believing that democracy, often measured through the rights that it distributes, can bring freedom to Black people. For her, it is an inconsistent logic to think that "the selective recognition of sameness guarantees the identity of right and privileges, while difference determines rights in accordance with one's place in society."[41] She explains further:

> One is left to wonder what exactly equality does entail and, by the same token, what constitutes a violation of equal protection. Did blacks constitute a different class of individuals or were all men of one class? The vacillation between the disavowal and recognition of difference encapsulates the predicament of equality.[42]

In addition, Joy James warns us not to equate democracy and its various technologies (rights, law, etc.) with freedom. This is useful as we think about Black geographical projects that allow for new ways of being. James explains that "in fantasies of democracy, the enslaver rescues the savage from barbarity, and the abolitionist saves the savage from the enslaver," but the truth of the matter is that "both forms of salvation are captivity."[43] James's point serves as a reminder of the ways in which the political state and its apparatus create the conditions for our suffering and at the same time demarcate the limits of our political action. It is important to remain aware of how the political state also works to regulate itself in order to keep us in its fold. James encourages us to consider how thinking in the familiar terms of visibility/invisibility and exclusion/inclusion limits our *political* imagination to Black incorporation and facile ideals of democracy, ensuring at the same time that Black geographies of resistance become captive of geographies of domination. A different political imagination, one that eschews visibility and inclusion as the foremost ends, is evident in the history of Black resistance.

Another important reason why antiblackness was not addressed in the debate on the charter, especially as it applies to mainstream groups organizing against it, was the priority given to "unity" to defeat the charter. Addressing antiblackness in particular was seen as a potential threat to that illusory unity. As Tamara K. Nopper has argued, "It can be difficult at times to draw attention to inequalities among people of color because it disrupts a desire for multiracial coalition."[44] A relevant question that she raised as we reflect on antiracist activism in Quebec during and after the debate on the charter is "how does our own desire to recognize diversity possibly contribute to a progressive color-blind racism in which we have no basis of comparison?"[45]

A common argument at the time was that using a black-white binary was not appropriate in the case of organizing opposition to the charter because the Muslim imagined at the center of the charter was Arab. Indeed, Islamophobia is too often understood as a white-on-brown form of violence. In the experience I described at the onset of this article, casting aside a black-white binary does not lead to a more robust understanding of racism, as many purported antiracist activists may maintain in such instances. Instead, blackness is cast aside completely, no longer relevant. What I am arguing is that that precise eviction, as in the statement "what are you doing here, this is not an issue that involves Black people, it's about [white] Quebecois and Arabs," is a form of antiblackness that maintains itself as antiracism. Here again, it is useful to go back to Sexton's explanation as to what lies behind these types of assertions:

First, [such opposition to a black-white binary] often serves to expunge critical discussions of black history altogether rather than expand the discourse as it supposedly claims to do. Second, it relies upon an insidious notion of black empowerment vis-à-vis other oppressed groups to make its claims about the exclusion of nonblack people of color by both whites and blacks. It thereby rationalizes the aforementioned expunging.[46]

Anthropologist João Costa Vargas has written much about the resistance that Black scholars encounter when they explain the specificities of Black suffering and death. Costa Vargas explains that this resistance is often articulated as an accusation of playing "oppression Olympics," whereby "our supposedly unwarranted focus on anti-blackness amount[s] to the unethical attack against and even erasure of the experiences of non-white and non-heteronormative allies."[47] When Black scholars and activists engage in multiracial solidarity movements, Costa Vargas proposes that we scrutinize further this seamless transition from Black focus to a people-of-color framework. Though he emphasizes that negating these kinds of coalitions altogether would be unsustainable, he points out that they must be considered a possibility rather than a requirement. For Costa Vargas, an unwavering belief in multiracial alliances puts "an immense moral, analytical, and political burden on blacks, not the least of which was the requirement that we unconditionally love the non-black."[48] In a world where Black life is always on the edge, our own vision of the future must remain at the center of our collective action.

In the case of Quebec, we can see how the idea that the debate on the charter was about white and Arab people helps evade the continued history of antiblackness more than it helps anyone to move or think "beyond" it. In a talk at McGill University earlier this year, Rinaldo Walcott argued that the white citizenry needs brown Muslims to do a certain kind of work in the process of racialization. He explained that post 9/11, brown Muslim people were in many ways shocked to realize that they were experiencing some of what Black people have been going through for centuries. But in that realization, they also made a move to disappear Muslim Black peoples. In a place like Quebec that readily erases its own history of antiblackness and slavery, it is no surprise that an attempt at disappearing Black people would be a welcome move.

In addition to Québec Inclusif, several Muslim groups were also formed to mobilize against the charter, and their general line did not stray from that of their white allies. One of them was the group Québécois musulmans pour les droits et libertés, or "Muslim Quebecers for rights and liberties." A point that this coalition of fifty Muslim groups reiterated in the media was that "Québec has made great leaps forward for its citizens and its institutions thanks to the Quiet Revolution, but this Charter creates quibbles between Québécers and we do not want to move backwards."[49] We can see here the type of respectability politics that is at play in opposing the charter through supporting Quebec national politics: we are supposed to believe that since the 1960s, Quebec has been a model antiracist society, a safe beacon in a dangerous Anglo-American world. Gone are the long history of antiblackness and everyday forms of anti-Black violence. These kinds of nationalist arguments were prevalent in the discourses against the charter and, intended or not, served to consolidate a liberal (and deeply oppressive) state.

Groups and individuals who had mobilized against the charter breathed a sigh of relief on April 7, 2014, when the PQ was defeated in the provincial election and the proposed charter was subsequently laid to rest by the incumbent government. While we can all be glad that the thousands of Muslim women in Quebec who wear the hijab do not have to choose between their faith and their livelihood, I do not read the defeat of the charter as an antiracist victory. Instead, I would like to revisit the charter debate through an Afro-pessimist lens and analyze the experience that I had as a Muslim Black feminist organizing against it. As Nicholas Brady so poignantly wrote, the reality of engaging in struggle in an anti-Black world is that anti-blackness is an ontological question that arrives always too early or too late for consideration. "Contrary to the feeling of some," offers Brady, "there has never been a black time, only an anti-black world where black people exist as its absent center, always too loud, needing to be silenced, yet always remaining unthought and hyper-present."[50]

Another consequence of antiblackness is the (im)possibility of political reform. Since the problem of an anti-Black world is ontological, in that Black people are cast outside the category of the human, it cannot be reformed. For example, Frank Wilderson III, one of Afro-pessimism's prominent intellectuals, argues that all attempts to reform society are bound to fail for Black people, since society itself is fundamentally anti-Black. The only acceptable solution, according to Wilderson (and other Afro-pessimists), is the creation of an entirely new world. In a recent interview, Wilderson explains what is at stake in rejecting Black incorporation and/or integration: "They're trying to build a better world. What are we trying to do? We're trying to destroy the world. Two irreconcilable projects."[51] In other words, Black people's experiences can only be transformed through the destruction of the current social order. This echoes James's ideas about the spatiality of Black political imagination and resistance. For them too, what makes Black political projects is their transformative possibilities and not their ability to integrate Black communities into racist societies.

Both the charter and the mobilization against it revealed who is a political subject in Quebec. The movement against the proposed bill proceeded by mobilizing only those who were identified as political subjects. It did so through a consideration of whose political subjecthood was threatened or problematized. It was even more apparent in the way that Black people's participation in the debate served a particular purpose: they were either an example of what no one wants to become (i.e., Black) and/or an example of an antiracist struggle that is now relegated to the past. "Multiethnic" coalitions in Quebec work in such ways that Black struggles only appear as a cautionary tale. Jabari's warning to white Quebecers that non-Black Muslims will not be "the negroes of Quebec" is a clear illustration.

Further, one must not read Professor C's comments as simply ignorant, for he did recognize that Muslim Black people exist. Instead, his position is akin to what Nopper has called the "'stay in your lane approach' which confines how Black people should trace and confront slavery and its afterlife."[52] This approach is one that is prevalent in how non-Black Muslim activists in Quebec as well as their allies such as Professor C do not recognize Islamophobia as a marker of the afterlife of slavery for Muslim Black people. Although Professor C reluctantly agreed that there are Muslim Black people, he dismissed the possibility of them being political subjects in this specific struggle for justice.

Professor C's remarks spoke less of my invisibility and undesirability than of my disposability within coalition politics. Usually, in the groups that I have been involved with politically, my role has been that of the token Black woman. I was always asked by these groups when and how I was planning on bringing in other Black folks. But this time around, I was being dismissed because my social and cultural network was useless. Far from being asked to bring in other Black folks, my own presence seemed unnecessary and contaminating. To Professor C, I was excess—a familiar view of Black people that Denise Ferreira da Silva describes as racial violence, whose precise calculus is "black body = value + excess."[53] To be seen only in terms of value and excess, not just by the racial state but by so-called antiracist activists, raises important questions about the relationship between antiracism and anti-Black racism—or, indeed, the antiblackness of antiracist politics. The visibility of the Black body is used to perform a specific kind of politics within coalitions. The question that we should take more seriously is the following: what precisely are the conditions of possibility and impossibility for Black people in ostensibly antiracist coalition politics?

It would be useful to bring into this argument other scholars of antiblackness to reflect further about how Muslim Black people in Quebec occupy the position of the unthinkable and how that made opposition to the charter insufficient to address their suffering. In his 2014 article "Neither Humans nor Rights: Some Notes on the Double Negation of Black Life in Brazil," Jaime Amparo Alves explains that while it remains crucial to recognize the power of the creative to fuel Black life amid the perpetual state of terror that our communities across the globe continue to live, it remains paramount that we challenge our political imagination and "push forward a radical agenda that demystifies concepts such as freedom, human rights, and civil society" and, I would add, justice.[54] Alves's ideas are helpful because when I make the critique that the charter and the debate around it revealed Black people's status outside of the human, the common response is for Black people in Quebec to work toward being "recognized" or "included" in that category. Instead, I propose that we imagine and build toward other and more creative ways of being. So far, and as the previous examples have shown, because the discourses and goals that were mobilized by opponents to the charter retained an anti-Black logic within which Black religiosity remained unimaginable and Black suffering in general was invisible, the project that they espoused could not lead to a place of Black freedom. To transform our coalitional organizing would require that we forego our investment in a justice that is distributed and recognized by the state. To consider their organizing as the site of possibility for Black people would be, as Calvin Warren put it, "to place our hope in a future politics that avoids history, historicity, and the immediacy of black suffering."

What Does Justice Look Like?

In the context of Quebec, where naming blackness alone is considered as an attack on the nation-building project, I made a point to dedicate much of this article to naming the racial violence that the charter enacted on Muslim Black people. I took on Hartman and Wilderson's provocation to not "consciously or unconsciously peel away from the strength and the terror of [the] evidence in order to propose some kind of coherent, hopeful solution to things."[55]

One could only approximate what justice looks like because the Black subject occupies a position for which there is no grammar of suffering available.

On the other hand, white and other non-Black people can reference a grammar of civility they can deploy, as Tryon Woods has explained, a discourse of the nation-state in a manner that makes them legible as subjects within that social formation.[56] Borrowing from Wilderson and Sexton, this could be the difference between a justice that seeks to repair a suffering that is contingent (rights being infringed) and justice that targets structural suffering (a violence that is gratuitous, that knows no limit nor logic).[57] Does justice look the same for Black and non-Black subjects? In the case of the charter, I have demonstrated in this article that the proposed bill did not solve the eviction of Muslim Black people from the religious.

Moving forward, I argue that obliterating the roots of antiblackness from the charter is due less to Muslim Black people being a small numeric minority in Quebec than about the ways in which antiblackness structures, on the one hand, commensurability between religion and humanity and, on the other, Black religiosity as unthinkable.[58] It is important to observe public policies and legislation just as much as the discourses and strategies that are deployed at the grassroots level because civil society plays a particularly salient role in (re)producing antiblackness.

One could argue that groups such as those I have just presented often do not realize how their platforms and their goals are rooted in antiblackness. But it is important to pay closer attention to dreams and projects that cannot imagine Black life. What I have learned from my involvement with the Indépendantistes is that I cannot work side by side with people who are not able to imagine what joy would look like for me in a new world. Coalition politics are often premised on the idea that when coming together, all parties must be ready to compromise. Yet, under these premises, Black people have the most to lose. What would coalitions look like if they were not premised on loss? What is commonly called "throwing people under the bus" could be better defined as "necessary death." When a coalition comes together, those who are not in its dreams are the first people we throw under the bus. The danger with the "politics of necessary death" is that the coalitions that are borne out of them can only eliminate those whose future is inconceivable.

DÉLICE MUGABO is a Black feminist activist. A Muslim of Rwandan origin, she was born in the Republic of Congo, and immigrated to Quebec at five years old. For almost a decade, she worked for an antipoverty and housing rights community organization where she developed an understanding and a critique of Quebec politics. In 2013 she participated in organizing "'Create

Dangerously': Congress of Black Writers and Artists," an event marking the forty-fifth anniversary of the Congress of Black Writers and Artists that was also held in Montreal. She then went on to cofound the Black Intellectuals Reading Group in 2014. Although now based in Halifax, her work remains committed to the Third Eye Collective, a Black feminist group in Montreal that focuses on gender violence within Black communities and transformative justice.

NOTES

I would like to acknowledge Samah Affan for inspiring my work on anti-Black Islamophobia, and to thank Nathalie Batraville, Ted Rutland, and K. Wayne Yang for commenting on previous versions. I am particularly grateful to Darryl Leroux for supporting me to develop my ideas. An earlier version of this paper was presented at the Canadian Black Studies Association conference in May 2015 at Dalhousie University.

1. Michel-Rolph Trouillot, *Silencing the Past: Power and the Production of History* (Boston, Mass.: Beacon Press, 1995), xix.

2. Denise Ferreira da Silva, "Before Man: Sylvia Wynter's Rewriting of the Modern Episteme," in *The Realization of Living: Sylvia Wynter and Being Human,* ed. Katherine McKittrick (Durham, N.C.: Duke University Press, 2015), 49.

3. Leïla Benhadjoudja, "Vivre ensemble au-delà du soupçon à l'égard de l'Autre," in *Le Québec, la Charte, l'Autre: Et après?,* ed. Marie-Claude Haince, Yara El-Ghadban, and Leïla Benhadjoudja (Montreal: Mémoire d'encrier, 2015).

4. Sovereigntists advocate for Quebec to become a state independent from Canada. The first referendum on that option was held in 1980 and a second one in 1995. Because various groups, political parties, and an important segment of the population remain invested in the sovereignty project, the issue continues to influence many other debates in Quebec.

5. I am basing this on e-mail exchanges with group members. They state on their website that "Indépendantistes pour une laïcité inclusive (IPLI) held its first meeting on February 7, 2013, and became registered with the Québec Entreprise Register on September 16, 2013." See http://ipli.info/qui.php. All translations are mine unless otherwise noted.

6. "Rassembler plutôt qu'exclure: Déclaration des Indépendantistes pour une laïcité inclusive sur la Charte des 'valeurs québécoises,'" http://www.ledevoir.com/documents/pdf/rassemblerplutotquexclure.pdf.

7. Jared Sexton, "The *Vel* of Slavery: Tracking the Figure of the Unsovereign," *Critical Sociology* (2014): 1–15, doi:10.1177/0896920514552535.

8. Jared Sexton, "People-of-Color-Blindness: Notes on the Afterlife of Slavery," *Social Text* 28, no. 2 (2010): 31–56, doi:10.1215/01642472-2009-066.

9. Saidiya Hartman, *Lose Your Mother: A Journey along the Atlantic Slave Route* (New York: Farrar, Straus and Giroux, 2007), 6.

10. Ibid.; Frank B. Wilderson III, *Red, Black, and White: Cinema and the Structure of U.S. Antagonisms* (Durham, N.C.: Duke University Press, 2010); Tiffany Lethabo King, "In the Clearing: Black Female Bodies, Space and Settler Colonial Landscapes" (PhD diss., University of Maryland, 2013).

11. João H. Costa Vargas, *Never Meant to Survive: Genocide and Utopias in Black Diaspora Communities* (Lanham, Md.: Rowman & Littlefield, 2011); Jaime Amparo Alves, "Macabre Spatialities: The Politics of Race, Gender and Violence in a Neoliberal City" (PhD. diss., University of Texas at Austin, 2012); Egbert Alejandro Martina, "The Netherlands and Its Discontents, or: How White Dutch Folks Started Worrying and Urged 'Us' to Take Rioters Seriously," *Processed Life Blog,* September 10, 2014, https://processedlives.wordpress.com/2014/09/10/the-netherlands-and-its-discontents-or-how-white-dutch-folks-started-worrying-and-urged-us-to-take-rioters-seriously/.

12. Sherman Jackson, "9/11 a Decade Later: The Ironic Impact of Islamophobia," *Huffpost Religion,* September 8, 2011, http://www.huffingtonpost.com/sherman-a-jackson/911-a-decade-later-islamophobia_b_952154.html.

13. Tariq Ramadan, "Even Now, Muslims Must Have Faith in America," *Washington Post,* September 12, 2010; Amir Saeed, "9/11 and the Increase in Racism and Islamophobia: A Personal Reflection," *Radical History Review* 111 (2011): 210–15.

14. Serif Onur Bahçecik, "Internationalizing Islamophobia: Anti-Islamophobia Practices from the Runnymede Trust to the Organization of Islamic Cooperation," *Ortadogu Etutleri* 5, no. 1 (2013): 141–65; Vashti Kenway, "The Hidden History of Islamophobia," *Marxist Left Review,* no. 9 (2015).

15. Edward Said, *Orientalism* (New York: Random House, 1977).

16. Junaid Rana, "The Story of Islamophobia," *Souls: A Critical Journal of Black Politics, Culture, and Society* 9, no. 2 (2007): 153.

17. Ibid., 157.

18. Sherene Razack, *Casting Out: The Eviction of Muslims from Western Law and Politics* (Toronto: University of Toronto Press, 2008).

19. Rinaldo Walcott, "Black Queer and Black Trans: Imagine Imagination Imaginary Futures," *Equity Matters,* October 27, 2011, http://www.ideas-idees.ca/blog/black-queer-and-black-trans-imagine-imagination-imaginary-futures.

20. Ibid.

21. Ibid.

22. Samah Jabbari, TV interview by Stéphane Gendron, *Racisme envers les musulmans,* Montréal, February 23, 2015, http://adr.tv/webtv.php?type=extraits&webtv=racisme-envers-les-musulmans&id_episode=820&nom.

23. Jabbari's statement caused an uproar on social media among the Black community and brought her to issue an apology through her Facebook page. What is interesting is that along with her apology, Jabbari posted several pictures of herself standing along Black girls and women at social events. One must ask what the unnamed and silent Black bodies in those pictures were meant to perform, stand in for, and cover. Neither Jabbari's apology nor her subsequent public statements present or explain where and how Black people in general and particularly those who are Muslim fit into the political vision and agenda of the organization that she represents.

34. Zakiyyah Iman Jackson, "Waking Nightmares—On David Mariott," *GLQ: A Journal of Lesbian and Gay Studies* 2, no. 3 (2011): 360, doi:10.1215/10642684-1163445.

35. Calvin Warren, "Onticide: Toward an Afro-pessimistic Queer Theory" (paper presented at the American Studies Association Annual Meeting, Washington, D.C., November 21, 2013).

36. Jared Sexton, "The Obscurity of Black Suffering," in *What Lies Beneath: Katrina, Race, and the State of the Nation,* ed. South End Press Collective (Cambridge, Mass.: South End Press, 2007), 124.

37. Québec Inclusif, "Manifesto for an Inclusive Quebec," September 12, 2013. Quotations are from the version I accessed in April 20, 2015, at http://quebec-inclu sif.org/427-2/?lang=en. A slightly modified version now appears at http://www .socialist.ca/node/1903.

38. Ibid.

39. Ibid.

40. Rachida Azdouz, radio interview, *Dimanche* magazine, April 28, 2013, http:// ici.radio-canada.ca/emissions/dimanche_magazine/2012-2013/chronique.asp?idC hronique=289027&autoPlay=##commenter.

41. Saidiya V. Hartman, *Scenes of Subjection: Terror, Slavery, and Self-Making in Nineteenth-Century America* (New York: Oxford University Press, 1997), 180.

42. Ibid.

43. Joy James, "Afrarealism and the Black Matrix: Maroon Philosophy at Democracy's Border," *Black Scholar* 43, no. 4 (2013): 125.

44. Tamara K. Nopper, "Where Do We Go When We Go 'Beyond Black and White'?," November 3, 2009, http://tamaranopper.com/2009/11/03/where-do-we-go -when-we-go-beyond-black-and-white/.

45. Ibid.

46. Sexton, "Obscurity of Black Suffering," 129.

47. João Costa Vargas, "Clyde Woods: Life after Black Social Death," *Antipode* (2012): 5, https://radicalantipode.files.wordpress.com/2012/12/woods_4_costa-vargas .pdf.

48. Ibid., 13.

49. Samira Laouini, radio interview by Geneviève Asselin, *Téléjournal Midi,* September 25, 2013, http://ici.radio-canada.ca/widgets/mediaconsole/medianet/6838336.

50. Nicholas Brady, "The Void Speaks Back: Black Suffering as the Unthought of the American Studies Association's Academic Boycott of Israel," *Out of Nowhere Blog,* December 23, 2013, https://outofnowhereblog.wordpress.com/2013/12/23/the -void-speaks-back-black-suffering-as-the-unthought-of-the-american-studies -associations-academic-boycott-of-israel/.

51. Frank B. Wilderson III, radio interview by Jared Ball, Dr. Hate, and Todd Steven Burroughs, "'We're Trying to Destroy the World': Anti-blackness and Police Violence after Ferguson," October 1, 2014, 20, http://sfbay-anarchists.org/wp-con tent/uploads/2015/01/frank-b-wilderson-iii-were-trying-to-destroy-the-world-anti blackness-police-violence-after-ferguson.pdf.

52. Tamara K. Nopper, "On Terror, Captivity, and Black-Korean Conflict," *Decolonization: Indigeneity, Education & Society,* September 24, 2015, https://decoloniza tion.wordpress.com/2015/09/24/on-terror-captivity-and-black-korean-conflict/.

53. Denise Ferreira da Silva, "To Be Announced: Radical Praxis or Knowing (at) the Limits of Justice," *Social Text* 1 (2013): 48.

54. Jaime Amparo Alves, "Neither Humans nor Rights: Some Notes on the Double Negation of Black Life in Brazil," *Journal of Black Studies* 45, no. 2 (2014): 145.

55. Saidiya V. Hartman and Frank Wilderson III, "The Position of the Unthought," *Qui Parle* 13, no. 2 (2013): 183.

56. Tryon Woods, "The Fact of Anti-blackness: Decolonization in Chiapas and the Niger River Delta," *Human Architecture: Journal of the Sociology of Self-Knowledge* 5, no. 3 (2007): 319–30.

57. Frank B. Wilderson III, "Gramsci's Black Marx: Whither the Slave in Civil Society?," *Social Identities* 9, no. 2 (2003): 225–40; Sexton, "People-of-Color-Blindness."

58. In Canada and the UK, policies toward Black immigrants have been more restrictive due to apprehensions about Black people igniting "social unrest." Vilna Bashi, "Globalized Anti-blackness: Transnationalizing Western Immigration Law, Policy, and Practice," *Ethnic and Racial Studies* 27, no. 4 (2004): 584–606.

The Racial Limits of Social Justice

The Ruse of Equality of Opportunity
and the Global Affirmative Action Mandate

DENISE FERREIRA DA SILVA

[I]n the wake of the verdict, I know those passions may be running even higher . . . But we are a nation of laws, and a jury has spoken.

—U.S. President Barack Obama, 2013

[This generation can't process] how can you be walking home from a store and end up dead, and how six women, five mothers, can't find it within the justice system to see that a life has been taken, that Trayvon Martin's life had value.

—Roslyn Brock, chairwoman of the NAACP, 2013

Both George Zimmerman's acquittal for the murder of Trayvon Martin and Ferguson's Grand Jury's refusal to indict Darren Wilson for killing Michael Brown reminded us (once again) that equal protection of the law remains elusive for Black people in the United States, and that these juridical decisions are grounded on an ethical grammar that actualizes G. W. F. Hegel's often-cited postulate—recalled in Roslyn Brock's above statement—that the "Negro" is an "object of no value."[1] For if the ethical mandate of the liberal state (under the rule of law) is to protect the lives, liberty, and property of its citizens, these decisions further confirm Black Lives Matter's charge that, before the laws of President Barack Obama's nation, Black and Latino people are persons without value, or "nobodies"—that is, ethical-juridical subjects without right to the formal (negative) protection of the law. If that is so, why is it that over the past fifty years or so there has been an expectation that the U.S. juridical architectures authorize substantive (positive) actions in favor of its Black citizens? More importantly, since the particularities of the U.S. racial situation have been inscribed in the sociological account of racial subjugation, how do we account for two apparently contradictory developments of the past two decades: as the United States slowly but decisively dismantled its racial justice architectures, throughout the globe, countries like Brazil have been busy designing and implementing affirmative action measures designed to correct racial inequality. In this article, I return to the question of im/possibility of global/racial justice by attending to the workings of raciality under the present figuration of state capital.

My reading of the global affirmative action mandate focuses on the simultaneous deployment of social inclusion and security programs to describe how raciality, through the *logic of exclusion* and the *logic of obliteration,* aids the state's current work for global capital. Whereas the pervasiveness of the *logic of exclusion,* through the thesis of discrimination, allows for a celebration of social inclusion measures to mark states' commitment to equality of opportunity, the *logic of obliteration* continues to perform a decisive role, as the unacknowledged justification for a security apparatus designed to curb political and social unrest that expose the modalities of economic expropriation—namely, elimination of social provisions, poor quality of social services, and expropriation of land and resources—characterizing global capitalism. What I show is how, through these logics, raciality resolves the contradictory demands the state has to meet for claiming success on these two disparate tasks because of how it checks demands for justice—in the global (ethical-juridical) context, in which the human rights framework is governed by the human and its principles, namely liberty, equality, and more recently security.

Following the trajectory of the notions that support social justice programs, namely the thesis discrimination and ethical principle of equality of opportunity, from President Kennedy's 1963 speech to the NGO Global Rights' report, I expose how effectively they exorcize the radical transformative potential of affirmative action. Focusing on consolidation of human rights as the guiding global ethico-juridical framework, I situate affirmative action in the context of an economic development program that relies on the expansion of consumer markets, financialization, as well as modalities of surplus-value expropriation, very similar to past colonial expropriation of the productive capacity of native lands and slave labor. What I find is that, rather than attending to the ethical mandate for racial justice, Brazil's affirmative action policies—as it was the case in the United States—have been grounded on a "compelling state interest" in meeting the needs of global capital.

My itinerary is simple. First, I provide a brief analysis of the mandate of the 1964 Civil Rights Act, in John Rawls's rendering and the U.S. Supreme

Court's interpretations. Second, I examine the global affirmative action mandate, targeting the construction of social justice organizing in the global ethical text. Finally, I turn my attention to the Brazilian case, in particular to describe how, when one attends to concomitant government equality (those designed to comply with the human rights framework, to alleviate poverty) and security programs, it becomes evident that "compelling state interest" is the sole force behind affirmative action and other similar measures. Still, because this article heeds the anticolonial trust of political movements that forced legislations and policies of the 1960s and 1970s that interpreted Title VII's wording as a green signal for reforms meant to address the effects of colonial expropriation and racial subjugation, its bet is the capacity of our critical engagements to contribute to a radical reimagining of global existence, where the principle of liberty (in all its guises) no longer justifies the racial (total and symbolic violence) capital needs to thrive.

"WE PREACH FREEDOM AROUND THE WORLD"

On June 11, 1963, fifty years before President Obama's speech in the aftermath of Trayvon Martin's killing, President John F. Kennedy told U.S. citizens that it was time to address the urgent "moral crisis" facing the country.[2] On July 2, 1964, taking up the pledge after Kennedy's assassination, President Lyndon B. Johnson signed the Civil Rights Act (the Act). Framing the mandate to bring about equal opportunity, to meet the call for "abundance and liberty for all" and to the "end of poverty and racial injustice," the document includes a phrase, "order such affirmative action," that animated substantive measures for addressing racial discrimination in all areas, but in particular in employment and education. The Act was just the first measure of the Johnson administration's social reform program known as the Great Society. Less than two decades later, however, substantive racial remedies took a blow. The 1978 *Bakke* decision, which limited the call for equal opportunity, was enshrined within the narrow construction of "compelling state interest." That was a first but definite setback to any hope for substantive redress for centuries of racial subjugation in the country.

What accounts for the failure of equality of opportunity to support racial redress is the fact that it presupposes the principle of liberty and its correlated thesis of discrimination. Following the operations of the principle of liberty in racial knowledge and moral philosophy, I find how it cannot but yield a thesis of discrimination, which operates as the fail-safe device in measures designed to ensure both formal (equal protection of the law) and substantive (redress) racial justice. The discussion of racial knowledge identifies a "racial dialectics" that disappears with colonial expropriation and racial (symbolic and total) violence by resolving them into two logics of racial subjugation, namely exclusion (which attributes it to individual acts of discrimination) and obliteration (which attributes it to the racial subaltern's intrinsic mental [intellectual and moral] deficiency). My reading of Rawls's version of equality opportunity focuses on how the thesis of discrimination and the principle of liberty render it a useless basis for racial redress. Returning to articulations of the thesis of discrimination in racial knowledge and contemporary moral philosophy, I find, helps situate landmark U.S. Supreme Court decisions on affirmative action cases' finding that "compelling state interest" is the sole acceptable principle for racial redress.

Exposing How the Principle of Liberty Works

Through the notions of liberty and necessity it is possible to dis-mystify the apparently contradictory role of modern juridical entities, such as law and the state. Moreover, the articulation of necessity and violence provides clues for grasping how raciality delimits the modern notion of justice, by producing affectable (racial subaltern) subjects to whom dear modern universal principles (liberty and equality) do not apply because they are governed by necessity—that is, by violence. All I do here is describe racial knowledge in such a way that exposes how the principle of liberty works through an articulation of necessity that results in two logics of racial subjugation, namely *exclusion* and *obliteration*.

Before doing so let me say a bit more about how necessity appears in descriptions of modern juridical and ethical order. Liberal sociology provides our most basic image of the post-Enlightenment capitalist social context, as one inhabited by rational individuals who decide and act on the basis of the principle of liberty. Though participating in its constitution by choosing their representatives (legislative branch) and welcoming the protection of the law and the state, they resent any state beyond enforcement of the law and protection of rights (executive branch) and administration of justice (judiciary branch). Looking back at classic versions of the liberal text, such as Thomas Hobbes's and John Locke's, we find that they base their descriptions of the proper modern juridical order on the *necessity* to protect the rational and self-interested individual *liberty* (body and property) always under threat of violence (theft, enslavement, or death) from other self-interested individuals. Consistently, this "originary violence" would be deployed in later major philosophical writings of the modern ethical order, in statements that write morality as an interiorized constraint necessary to curb "originary violence": as in Immanuel Kant's argument that, though apparently contradictory, the moral law protects freedom (liberty) because it alone preserves what distinguishes the rational subject, that is, its dignity (intrinsic value); and Hegel's, which articulates ontological violence in the Lordship and Bondsman passage, where the life-and-death struggle signals an "original" situation, a sort of pre-ethical moment before the subject finds moral unity in the participation in spirit. This description of the modern ethical order is repeated in nineteenth-century sciences of man and society, in particular in Émile Durkheim's formulation of the science of morality (sociology), where he offers the notion of culture (collective consciousness) to capture the moral bounds (constraints) necessary for collective life.

Let me focus on the two basic images of the postbellum U.S. social context presented in sociological studies: first, the *ideal* one, which is that of a transparent (modern) society, populated with self-interested individuals, in free competition, who enjoy the protection of the law and the state; and second, the *actual* one, which is an affectable (modern) society, populated with self-interested but racially identified individuals, where discrimination (as well as racial conflict and competition) rather than liberty or equality prevail. For social scientists studying the second image the task was to fix that—the racial problem—which made it depart from the ideal of a transparent society.

The Racial Dialectic Works through the Race Relation Cycle

When I turn to these studies I find a redeployment of "originary violence" that describes an ethical order in the moment Hegel describes in his Lordship and Bondage passage.[3] A perverse racial dialectic, which combines two socio-logics, namely *exclusion* and *obliteration* and their effects of signification, is the naturalization of social subjugation and of blackness as a signifier of violence. The racial dialectic works through the "race relation cycle" (conflict => competition => assimilation => amalgamation) and the "theory of racial and cultural contacts," which write the colonial architectures and their effect of power (the expropriation of the productive capacity of native lands and slave labor) as effects of the naturally violent encounter between racially different collectives.[4] How does it work? It transmutates (a) the **economic debt** resulting from an extreme economic expropriation (as white Americans continue to hold virtually all the wealth produced by slave labor) into (b) a **moral deficit** (which the sight of blackness causes in whites' minds, as Black economic dispossession becomes an effect of the exclusionary ideas and actions blackness entails), which is then returned as (c) the racial other's **mental deficiency** (as economic dispossession and the social conditions it breed produce a pathological subject unable to thrive on equal foot in a free, competitive society). Its primary effect is to *occlude* colonial expropriation of the productive capacity of native lands and slave labor by explaining racial subjugation: a solely whites' **moral deficit** (discriminatory actions) explains the racial others' **moral deficiency**, while the **economic debt** can only result from the subaltern **racial difference**, which causes whites' **moral deficit**.

Two basic accounts of racial subjugation in the United States derive from this dialectics. On the one hand, there is the partial reading, in which **(a) is sublated into (b)**, renders the *logic of exclusion*, or the thesis of discrimination, which figures racial discrimination/inequality as a stain in the otherwise transparent U.S. social context, and assumes that this anomaly would disappear with the elimination of racial beliefs—through education and improving Black people's conditions, through mechanisms to bring about equality of opportunity. On the other hand, we have the full reading, which **does not sublate (a) into (b)**—that is, a juridico-economic element (colonial expropriation) is not translated into an ethical one (irrational prejudice and false beliefs) that colonial expropriation is at the "origin" of the **economic debt** plaguing the racial "others of Europe." Because it attends to how racial difference as signifier of mental capacity (**mental deficiency**) is a product of nineteenth-century racial knowledge and not the effect of white "prejudice" (**moral deficit**), this reading highlights the **explanatory primacy** of the logic obliteration, registered in the first (conflict) and the last (miscegenation) moments of the "racial relations cycle"; both refigure the trust of colonial expropriation (conquest, settlement, and slavery), which is the expropriation of the total value yielded by native land and slave labor, something that consistently bet on an ethical indifference to the annihilation of the native and the enslaved.

The Limits of Justice

Let me highlight two aspects of this account of racial subjugation that interest me. First, because it presupposes the ideal U.S. social context, the thesis of discrimination (through the *logic of exclusion*) only authorizes the kind of state action described in the classical texts, that is, to protect liberty and property. Second, the explanatory primacy of *logic of obliteration* recalls how it is a sociological reiteration of the moral philosophical statements, such as in Hegel, that postulate that post-Enlightenment white/Europe(ans) monopolize modern ethical principles, such as liberty and dignity. Put differently, through the thesis of discrimination, raciality works from within the liberal text checking the ethical claims and the juridical strategies available to those demanding remedies to address the effects of racial subjugation. First, as a sociological tool of raciality, the thesis of discrimination *occludes* the fundamentally political (juridico-economic) character of racial subjugation, as it inherits the naturalization of colonial expropriation into the "theory of racial and cultural contacts." Second, because it derives from a partial reading of the "race relations cycle," which renders the racial subaltern's racial (mental and physical) difference as the primary cause of their subjugation, discrimination easily accommodates *oblivion* (in/difference) as an acceptable moral response to harm done to the racial subaltern, for ultimately their plight results from how *nature* (both in its divine and scientific rendering) governs their (bodily, mental, social) conditions of existence. In the global juridical architectures, raciality works through the notions of the human and *naturalized* cultural (intellectual and moral) difference. Whenever the post-Enlightenment notion of the human is deployed in a juridical context, it combines with cultural difference to enable the statement that (a) the idea of the human conveys a unity of diversity, (b) the ethical principle of dignity (the sanctity of human life), but also that (c) the view that the "cultures" of the racial subaltern ("nobodies") do not respect the latter principle. Not surprisingly, whenever the U.S. state's self-protecting forces (the police or the military) deploy (or authorize) total violence against Black, Latino, Arab, or Muslim persons, they consistently (and more often than not successfully) justify these actions on the basis that these persons constituted a threat to those who killed them because these "nobodies" have no respect for the sanctity of human life.[5] No wonder then, in the absence of a "compelling state interest," before the liberal halls of justice, the racial subaltern becomes consistently *nobody*, a person without value. Both in moral and legal interpretations of equality, the thesis of discrimination reproduces the *occlusion* of colonial expropriation and *oblivion* to injuries to racial subaltern collectives—as such, it acts as an ethical check on state-mandated or state-supported remedies beyond the protection of the right to equality before the law.[6]

"The Rights Secured by Justice"

Though equality of opportunity, as the remedy to racial discrimination, was already circulating in sociological treatises, political speeches, and juridical frameworks, John Rawls's celebrated 1971 volume, *A Theory of Justice*, is unquestionably the authoritative articulation of this moral concept in contemporary liberal philosophy.[7] My interest in revisiting Rawls's articulation of equality of opportunity lies in how it reproduces the effects of the racial dialectic, that is, *occlusion* of colonial expropriation and *oblivion* to racial subjugation. More particularly, I am interested in the consequences of his placing of social justice in a picture of the "basic structure of society," in which economic inequalities are contingent upon the decision about how major social institutions (family, economic, political) should function. Because it subsumes equality to liberty, his formulation settles the thesis of discrimination at the core of equality of opportunity, as a fail-safe device that undermines ethical (moral) arguments in support of substantive measures able to redress the **economic debt** resulting from colonial expropriation and perpetuated by racial subjugation.

How so? When presenting his theory of justice, Rawls's decisive move is to ground social justice on the principle of equal liberty, in a portrait of the ideal liberal capitalist context. From this, individuals' self-interested decisions, and not colonial expropriation (of lands and labor), racial (symbolic or total) violence, or heteropatriarchal subjugation, explain the social inequalities pervasive in his picture of the "basic structure of society." The defining statement is that what is at stake in social justice is not the actual structure but how the social subject navigates in it. For this reason, the task of the decision makers concerned with promoting equality is not to change the "basic structure of society" but to follow principles (of justice) that ensure that no social subject is stuck in the "least advantageous positions." Not surprisingly, both principles of justice articulate the thesis of discrimination, which can only be corrected by the principle of liberty: (I) "Each person is to have an equal right to the most extensive basic liberty compatible with a similar liberty for others" and (II) "Social and economic inequalities are to be arranged so that they are both (a) reasonably expected to be to everyone's advantage, and (b) attached to positions and offices open to all."[8] Furthermore, he reiterates this subsumption of equality to liberty by highlighting that "a departure from the institutions of equal liberty required by the first principle cannot be justified by, or compensated for, by greater social and economic advantages. The distribution of wealth and income, and the hierarchies of authority, must be consistent with both the liberties of equal citizenship and equality of opportunity."[9] From that he derives a formulation of social justice based on a principle of equality without historical or structural reach.

My point is that Rawls presents a naturalized view of economic inequality in the formula "original position": namely, the unequal positioning (because of the play of conflicting and mutual interests) of the rational self-interested individuals, who recognize their mutual interest in liberty, when deciding on the principles of justice under the "veil of ignorance." Inequality describes a static social arrangement, in terms of already given social positions, where change relates to the decision on how individuals should move through these positions. Consistently, equality of opportunity derives its moral necessity when in correspondence to liberty; that is, opportunity means the freedom to enjoy social mobility—not to be discriminated against in situations of competition. Such a view of social justice could not be further removed from the account of social inequalities in denunciations of colonial expropriation, racial violence, and patriarchal domination articulated in 1960s civil rights women's movements, for instance. And yet equality of opportunity would be the prevailing basis for supporting affirmative action as an instrument for social redress.

"COMPELLING STATE INTEREST"

Nearly fifty years later, then president of the NAACP Legal Defense and Educational Fund Sherillyn Ifill's remembrance of the "promise of racial equality and justice for all" in the wake of the Zimmerman decision echoes President Johnson's 1965 speech to Howard University's students and faculty, in which he reminded them that "freedom is not enough," that what was needed was substantive equality, tangible, measurable results, such as educational achievement.[10] Throughout the 1960s and in the early 1970s this pledge seemed to hold, when a number of substantive measures for remedying racial inequalities, in particular in education but also in employment, were put into place. The backlash that followed had many political determinants, such as the FBI and COINTELPRO's virtual decimation of internal radical fronts and the end of the imperial misadventure in Vietnam. Evidently, though mentioned in President Kennedy's June 1963 address, the political context does not enter in the *Bakke* court's considerations when it used failure to prove a compelling state interest to decide against substantive affirmative action measures.

Under the umbrella of President Johnson's "Great Society," the wording in Title VII of the 1964 Civil Rights Act allowed for a series of legislation and policies, in particular but not only in education, that were termed attempts to address the effects of slavery upon Black people in the United States. Nevertheless, though publicly celebrated as a decisive statement on the U.S. commitment to racial justice, the Act includes a fail-safe device, the thesis of discrimination, which undermines claims for substantive racial remedies and works, on two levels: (1) Juridically, in regard to both the law and the state, the very structure of the Act situates it in the "checks and balances" frame that organizes the U.S. political architecture. In other words, because the state is construed as a self-interested party—always prone to abuse its legal authority, that is, to intervene in order to limit its citizens equal liberty—its actions must be also subjected to judicial review. (2) Ethically, because the principle of liberty supersedes equality of opportunity (its correlated thesis of discrimination); as we saw in Rawls's moral philosophical articulation, the latter alone cannot withstand moral scrutiny. Under this supremacy of the principle of liberty, aided by the "racial dialectic" (its naturalizing of the effects of past and present economic expropriation and juridical domination), it is no surprise that the even relatively timid social reforms implemented in the 1960s and 1970s, under the guidance of the Act, would not survive scrutiny when they came before the U.S. halls of administrations of justice. What landmark U.S. Supreme Court's decisions on affirmative action initiatives in higher education expose is that equal opportunity holds racial redress to a narrow legal construction of equality as equal protection before the law or to the argument of a "compelling state interest."

U.S. Liberty versus Substantive Racial Equality

When the U.S. Supreme Court reviewed *Regents of the Univ. of California v. Bakke* (1978) and *Grutter v. Bollinger* (2003), it activated the fail-safe device, the thesis of discrimination, at the very structure of the 1964 Civil Rights Act and proved the frailty of even modest racial remedies, such as affirmative action programs in higher education.[11] In both landmark decisions, we find the principle of equality of opportunity crumbled before the courts' argument that affirmative action remedies constituted an "exercise of preferential treatment" (*Bakke* decision) or "unlawful interest in racial balancing" (*Grutter* decision). In both, what President Johnson presented as a measure to bring about racial equality was interpreted as a violation of the Fourteenth Amendment (Equal Protection), that is, *discriminatory* policies, which could only be upheld if meeting a "compelling state interest."

In the *Bakke* case, a five-way divided U.S. Supreme Court applied the strict scrutiny standard to decide in part in favor and in part against UC Davis Medical School's claim to the lawfulness of its 1973 admissions program for admitting a specified number of "students from certain minority groups."[12] The *Bakke* court judges applied strict scrutiny to decide whether there was a "compelling state interest" in the petitioner's goals: (i) "reducing the historic deficit of traditionally disfavored minorities in medical schools and in the medical profession," (ii) "countering the effects of societal discrimination, (iii) "increasing the number of physicians who will practice in communities currently underserved," and (iv) "obtaining the educational benefits that flow from an ethnically diverse student body." After reducing the goal of "reducing historic deficit" and "countering effects of societal discrimination" to exercises in preferential treatment and discrimination, the *Bakke* court ruled for the illegality of such exercises in substantive equality, as a violation of the Fourteenth Amendment (and also Title VI of the Civil Rights Act)—which establishes the formal (negative) right to equal protection under the law. Consistently, the split decision upheld the last goal, diversity of the student body, as exercising academic freedom (the principle of liberty), which has grounds in the First Amendment. Taking substantive equality with one hand, by rendering remedies for past discrimination *illegal* (as a violation of equal protection or acts of discrimination) and upholding liberty (protection of academic freedom) with the other, the *Bakke* decision activated the fail-safe device in the Civil Rights Act, the thesis of discrimination, which consistently threatens any positive measures for remedying past or present racial injustice.

When reviewing *Grutter v. Bollinger* in 2003, the U.S. Supreme Court managed to uphold the University of Michigan Law School's affirmative action program, without reversing the *Bakke* decision. Citing the *Bakke* decision as "the touchstone for constitutional analysis of race-conscious admission policies," it declared the *legality* of the University of Michigan Law School's goal of achieving a diverse student body, against Grutter's claim that the law school discriminated against her on the basis of race, thus violating the Fourteenth Amendment. Nevertheless, also in this decision, the fail-safe device was activated once again to curb substantive racial remedies. Delivering the court's opinion, Justice Sandra Day O'Connor recalls that in the *Bakke* decision, Justice Lewis F. Powell Jr. "rejected an interest in 'reducing the historic deficit of traditionally disfavored communities in medical schools and in the medical profession' as an un-lawful interest in racial balancing" and "an interest in remedying societal discrimination because such measures would risk placing unnecessary burdens on innocent third parties who bear no responsibility for whatever the harm the beneficiaries of the special admissions program are thought to have suffered." Nevertheless, upholding liberty again, now under the guise of *diversity,* the *Grutter* court finds a "compelling state interest" appropriate to the times. "Major American businesses have made clear," Justice O'Connor notes, "that the skills needed in today's increasingly global marketplace can only be developed through exposure to widely diverse people, cultures, ideas, and viewpoints. High-ranking retired officers and civilian military leaders assert that a highly qualified, racially diverse officer corps is essential to national security."[13] This (yet another) bittersweet victory for the project of racial justice comes along the U.S. global economic and military needs. These legal interpretations cannot be solely attributed to racial interests of conservative justices because when affirmative action cases are brought before U.S. courts, they carry in themselves a principle, namely *equality of opportunity*, which functions as a fail-safe device because when under judicial review, the phrase activates its correlate, the thesis of discrimination—that is, *unequal liberty* (Justice O'Connor's "racial balancing") or preference (Justice Powell's "preferential treatment").

Two aspects in this juridical legacy of affirmative action deserve attention. On the one hand, they limit state action to the "compelling state interest" criterion and effectively render *illegal* (that is, discriminatory or a violation of the Fourteenth Amendment) any substantive (positive) measures targeting the "basic structure of society"—as the *Bakke* court said was the intent of the UC Davis Medical School's admissions program. On the other hand, because it relies on a translation of substantive remedies into *discrimination* (unequal liberty), these decisions expose how the only acceptable grounds for racial remedies in higher education are the state's economic and military needs, as the *Grutter* court noted as the laudable outcome of the University of Michigan Law School's *diversity* goals. Hence, the most important aspect of the 1964 Civil Rights Act's fail-safe device is to limit the state's ability to interfere with the modern liberal capitalist "basic structure of society." Any attempt to do so is deemed an *illegal* action against freedom, that is, discriminatory, possibly politically motivated, or in the service of particular interests—in sum, a downright violation of citizens' formal (negative) right to equal protection. Now, if any substantive state action toward social reform is inherently suspicious, how do we account for the fact that, over the past two decades, affirmative action has entered the global ethico-political agenda as a gauge for a state's performance in the global stage?

"THE OBLIGATION TO TAKE ACTION"

Looking into how Brazil has heeded the global affirmative action mandate, I focus on how a promotion of a social inclusion agenda, which includes poverty alleviation programs, coincides with an economic development project based on old colonial staples (large-scale agriculture and natural resources exploitation) as well as with the assembly of a security apparatus that targets the same racial subaltern and economically dispossessed population. Moving toward exposing their interconnections, I begin with a brief discussion of the global affirmative action mandate, in which I highlight the ways in which it reproduces the legacy previously discussed. Following is a discussion of Brazil's economic and social inclusion programs, which includes a description of major legal and policy shifts, and also a review of the social inclusion and security policies of the last three presidents, Fernando Henrique Cardoso, Luiz Inacio (Lula) da Silva, and Dilma Rousseff.[14] My sole objective in this section is to indicate how within the Brazilian affirmative action experiment, in spite of obvious differences with the United States— well, perhaps because of them—the compelling state interest criterion is also met in terms of meeting the security needs of global capital.[15]

"Options to Redress"

A typical articulation of social inclusion and development is the 2008 World Bank report *Social Inclusion and Mobility in Brazil,* which, according to its authors, was designed to fill a gap in investigations of how social "exclusion constrains socieconomic mobility." The volume, which amassed findings on Brazilians' perceptions on income, inequality, and poverty, is just one example of how International Financial Institutions (such as the World Bank and the IMF) and multilateral organizations (such as the UN and the WTO) participate in designing the social reform (ethical and juridical) plans that usually accompany global economic strategies. The current social inclusion plan combines the determination for poverty alleviation as well as the creation of antidiscriminatory apparatuses and measures designed to address social (racial, gender-sexual) inequalities. "Social exclusion," the authors clarify, "refers to processes that increase the exposure to risks and vulnerability of certain social groups. . . . Exclusion works through institutional-procedural processes that limit the opportunities of certain groups to exercise their rights to have equal access to markets, services and means of political participation and representation based on built-in features of the functioning of those institutions."[16] Among these measures, affirmative action programs appear as the most curious to anyone who has followed the trajectory of affirmative action in the United States. For one thing, global instruments return to the vision President Johnson articulated, which is that the role of social inclusion measures is to correct the effects of past and current discrimination as well as to facilitate social equity.

Not surprisingly, the thesis of discrimination also plays a crucial role in the global affirmative action platform. To be sure, the thesis of discrimination has been circulating in international instruments since the 1948 UN charter. Within two years of the release of the 1964 Civil Rights Act, the United Nations' General Assembly released two significant resolutions, namely the International Convention on the Elimination of all Forms of Racial Discrimination (CERD, 1965) and the International Covenant on Civil and Political Rights (ICCPR, 1966). Entering into force in 1969, article 1 of the CERD provides a full articulation of the thesis of discrimination "as any distinction, exclusion, restriction or preference based on race, color, descent or national or ethnic origin which has the purpose or effect of nullifying or impairing the recognition, enjoyment or exercise, on the equal footing, of human rights and fundamental freedoms in the political, economic, social, cultural or any other field of public life." This articulation is tamed by the ICCPR, which entered into force in 1976, with a narrow legal definition of equality. Its article 26 interprets discrimination as limiting of liberty—perhaps resonating the 1973 *Bakke* decision discussed earlier—that is, in terms of the denial of equal treatment of citizens before the law, of the legal rights that guarantee it.

From the mid-1990s, on the tails of the 1992 United Nations Conference on the Environment and Development (Rio de Janeiro)'s attention to human development and the 1993 UN World Conference on Human Rights (Vienna)'s renewed commitment to the "protection and promotion" of Human Rights, the thesis of discrimination would make its way into most multilateral instruments, but with even more force in the first decade of the twenty-first century. Though it is impossible (and undesirable) to fix one cause for this development, it certainly reflected the work of international nongovernmental organizations (NGOs), which took up where the 1980s social movements left off and grabbed onto the Human Rights Framework in their social justice crusade. Furthermore, it also helped that social scientists have amassed a nonnegligible amount of data showing the persistence of economic inequalities in spite of celebrated promises of the global economic arrangement. From the outset, INGOs and social scientists have worked closely together—often in the production of reports—toward the goal of impressing upon multilateral bodies and governments the twin need for addressing discrimination and promoting social exclusion.

Today we observe proliferation of affirmative action programs across the globe, but in particular in Latin America, Asia, and Africa, a phenomenon that owes much to the work of INGOs such as Global Rights.[17] In its 2005 report, "Affirmative Action: A Global Perspective," Global Rights provides an agenda based on its assessment of the state of affirmative action policies across the globe.[18] This country-by-country evaluation of affirmative action legislation and programs is introduced by a discussion of the relevant human rights instruments as well as the resolutions from the major human rights conferences of the previous twenty years or so. The thesis of discrimination is articulated in Global Rights' framing of the best practices regarding affirmative action. Regarding its activities in Latin America, Global Rights' executive director, Gary MacDougall, says that it "works to strengthen the collaboration between social justice groups in different countries working on similar concerns and, among other things, aims to link organizations defending the rights of people of African descent across the Americas. Global Rights is also leading a campaign to draft and adopt a regional human rights treaty combating racial discrimination throughout the Americas." Now, instead of the principle of equality of opportunity, another concept guides the Human Rights Framework: "Non-discrimination is a cornerstone concept in international human rights, as international norms are virtually unanimous in requiring that states take specific steps to support the right to nondiscrimination and equality before the law."[19] Undoubtedly, this reflects the narrow construction of discrimination—as a violation of the right to equal protection of the law, which follows closely the *Bakke* decision—presented in article 26 of the ICCPR. What is curious, however, is that this narrow concept of nondiscrimination can become the basis for affirmative action by Global Rights' executive director: "Non-discrimination provisions are fundamental to major international human rights norms, and these norms compel affirmative action in certain cases."[20]

The legacy of U.S. affirmative action has mapped the ethical-juridical terrain for this global mandate for social inclusion (nondiscrimination and affirmative action). How does Global Rights deal with this limitation? In its reading of the body of international law, Global Rights' major move is to show how in the existing international instruments, "certain norms specify that race-conscious affirmative action policies do not violate nondiscrimination provisions, while others explicitly call for affirmative action to combat discrimination" and to include an explicit mandate that states take action to implement their provisions, including nondiscrimination and affirmative action policies.[21] For instance, it finds that the International Convention on the Elimination of Racial Discrimination allows for race conscious affirmative action:

Article 1, paragraph 4, states that "special measures" adopted only to secure "adequate advancement" of marginalized racial or ethnic groups requiring such protection, and to ensure equal enjoyment of human rights and basic freedoms, do not constitute invidious racial discrimination. The same provision sets forth limitations on such special measures, noting that they must not result in "the maintenance of separate rights for different racial groups," and that the measures shall cease when the objectives that led to their creation have been achieved.[22]

The report then moves on to list the various ways in which the provisions have been met by states across the globe with programs that seek to (a) eliminate present discrimination, (b) remedy past discrimination, (c) equalize opportunities between groups, and (d) embrace and promote diversity. Certainly, the range of affirmative action goals and provisions listed in the report indicate a racial justice program well beyond what was achieved in the United States, even before the U.S. Supreme Court disavowed the goal to remedy past discrimination.

However, because they are anchored in the principle of nondiscrimination, these programs would only find support in the criterion liberal juridical structures found acceptable in cases when the state engages in social reform. As I will next discuss, in the case of Brazil this compelling interest was the same noted in Justice O'Connor's majority opinion in the *Grutter* case, namely the economic and security needs of a development program that attends to the interest of global capital.

The Duty to Include

When considering how the last three administrations—Fernando Henrique Cardoso's, Luiz Ignacio (Lula) da Silva's, and Dilma Rousseff's—have responded to the global mandate for social inclusion,[23] a very particular question comes to mind: how does the state fulfill its classical function, the protection of its citizens' liberty and security, while attending to global capital's need for a larger consumer market and smaller labor force? How can it do so when the juridico-economic architecture does not provide for the majority of the population—either through employment or welfare provision—the conditions for obtaining the financial resources necessary for consumption? Global (financial) capital, I admit, seems to solve this problem, to ensure its survival, by betting on debt and blackmail.[24] What about its twin, the state? How do states reconcile global capital's demand for consumers (of things and debt) and the growing numbers of unemployed or those working precariously and dangerously under dire conditions?

Before the economic recession that crippled the country's economy in 2015, Brazil was widely celebrated as the latest addition to the select club of global economic powers. During the heyday of this latest economic "miracle," Lula's and Rousseff's administrations enjoyed praise for an economic development project that places the extraction of natural resources and large-scale agricultural production as the main sites of economic activity, accounting for 22 percent of the GDP in 2011. This (re)turn to colonial modalities of economic expropriation entailed a "recolonization" of the Amazon and the central regions of the country with the setting up of large plantations of soy, sugar cane, and other sources of renewable energy as well as the construction of mega-dams to meet the needs of these energy hungry economic projects.

Though the country has not significantly reduced its infamously high levels of economic inequalities, both President Lula and President Rousseff have proudly paraded their social inclusion and antipoverty programs in the media, a shift that began in 1995 in a clear response to the 1993 Vienna World Conference on Human Rights mandate, when President Cardoso created a task force for the National Human Rights Plan on the same day as Black Brazilian Movement and other social movements joined leftist parties and anarchists to protest against his agenda of economic liberalization and cuts to social provisions, in Brasília, the country's capital.[25] A number of racial inclusion and antiracism legislation, programs, and platforms have been put in place since then, such as the creation of a Secretary for the Promotion of Racial Equality (Secretaria de Políticas de Promoção da Igualdade Racial, SEPPIR) in 2003,[26] and the signing into law of the Racial Equality Statute in 2010, which consists of a comprehensive program for racial inclusion, covering health, education, media, and employment.[27]

After many years of legal challenges by white academics and politicians, in 2013 the federal government added to its racial inclusion accomplishments the Supreme Federal Tribunal's landmark decision on the legality of the University of Brasília's affirmative action program, thus upholding affirmative action in higher education as the law of the land. In stark contrast to the position taken by the U.S. Supreme Court, Brazilian justices supported the state's "obligation to action," to address the effects of past and present discrimination.[28] For instance, Justice Rosa Weber stated that the state would "correct concrete inequalities so as formal equality can once again play its beneficial role."[29] Justice Carmen Lucia Rocha defended the legality of the university's quota system but affirmed that "affirmative action policies are not the best option, but a step. It would be better if all were free and equal," and that they are linked to the state's possibility to promote equality.[30] Meanwhile Justice Joaquim Barbosa, who served as the first Black president of the Brazilian Supreme Federal Tribunal, recalled that we "should not overlook the fact that universal history does not register, in the contemporary era, another example of a nation which had moved from peripheral position to that of an economic and political power, respected in the international scene while adopting internally, exclusionary policies against a significant part of its population."[31]

In mid-2013, television and newspaper newscasts revealed, in action, the security apparatus that the last two Brazilian governments assembled while advancing social inclusion reforms. Throughout this time, as with drug trafficking and terrorist networks, the global security industrial complex has become the main justification for the U.S. deployment of its military in South Asia and Central and South America. This security apparatus is more frequently and consistently deployed—including as part of the foreign aid agenda—against precisely the racial subaltern populations protected by the principle of nondiscrimination. This security architecture has been built to protect everyone else against the very subjects the Human Rights Framework protects: African and people of African descent, indigenous peoples, migrants, and refugees.[32] While it continued to do its normal law enforcement in the favelas (slums), Brazil's security apparatus was also deployed to repress young protesters in major cities and Indigenous protesters in rural areas.[33] During the month preceding the June protests, President Rousseff had sent National Security Force troops to accompany the Minister for Justice's meeting with the Terena leaders who, tired of waiting for the fulfillment of an order of land reclamation, had occupied a farm in the State of Mato Grosso do Sul.[34] The minister's visit followed the killing of an Indigenous protester by the local military police. This is only one instance of indigenous mobilization against Brazil's "recolonizing" move. In the month before, the federal government had deployed the National Security Force and the Federal Police to the site of construction of the Belo Monte Dam to fulfill a state court order by removing Indigenous protesters from several groups—Mundurucus, Jurunas, Caiapós, Xipaias, Curuaias, Asurinis, Paracanãs, and Araras—that had occupied the site on May 2, 2013.[35] This deployment of the state's repressive apparatus to curb social protests against President Rousseff's economic development model only give an inkling of the role this security apparatus performs. Elsewhere I have described the choreography of police and military occupations of Rio de Janeiro's favelas, highlighting how the state deploys its deadly powers in these neighborhoods to show the ways in which security does the work of racial power, as raciality allows for the in/distinction between drug dealers and other favela residents and justifies the killing of the latter when resulting from state actions to recuperate territory.[36] More recently, the new policing strategy, the Unities of Pacification Police, has taken control of some favelas in the Zona Sul of the city while in the periphery, neighborhoods dominated by drug trafficking are still living with threats, such as stray bullets in gun fights between gangs or between gangs and the police, and temporary police occupations, which kill young people whom they argue are suspects who have resisted arrest.[37] In sum, the joint deployment of equality (social inclusion) measures and the security apparatus—targeting the same populations—does not mark a contradiction but actually gives us the opportunity to appreciate the level of entanglement of state capital; that is, the global mandates for equality and for security belong in the state's agenda in support of global capital.

What I am highlighting is how in the global present, a compelling state interest has two very different modalities: the duty to include and the duty to (self-) preserve—both sustained by the racial dialectics—for responding to demands for social justice. Regarding affirmative action as an aspect of the equality (social inclusion) mandate, it is evident how perverse "racial dialectics" hide (a) how the dismantling of the welfare state left these neighborhoods available to the control of kids with guns; (b) that drug-related violence, including racial (state) violence, serves the needs of global capital as it takes care of an excess population, which is no longer necessary for maintaining or increasing the margins of profit; and further, (c) there is a compelling economic interest in the latest inroads into Indigenous lands, as exemplified by Belo Monte and other mega-dams but also by large plantations for crops designed to be used as biofuel. My point is that raciality here mediates between the mandate for equality and the mandate for security. How? Because its construction of the racial other as an affectable subject checks the liberty attributed to the ethical figure of the human. The constructed racial other authorizes the state to deploy its forces of self-preservation in Black spaces in the same way that it authorizes U.S. citizens like Zimmerman to deploy total violence against an unarmed seventeen-year-old because he was wearing a piece of clothing, a *hoodie*, which in the postracial United States has become a (racial) signifier of crime. Put differently, raciality, as it did in mid-July 2013, in that Florida court, collapses administration of justice and law enforcement, thus rendering it possible that the state (and other) deploy its instruments of total violence without unleashing an ethical crisis or a guilty verdict.

CONCLUSION

My goal here has not been to accuse liberal juridical architectures of doing what they are designed to do, which is to support the workings of capitalism. My desire is to offer a critical engagement with the global present, in particular targeting formulations of social justice supporting equality (social inclusion) programs that states advance in response to mandates from multilateral organizations, INGOs, International Financial Institutions, and also, of course, their economically dispossessed constituencies. What this consideration of the principle governing projects of social justice, namely equality of opportunity, shows is how its ethical fail-safe aspect, the thesis of discrimination, undermines projects of social (substantive) justice. This is accomplished because the discrimination (or exclusion) has been articulated in the account of racial subjugation, the racial dialectics, which effectively disavow colonial expropriation and racial (symbolic and total) violence as the moments of racial subjugation.

This perverse dialectics of raciality works as the logic of obliteration (for self-determination to hold the colonial/racial other cannot exist) resolves the logic of exclusion (their existence undermines self-determination and turns rational and free whites/Europeans into affectable subjects) back into itself (the resulting whites/Europeans' unbecoming actions negatively affect the racial Other, rendering them unable to live in the rational free societies Europeans have built) without ever exposing its operation. Exposing these workings of raciality shows how urgently an ethical-political program (a plan for racial/global justice) that does not rely on self-determination, under its many names, such as liberty or equality, is needed, because the arsenal of raciality has inscribed violence (at the core of its account of racial subjugation) in the very fabric of global political (economic, juridical, and ethical) architectures. For this reason, any global ethical program designed to dissolve the effects of the power of raciality must target the governing logic of obliteration. Under the rule of the figure of the human, racial subjugation is not about exclusion from universality. When the tools of scientific reason restate modern philosophical statements and produce the racial other's mind as one unable to conceive or comprehend the universal, they are not dys-selecting—and here is how my reading of the human differs from Sylvia Wynter's—or excluding, or discriminating, but producing a kind of human being with mental attributes that are mapped on their bodies and places of origin. For this reason, they produce the global space as the context of humanity, as a diverse unity (that is, differentiated ethical figures), in such a way as every text that deploys its tools never fails to find neatly distinguishable *persons* and *places* of transcendentality (liberty) and affectability (necessity).

The violence Frantz Fanon finds defining the colonial space is not intrinsic to the colonized and their places of residence; instead, it is the very mode of operation of colonial and racial power; it is the violence the tools of raciality reproduce onto the global space. However, it fuses so well with the state's function of protecting the subjects of liberty (self-determination) that it is easy to lose sight of this otherwise evident fact. What the demand for self-determination does is erase the founding colonial juridical-economic architectures (conquest, settlement, and slavery) that birthed capitalism and modernity. Precisely this *occlusion*—an effect of historicity—sustains the disavowal of affirmative action as a mechanism for addressing the effects of racial power that has prevailed in the U.S. Supreme Court decisions discussed earlier. Working in tandem with obliteration (an effect of scientific universality), occlusion also responds to the general moral stance before racial violence, which I term "oblivion." Though my argument in this article faces off historical materialism, it is directed toward clearing the terrain for an ethical program that begins with acknowledgment of the founding violence of modern representation but recalls the need for another point of departure for describing global existence without self-determination (freedom or liberty) and the account of affectability and necessity it demands.

DENISE FERREIRA DA SILVA is the director of the Social Justice Institute (GRSJ) at the University of British Columbia. Her work describes how raciality maps the global (juridical, economic, and symbolic) configuration, as it seeks a new ethical basis for global justice. Her publications include *Toward a Global Idea of Race* (2007) and the coedited (with Paula Chakravartty) volume *Race, Empire, and the Crisis of the Subprime* (2013).

NOTES

1. G. W. F. Hegel, *The Philosophy of History* (Kitchener, Ont.: Batouche Books, 2001), 113. Barack Obama and Roslyn Brock are both quoted in Yamiche Alcindor and Larry Copeland, "After Zimmerman Verdict, Can Nation Heal Racial Rift?," *USA Today*, July 15, 2013.

2. "Today we are committed to a worldwide struggle to promote and protect the rights of all who wish to be free. And when Americans are sent to Viet-Nam or West Berlin, we do not ask for whites only. It ought to be possible, therefore, for American students of any color to attend any public institution they select without having to be backed up by troops. . . . The heart of the question is whether all Americans are to be afforded equal rights and equal opportunities, whether we are going to treat our fellow Americans as we want to be treated. If an American, because his skin is dark, cannot eat lunch in a restaurant open to the public, if he cannot send his children to the best public school available, if he cannot vote for the public officials who represent him, if, in short, he cannot enjoy the full and free life which all of us want, then who among us would be content to have the color of his skin changed and stand in his place? Who among us would then be content with the counsels of patience and delay? . . . We preach freedom around the world, and we mean it, and we cherish our freedom here at home, but are we to say to the world, and much more importantly, to each other that this is a land of the free except for the Negroes; that we have no second-class citizens except Negroes; that we have no class or cast system, no ghettoes, no master race except with respect to Negroes? Now the time has come for this Nation to fulfill its promise." John F. Kennedy, "Address on Civil Rights" (speech, Washington, D.C., June 11, 1963), Miller Center, http://millercenter.org/president/speeches/detail/3375.

3. G. W. F. Hegel, *Phenomenology of Spirit* (Oxford: Oxford University Press, 1977), 114–18.

4. For a discussion of the logics of racial subjugation, "theory of racial and cultural contacts," and the "race relation cycle," see Denise Ferreira da Silva, *Toward a Global Idea of Race* (Minneapolis: University of Minnesota Press, 2007), 153–70.

5. See Denise Ferreira da Silva, "Many Hundred Thousand Bodies Later: An Analysis of the 'Legacy' of the International Criminal Tribunal for Rwanda," in *Events: The Force of International Law*, ed. Sundhya Pahuja, Fleur Johns, and Richard Joyce (New York: Routledge, 2010), 165–76.

6. With the term "occlusion" I capture the signifying process through which historicity (interiority/ temporality) folds colonial practices—expropriation of the productive capacity of land and bodies—into the self-producing trajectory of spirit, and in doing so engulfs coloniality and the violent relationships of power that characterize it.

7. "The basic structure," Rawls describes, "is the primary subject of justice because its effects are so profound and present from the start. The intuitive notion here is that this structure contains various social positions and that men born into different positions have different expectations of life determined, in part, by the political system as well as by economic and social circumstances. In this way the institutions of society favor certain starting places over others." Then, he goes on to say, "These are especially deep inequalities. . . . It is these inequalities, presumably inevitable in the basic structure of any society, to which the principles of social justice must in the first instance apply. These principles, then, regulate the choice of a political constitution and the main elements of the economic and social system." In sum, for Rawls, "the justice of a social scheme depends essentially on how

fundamental rights and duties are assigned and on the economic opportunities and social conditions in the various sectors of society." John Rawls, *A Theory of Justice* (1971; repr., Cambridge, Mass.: Harvard University Press, 1999), 7.

8. Ibid., 60.

9. Ibid., 61.

10. Ifill is quoted in Alcindor and Copeland, "After Zimmerman Verdict." "You do not wipe away," Johnson stated, "the scars of centuries by saying: Now you are free to go where you want, and do as you desire, and choose the leaders you please. . . . To this end equal opportunity is essential, but not enough, not enough. Men and women of all races are born with the same range of abilities. But ability is not just the product of birth. Ability is stretched or stunted by the family that you live with, and the neighborhood you live in—by the school you go to and the poverty or the richness of your surroundings." Lyndon B. Johnson, "Remarks at the Howard University Commencement" (speech, Washington, D.C., June 4, 1965), Miller Center, http://millercenter.org/president/speeches/speech-3387.

11. The argument in this article was written two years before the U.S. Supreme Court reviewed *Fisher v. University of Texas at Austin,* 570 U.S.__ (2013), which supports this analysis. Furthermore, Justice Antonin Scalia's comments on how young Black people are unprepared for attending elite universities suggest how U.S. juridical decision makers share in an overall devaluing of Black persons. See http://www.supremecourt.gov/oral_arguments/argument_transcripts/14-981_p8ko.pdf.

12. For Justice Powell, "Preferring members of any one group for no reason other than race or ethnic origin is discrimination for its own sake. This the Constitution forbids. The State certainly has a legitimate and substantial interest in ameliorating, or eliminating where feasible, the disabling effects of identified discrimination. But we have never approved a classification that aids persons perceived as members of relatively victimized groups at the expense of other innocent individuals in the absence of judicial, legislative, or administrative findings of constitutional or statutory violations." *Regents of Univ. of California v. Bakke,* 438 U.S. 265 (1978), https://supreme.justia.com/cases/federal/us/438/265/case.html.

13. *Grutter v. Bollinger,* 539 U.S. 306 (2003), https://supreme.justia.com/cases/federal/us/539/306/case.html.

14. For an expanded analysis of Brazil's security apparatus, see Denise Ferreira da Silva, "No-bodies: Law, Raciality and Violence," *Griffith Law Review* 18, no. 2 (2009): 212–36.

15. Read, for instance, Dilma Rousseff's speech to agribusiness leaders in 2011: "Undoubtedly, the National Confederation of Agriculture and Livestock is of great importance to the Brazilian agricultural sector, that is, with, as all of you know, 22.4% of our Gross Domestic Product and accounts for 37% of our exports. Undoubtedly Brazil is proud to have one of the most productive agricultures, more efficient and more competitive, among the best in the world. . . . In addition to producing most of the food our population consumes, we are the largest exporter of soy complex, meat, sugar and forestry products. In the world ranking, Brazil is the leading producer of sugar, coffee beans, orange juice; and the second position in soybeans, beans, beef, tobacco and ethanol. We export agricultural products to 214

international destinations. . . . In addition to this entrepreneurial character, the technological factor and our good climate also help our public policies to support agricultural development and livestock. I quote a single number: the current Agricultural and Livestock Plan has [US$] 107 billion available to fund the Brazilian agribusiness, almost four times the total applied to the crop ten years ago." "Discurso da Presidenta da República, Dilma Rousseff, durante cerimônia de encerramento do seminário "Os desafios do Brasil como 5a potência mundial e o papel do agronegócio" (speech, Unique Palace, Brasília November 23, 2011), http://www2 .planalto.gov.br/acompanhe-o-planalto/discursos/discursos-da-presidenta/dis curso-da-presidenta-da-republica-dilma-rousseff-durante-cerimonia-de-encerra mento-do-seminario-201cos-desafios-do-brasil-como-5a-potencia-mundial-e-o -papel-do-agronegocio201d. All translations are mine unless otherwise noted.

16. Estanislao Gacitúa Marió and Michael Woolcock, eds., *Social Exclusion and Mobility in Brazil* (Washington, D.C.: International Bank for Reconstruction and Development/World Bank, 2008), 12.

17. See the Global Rights website, http://www.globalrights.org/index.html.

18. Global Rights, "Affirmative Action: A Global Perspective," http://docslide.us/ documents/affirmative-action-global-perspective.html.

19. Ibid., 2.

20. Ibid., 3.

21. Ibid.

22. Ibid., 6.

23. This is articulated in Rousseff's speech in 2013: "What is the root of inequality?" she asks. "We know that each person is different from another. But we also know that the root of inequality is different opportunities. We want to ensure there is equal opportunity, [which] is to ensure that a child . . . and the poorer the child, the more it must have access to quality education, it must have access to the stimulus because it will develop and be able to compete for the opportunities that will occur throughout its life. The first is to teach how to read and write at the right age. The second is part of a generation of Brazilians who must have access to school fulltime." See "Discurso da Presidenta da República, Dilma Rousseff, durante cerimônia de repactuação do Programa Brasil sem Miséria com o RS Mais Igual e formatura do Programa Nacional de Acesso ao Ensino Técnico e Emprego (Pronatec)" (speech, Porto Alegre, April 12, 2013, http://www2.planalto.gov.br/acompanhe-o -planalto/discursos/discursos-da-presidenta/discurso-da-presidenta-da-repub lica-dilma-rousseff-durante-cerimonia-de-repactuacao-do-programa-brasil-sem-mi seria-com-o-rs-mais-igual-e-formatura-do-programa-nacional-de-acesso-ao-ensino -tecnico-e-emprego-pronatec.

24. See, for instance, Tayyab Mahmud, "Debt and Discipline," *American Quarterly* 64, no. 3 (2012): 469–94; Ofelia O. Cuevas, "Welcome to My Cell: Housing and Race in the Mirror of American Democracy," *American Quarterly* 64, no. 3 (2012): 605–24.

25. The mandate of the Task Force for the Advancement for the Black Population, which would later integrate into the National Human Rights Program, included proposing policies against racial discrimination, promoting the development and

participation of the Black population, gathering and publicizing information of interest to this population, examining the existing legislation, and proposing necessary changes to promote and consolidate Black citizenship. See "Programa Nacional de Direitos Humanos," http://www.dhnet.org.br/dados/pp/pndh/textointegral.html.

26. Its charges include "formulation, coordination and articulation of policies and guidelines for the promotion of racial equality" and the "formulation, coordination and evaluation of public policy statements promoting equality and protecting the rights of individuals and ethnic groups, with emphasis on the Black population, affected by racial discrimination and other forms of intolerance." SEPPIR, "A Secretaria," June 19, 2015, http://www.seppir.gov.br/sobre-a-seppir/a-secretaria.

27. The first two articles of the document delimit its mandate. Article 1: "This Law establishes the Racial Equality Statute, to ensure the Black population to the realization of equal opportunities, protection of ethnic, individual, collective and diffuse rights and the fight against discrimination and other forms of ethnic intolerance." Article 2: "It is the duty of the state and society to ensure equal opportunities, recognizing every Brazilian citizen, regardless of ethnicity or skin color, the right to participation in the community, especially in political activities, economic, business, educational, cultural and sports, defending their dignity and their religious and cultural values." Estatuto da Igualdade Racial, Presidência da República, Casa Civil, lei no. 12.288, July 20, 2010, http://www.planalto.gov.br/ccivil_03/_Ato2007-2010/2010/Lei/L12288.htm.

28. See Denise Ferreira da Silva, "The End of Brazil: An Analysis of the Debate on Racial Equity on the Edges of Global Market Capitalism," *National Black Law Journal* 21, no. 3 (2010): 1–18.

29. Publicado em Sexta, "Cotas raciais: Voto da ministra Rosa Weber," *Geledés.org,* April 27, 2012, http://www.geledes.org.br/areas-de-atuacao/educacao/cotas-para-negros/13970-cotas-raciais-voto-da-ministra-rosa-weber.

30. Ibid.

31. STF, "Cotas raciais: O voto do Ministro Joaquim Barbosa," *Geledés.org,* April 27, 2012, http://www.geledes.org.br/cotas-raciais-o-voto-ministro-joaquim-barbosa/#ixzz419DwjLwF.

32. Illegal trades in drugs and weapons are connected to the armed conflicts that have replaced anticolonial and Cold War–related hot wars throughout the Global South (South Asia, Southeast Asia, Africa, Latin America, and the Caribbean) and in the economically dispossessed locales in these regions, where the majority of residents are not of European descent. For the most part it acts in urban areas, in favelas, through invasions and occupations devised to retrieve the control of territory lost to drug gangs. Like other postcolonies of the Global South and the Global North, favelas and other economically dispossessed rural urban areas, with majority Black populations, are the primary site of operation of the illegal drug industry (cultivation and trade). See Do GI, "Protestos pelo país reúnem mais de 250 mil pessoas," *Globo.com,* June 18, 2013, http://g1.globo.com/brasil/noticia/2013/06/protestos-pelo-pais-reunem-mais-de-250-mil-pessoas.html.

33. Ibid.

34. Redação RBA, "Governo manda Força Nacional para região de conflito entre índios e fazendeiros," *Rede Brazil Atual*, June 5, 2013, http://www.redebrasilatual.com .br/cidadania/2013/06/forca-nacional-de-seguranca-vai-atuar-em-conflito-indigena -em-mato-grosso-do-sul-4417.html.

35. "Indígenas fazem nova ocupação de Belo Monte por consultas," *Xingu Vivo*, May 21, 2013, http://www.xinguvivo.org.br/2013/05/27/governo-nao-cumpre-palavra -e-indigenas-ocupam-belo-monte-novamente/.

36. da Silva, "No-bodies."

37. The disappearance of Amarildo de Souza in the favela Rocinha, in Rio de Janeiro, sparked a protest, which, on a rare occasion, united leftist protesters and favela residents. See Donna Bowater, "Where's Amarildo? How the Disappearance of a Construction Worker Taken from His Home by Police Has Sparked Protests in Brazil," *Independent*, August 4, 2013.

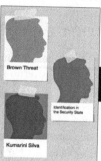